Azure Patterns for Real-World Apps: Resilient by Design

First Edition

Preface

In an era where digital services are the lifeblood of global businesses, the ability of systems to withstand and recover from failure is not just a technical necessity—it's a business imperative. *"Azure Patterns for Real-World Apps: Resilient by Design"* is your comprehensive guide to building applications that not only survive disruptions but thrive amid them. Whether you are an architect designing complex distributed systems or a developer integrating resilience into microservices, this book equips you with patterns, principles, and platform-specific guidance to succeed in Azure's vast cloud ecosystem.

The structure of this book is intentional. It begins with foundational concepts and design philosophies, gradually building toward specialized implementations and real-world case studies. From retry strategies to chaos engineering, every chapter emphasizes resilience at different layers—compute, data, messaging, observability, security, and deployment.

In **Chapter 1**, we lay the groundwork by exploring what resilience truly means in the context of modern applications and how Azure supports it with native services. In **Chapter 2**, we introduce key architectural patterns like circuit breakers and idempotency—essentials for any cloud-native system. **Chapter 3** discusses availability and disaster recovery at a global scale, helping you design with both redundancy and responsiveness in mind.

The middle chapters focus on practical design decisions, such as the trade-offs between stateless and stateful systems in **Chapter 4**, or how to ensure data durability and consistency in **Chapter 5**. **Chapter 6** dives into event-driven architectures, and **Chapter 7** teaches you how to make your systems observable and self-healing with telemetry, health checks, and automation.

Security is often overlooked in resilience planning, which is why **Chapter 8** emphasizes identity, secrets management, and governance under failure conditions. We then pivot to the DevOps pipeline in **Chapter 9**, ensuring that your deployments are just as resilient as your runtime systems. Real-world architecture reviews in **Chapter 10** offer practical insight into successful implementations across industries.

Finally, **Chapter 11** looks to the future—introducing advanced topics like chaos engineering, predictive resilience with AI/ML, and sustainable design principles to future-proof your architecture.

Whether you're working on greenfield applications or modernizing legacy systems, this book provides a toolkit to build resilient, robust, and reliable applications on Microsoft Azure. Let's build systems that bend but never break.

Table of Contents

Preface 2

Chapter 1: Introduction to Resilient Architecture on Azure 20

  Understanding Resilience in Modern Applications 20

    The Nature of Failure..20

    What Is Resilience? 20

    The Azure Advantage 21

    Core Concepts: Reliability vs Resilience 21

    Resilience by Design..21

    Mindset Shift: Embracing Failure..22

    When to Start Thinking About Resilience 23

    Summary 23

  The Azure Ecosystem and Its Resilience Capabilities 23

    Global Infrastructure Foundation..23

    Compute Services and Resilience 24

    Storage and Data Services 25

    Networking and Traffic Management..27

    Observability and Automation...27

    Identity and Secrets Resilience 29

    Governance and Compliance 29

    Service-Level Agreements (SLAs) 29

    Conclusion 30

  Core Principles of Cloud-Native Design 30

    Principle 1: Embrace Failure as a First-Class Concern 30

    Principle 2: Design for Horizontal Scalability 31

    Principle 3: Build with Disposable and Replaceable Components........................32

    Principle 4: Automate Everything 32

    Principle 5: Externalize State and Configuration...33

    Principle 6: Observability as a Feature..34

    Principle 7: Favor Event-Driven and Asynchronous Architectures.......................34

    Principle 8: Secure by Default 35

    Conclusion 36

  Why Resilience Matters: Real-World Failure Scenarios 36

    Scenario 1: The E-Commerce Holiday Crash...37

    Scenario 2: The Global SaaS Outage...38

Scenario 3: Microservice Chain Reaction 39

Scenario 4: Secrets and Configuration Leak 40

Scenario 5: Misconfigured Infrastructure as Code 41

Lessons Learned from Failures 42

Building a Culture of Resilience..42

Conclusion 42

Chapter 2: Foundational Patterns for Resilient Systems.......................44

Retry and Circuit Breaker Patterns...44

The Nature of Transient Failures 44

The Retry Pattern...44

The Circuit Breaker Pattern 46

Implementing Patterns in Azure Services 47

Best Practices 48

A Real-World Example 48

Conclusion 49

Bulkhead Isolation 49

Why Bulkheads Matter 49

Dimensions of Isolation 50

Implementing Bulkhead Isolation in Azure 50

Bulkhead Patterns in Messaging and APIs 53

Tenant and Domain Bulkheading...53

Monitoring and Testing Bulkheads 54

Common Pitfalls 54

Real-World Example 55

Conclusion 55

Timeout and Backoff Strategies 56

The Purpose of Timeouts...56

Timeout Strategy Principles 56

Configuring Timeouts: Language and Azure Examples 57

Understanding Backoff Strategies..58

Example: Exponential Backoff with Jitter (C# with Polly) 58

Example: Exponential Backoff with Jitter (Python)................................59

Azure SDK and Service Support for Backoff 59

Combining Timeout + Backoff for Maximum Resilience.......................59

Timeout and Backoff in Azure Functions 60

Best Practices 60

Real-World Scenario..61

Conclusion 61

Idempotency in Distributed Systems 62

Understanding Idempotency 62

Why Idempotency Is Critical in the Cloud 62

Strategies for Idempotency 63

Idempotency in Messaging Systems 64

Idempotency in Workflows and Durable Functions 65

Data Layer Idempotency 65

Testing and Validating Idempotency 66

Anti-Patterns to Avoid 66

Real-World Scenario...67

Conclusion 67

Chapter 3: High Availability and Disaster Recovery Strategies 68

Availability Zones vs. Regions...68

Azure's Global Infrastructure Hierarchy..68

What Are Availability Zones? 68

What Are Regions?...69

Availability Zones vs. Regions: Comparison 70

Designing for Availability with AZs..71

Designing for Resilience with Regions 71

Combined Strategy: AZ + Region..72

Cost Considerations...73

Monitoring and Testing 73

Real-World Scenario...73

Conclusion 74

Geo-Redundancy with Azure Services...74

What is Geo-Redundancy? 75

Geo-Redundancy in Azure Storage 75

Geo-Redundancy in Databases..76

Geo-Redundancy for Web Applications 78

Geo-Redundancy in Compute 79

Cross-Region Backup and Restore 80

Failover Planning and Automation 81

Testing Geo-Redundancy 81

Real-World Case Study 82

Conclusion 82

Building with Active-Active and Active-Passive Models 82

Active-Active Architecture 83

Use Cases for Active-Active 83

Designing Active-Active with Azure Services 84

Active-Passive Architecture 85

Use Cases for Active-Passive 85

Designing Active-Passive with Azure Services 86

Choosing Between Active-Active and Active-Passive 87

Automating Deployment and Failover 88

Monitoring and Observability 89

Testing Your Design 89

Real-World Case Study 90

Conclusion 90

Designing for Failover and Failback 90

Understanding Failover and Failback 91

Types of Failover 91

Failover Triggers 92

DNS and Traffic Routing for Failover 92

Handling Stateful Failover 93

Application-Level Failover 94

Automation of Failover and Failback 95

Validating Failback Conditions 96

Documentation and Runbooks 96

Testing Failover and Failback 96

Real-World Scenario 97

Conclusion 98

Chapter 4: Stateless and Stateful Design on Azure 99

Choosing Between Stateless and Stateful Architectures 99

What Is Stateless Architecture? 99

What Is Stateful Architecture? 100

When to Use Stateless Design 101

When to Use Stateful Design 101

Stateful Workflows in Azure Durable Functions 102

Hybrid Architecture: Combining Stateless and Stateful 103

Best Practices for Managing State in Azure 103

Common Anti-Patterns 104

Real-World Example 105

Conclusion 106

Session Management in the Cloud 106

Understanding Sessions in Modern Applications 106

Session Management Challenges in the Cloud 107

Common Session Management Strategies 107

Azure Solutions for Session Management 109

Hybrid Model: Client-Side + Server-Side 111

Session Expiration and Cleanup 111

Multi-Region and Global Session Management 112

Monitoring and Observability 112

Real-World Example 113

Summary Best Practices 113

Conclusion 114

Durable Functions and State Persistence 114

The Challenge of Orchestrating State in the Cloud 114

Durable Functions Overview 115

Core Components 115

Basic Orchestration Example 116

Persistence and Checkpointing 117

Common Orchestration Patterns 117

Durable Entities 119

Monitoring and Diagnostics 120

Real-World Scenarios 120

Resilience Considerations 121

Conclusion 121

Leveraging Azure Cache and Redis for Performance 122

Why Caching Matters 122

Azure Cache for Redis Overview 123

Core Caching Patterns 123

Integrating Redis with Azure Applications 126

Redis for Resilience and High Availability 127

Advanced Redis Features 128

Cache Invalidation Strategies 129

Real-World Case Study 129

Monitoring and Metrics 130

Best Practices Summary..130

Conclusion 131

Chapter 5: Resilience in Data Architectures 132

Azure SQL and Cosmos DB Resilience Features 132

Azure SQL Database: Overview and Availability Tiers 132

Resilience Features in Azure SQL 132

Azure Cosmos DB: Overview and Multi-Region Features 135

Resilience Features in Cosmos DB 135

Monitoring and Diagnostics in Cosmos DB...138

Best Practices for Resilient Data Architectures 138

Real-World Case Study 139

Conclusion 140

Replication and Partitioning Strategies 140

Understanding Replication 140

Replication in Azure SQL...141

Replication in Cosmos DB 142

Replication Considerations 143

Understanding Partitioning 143

Partitioning in Azure SQL 143

Partitioning in Cosmos DB 144

Combining Replication and Partitioning 145

Data Movement and Migration Tools 146

Best Practices 146

Real-World Example 147

Conclusion 147

Backup, Restore, and Data Retention Best Practices 147

Objectives of Backup and Retention 148

Azure SQL Database Backup 148

Azure Cosmos DB Backup 149

Azure Blob Storage Backup and Versioning 150

Automation and Backup Scheduling 151

Retention Policy Design...152

Security and Encryption 152

Backup and Restore for Azure Kubernetes (AKS) 153

Testing and Validation 153

Real-World Case Study 154

Best Practices Summary..154

Conclusion 155

Handling Eventual Consistency...155

What is Eventual Consistency? 155

Why Eventual Consistency is Needed 156

Eventual Consistency in Azure Cosmos DB 156

Designing for Eventual Consistency 157

Conflict Resolution..158

Compensating Transactions 159

Messaging Systems and Eventual Consistency..159

Testing Eventual Consistency...160

Monitoring and Observability 160

Real-World Scenario..160

Best Practices Summary..161

Conclusion 162

Chapter 6: Messaging and Event-Driven Patterns...................................163

Decoupling with Azure Service Bus and Event Grid 163

Why Decoupling Matters..163

Azure Service Bus Overview 164

Example: Decoupling Order Processing with Service Bus 164

Azure Event Grid Overview...166

Example: Serverless Processing with Event Grid.......................................166

Decoupling Patterns..167

Ensuring Reliability 168

Monitoring and Observability 169

Real-World Example 169

Best Practices Summary..170

Conclusion 170

Message Delivery Guarantees 171

The Three Core Delivery Guarantees..171

Delivery Guarantees in Azure Messaging Services 173

Azure Service Bus: Guarantee Details 173

Azure Event Grid: Guarantee Details..175

Azure Event Hubs: Guarantee Details 176

Designing for At-Least-Once 176

Designing for Exactly-Once...176

Real-World Example: Payment Processing System..177

Monitoring and Troubleshooting 178

Best Practices Summary..178

Conclusion 179

Handling Poison Messages 179

What Are Poison Messages?..179

Symptoms of Poison Messages 180

Azure Service Bus: Built-in Poison Message Handling 180

Manual Inspection and Reprocessing 181

Custom Dead-lettering Logic..182

Azure Event Grid and Poison Messages 183

Azure Event Hubs and Poison Message Handling 183

Poison Message Patterns and Strategies 184

Monitoring and Alerting 185

Real-World Case Study 186

Best Practices Summary..186

Conclusion 187

Event Sourcing and CQRS Patterns 187

What is Event Sourcing? 188

What is CQRS? 188

Event Sourcing + CQRS = Powerful Synergy 189

Implementing Event Sourcing in Azure 189

Implementing CQRS in Azure..191

Ensuring Consistency and Resilience...192

Versioning and Schema Evolution..192

Testing and Debugging..192

Real-World Use Case...193

Challenges and Considerations 193

Best Practices Summary..194

Conclusion 194

Chapter 7: Observability and Failure Detection...195

Designing for Monitoring with Azure Monitor and Log Analytics 195

What Is Observability?...195

Azure Monitor: The Central Hub...196

Architecture of Azure Monitoring...196

Log Analytics: Query-Driven Insight 197

Instrumenting Applications with Application Insights.............................197

Monitoring Infrastructure...198

Building Dashboards and Workbooks...199

Creating Alerts 199

Integrating with DevOps Pipelines...200

Monitoring for Resilience..200

Real-World Implementation Example 201

Best Practices Summary..202

Conclusion 202

Tracing with Application Insights..202

What is Distributed Tracing?..203

Application Insights Telemetry Model 203

Enabling Tracing in .NET Applications..204

Enabling Tracing in Azure Functions 205

Viewing Traces in Application Insights 206

Propagating Trace Context Across Services...206

Tracing Across Asynchronous Boundaries...207

Custom Telemetry and Enrichment 207

Integrating Traces with Logs and Metrics..208

Real-World Use Case..209

Best Practices Summary..209

Conclusion 210

Health Checks and Telemetry Pipelines 210

The Purpose of Health Checks..210

Application-Level Health Checks...211

Azure Services and Health Probes 212

Custom Health Checks for Dependencies 213

Building Telemetry Pipelines...214

Sample Pipeline: Application Insights to Alerting and Dashboard 214

Combining Health Checks with Telemetry 215

Auto-Healing and Automated Response 216

Real-World Use Case..216

Best Practices Summary..217

Conclusion 217

Automating Recovery with Azure Automation 217

The Case for Automated Recovery 217

What Is Azure Automation? 218

Types of Runbooks 218

Example Recovery Use Cases..219

Integrating Azure Automation with Azure Monitor 220

Securing Automation Runbooks..221

Building a Recovery Framework 221

Advanced Patterns 221

Real-World Example 222

Best Practices Summary...223

Conclusion 223

Chapter 8: Security and Compliance in Resilient Systems 225

Designing with Zero Trust Principles..225

What is Zero Trust?...225

Core Principles of Zero Trust 226

Applying Zero Trust on Azure 226

Network Segmentation and Micro-Perimeters 227

Data Security and Encryption...228

Monitoring and Analytics 229

Automation and Governance..229

Real-World Scenario...230

Best Practices Summary...230

Conclusion 231

Key Vault and Secrets Management...231

Why Secrets Management Matters 231

Azure Key Vault Overview 232

Key Vault Design Considerations 232

Storing and Accessing Secrets..233

Controlling Access with Azure RBAC 233

Secret Rotation and Expiration 234

Monitoring and Auditing 235

Integrating Key Vault into CI/CD Pipelines......................................235

Common Anti-Patterns to Avoid 236

High Availability and Resilience...237

Real-World Implementation Example 237

Best Practices Summary...238

Conclusion 238

Identity and Access Resilience..238

The Role of Identity in Resilience 239

Azure Identity Fundamentals...239

Designing for Authentication Resilience...240

Ensuring Authorization Resilience 241

Securing Application Access with Managed Identities.....................241

Monitoring Identity Health 242

Identity Backup and Recovery 243

Resilience for Federated Identities 243

Real-World Example 243

Best Practices Summary..244

Conclusion 245

Policy-Driven Governance and Compliance..245

Why Policy-Driven Governance? 245

Governance Architecture in Azure...246

Common Policy Examples..247

Azure Policy Initiatives..249

Auto-Remediation with DeployIfNotExists 250

Auditing Compliance...251

Blueprint-Based Governance 251

Real-World Governance Implementation 252

Best Practices Summary..253

Conclusion 253

Chapter 9: DevOps for Resilient Deployments 254

Infrastructure as Code with Bicep and ARM Templates......................254

Why Infrastructure as Code?...254

Bicep vs. ARM Templates 254

Basic Bicep Example...255

Designing Resilient Infrastructure with IaC 256

Automating Resilient Deployments 257

Idempotency and Drift Detection 259

Managing Secrets Securely 259

Resilient Design Patterns in Bicep 260

Real-World Use Case...261

Best Practices Summary...262

Conclusion 262

Safe Deployment Strategies (Canary, Blue/Green) 263

Why Safe Deployment Strategies Matter 263

Deployment Strategy Comparison 264

Blue/Green Deployment on Azure..264

Canary Deployments on Azure...265

Feature Flags and Targeted Rollouts 267

Safe Rollback Patterns...268

Monitoring During Deployment 268

Automation and Pipelines 269

Real-World Use Case 270

Best Practices Summary...270

Conclusion 271

CI/CD Resilience with Azure DevOps and GitHub Actions 271

Why CI/CD Resilience Matters...271

Azure DevOps and GitHub Actions Overview...272

Core CI/CD Resilience Patterns...273

Secrets Management and Resilience..274

Test Resilience in the Pipeline 275

Artifact Handling and Versioning 275

Deployment Validation Steps 276

Rollback and Re-deploy Safety Nets 276

Resilience for Long-Running Pipelines 277

Monitoring CI/CD Pipelines...278

Real-World Case Study 278

Best Practices Summary...279

Conclusion 279

Rollbacks and Rollforwards Best Practices 279

Rollback vs. Rollforward...280

Preparing for Rollbacks 280

Rollback Techniques by Platform 281

Rollforward Strategy 282

Database and Schema Changes 283

Monitoring and Alerting 283

Automating Rollbacks 284

Real-World Example 285

Best Practices Summary..285

Conclusion 286

Chapter 10: Real-World Case Studies and Architectural Reviews.............287

E-Commerce Platform at Scale 287

Business Requirements and Constraints 287

High-Level Architecture Overview 288

Resilience Strategy by Layer 288

Deployment and Operations...290

Failure Scenarios and Recovery 291

Observability and Alerting 292

Key Lessons Learned...292

Summary 293

Global SaaS Provider with Multi-Tenant Resilience 293

Platform Overview 293

Multi-Tenant Resilience Strategy 294

CI/CD and Tenant-Aware Rollouts 296

Observability at Scale 297

Failure Scenarios and Response 298

Business Impact 299

Key Lessons Learned...299

Summary 300

Real-Time Analytics Platform...300

Business Requirements 300

High-Level Architecture 301

Resilience Techniques by Layer 302

Handling Late or Out-of-Order Data...303

Scaling for Load Spikes 304

Observability and Failure Detection 304

Incident Response and Real-World Failures.................................305

Design Learnings...306

Summary 306

Lessons Learned from Post-Mortems..307

Purpose and Anatomy of a Post-Mortem 307

Incident #1: Azure Storage Key Rotation Breaks Downstream Access 308

Incident #2: Feature Flag Misfire Causes Partial Outage...............309

Incident #3: Intermittent DNS Resolution Failures in AKS 310

Cultural Learnings 311

Technical Meta-Lessons 312

Implementing a Post-Mortem Practice 312

Summary 313

Chapter 11: Future-Proofing Resilient Systems 314

Leveraging AI and ML for Predictive Resilience 314

The Shift from Reactive to Predictive 314

Key Capabilities of Predictive Resilience...315

Azure Services for Predictive Resilience 315

Building a Predictive Resilience Pipeline...317

Practical Example 318

Challenges and Considerations 318

Best Practices 319

Summary 320

Chaos Engineering on Azure 320

Why Chaos Engineering? 320

Principles of Chaos Engineering 320

Chaos Engineering Scenarios on Azure 321

Tooling for Chaos Engineering on Azure..322

Building a Chaos Engineering Practice...324

Example Use Case: API Dependency Outage 325

Measuring the Impact of Chaos Engineering..326

Best Practices Summary..326

Summary 327

Evolving with Azure's Roadmap and New Services 327

Why Architectural Evolution Matters...327

Categories of Azure Change..328

Principles for Evolution-Ready Architecture 329

Monitoring for Azure Platform Drift 331

Migration and Upgrade Strategies 331

Case Study: Transitioning to App Service Premium V3 332

Team and Process Alignment 332

Summary 333

Sustainability and Cost Optimization in Design...333

Why Sustainability and Cost Optimization Matter for Resilience 333

Foundational Principles 334

Azure Tools for Cost Optimization and Sustainability 338

Governance for Cost and Sustainability 339

Real-World Example 339

Design Patterns for Resilient Efficiency..340

Summary 341

Chapter 12: Appendices 342

Glossary of Terms 342

A 342

B 342

C 343

D 343

E 343

F...344

G 344

H 344

I..345

K 345

L..345

M 345

N 346

O 346

P 346

Q 347

R 347

S 347

T..348

U 348

V 348

W 348

Z..348

Resources for Further Learning 349

1. Official Microsoft Documentation 349

2. Microsoft Learn Modules 350

3. Books and Publications 350

4. Community and Expert Blogs 351

5. GitHub Repositories and Open Source Projects 351

6. Conference Talks, Videos, and Podcasts...352

7. Learning Platforms 352

8. Certifications...353

9. Newsletters and Community Updates 353

Summary 353

Sample Projects and Code Snippets...354

Sample Project 1: Resilient API with Azure API Management and Azure Functions
....354

Sample Project 2: Event-Driven Resilience with Azure Service Bus.....................356

Sample Project 3: Geo-Redundant Web App with Traffic Manager 358

Sample Project 4: Durable Functions for Workflow Resilience 359

Sample Project 5: Resilience Observability with Azure Monitor and Workbooks360

Sample Project 6: Infrastructure as Code (IaC) for Resilience............................361

Summary 362

API Reference Guide..362

Azure Resource Manager (ARM) API Basics 362

1. Azure App Service 363

2. Azure Functions..364

3. Azure Service Bus 365

4. Azure Cosmos DB 366

5. Azure Monitor (Log Analytics)...367

6. Azure Storage 368

7. Azure Bicep Example for Resilient Deployment...................................370

Summary 371

Frequently Asked Questions..371

Q1: What is the difference between high availability and resilience?.................371

Q2: How can I simulate a regional outage in Azure for testing?.........................371

Q3: What are best practices for implementing retries without causing cascading
failures?...372

Q4: How do I manage secrets securely and resiliently in Azure? 373

Q5: What is the role of Azure Availability Zones in resilience design? 373

Q6: When should I use active-active vs. active-passive architecture? 373

Q7: How can I ensure database resilience in Azure?...374

Q8: What's the difference between Azure Front Door and Azure Traffic Manager?
....374

Q9: What is the difference between Zone Redundant and Geo-Redundant
services? 375

Q10: How do I audit resilience configurations in my Azure subscription? 375

Summary 376

Chapter 1: Introduction to Resilient Architecture on Azure

Understanding Resilience in Modern Applications

Resilience, in the context of modern cloud-native applications, is the system's ability to recover from and adapt to failures in order to maintain continuous business operations. It is not merely about avoiding failure, but about designing systems that respond gracefully when failures occur. In a world where downtime equates to lost revenue, degraded user experience, or even legal risk, resilience must be considered a first-class architectural concern.

The Nature of Failure

Failures are inevitable. They may come from hardware faults, software bugs, network outages, configuration errors, or even third-party service unavailability. Consider some of the following real-world examples:

- A database cluster temporarily unavailable due to regional issues.
- An API throttled due to unexpected traffic surge.
- A microservice failing silently due to a memory leak.

In a monolithic era, a single point of failure often led to system-wide outages. In today's distributed systems, the complexity multiplies. Each dependency—internal or external—presents a unique risk. Thus, we shift from *if* failures occur to *when* they occur, and how we *respond*.

What Is Resilience?

Resilience is the umbrella term encompassing high availability, fault tolerance, graceful degradation, recoverability, and more. Key attributes of a resilient system include:

- **Redundancy**: Duplication of critical components.
- **Failover**: Automatic transition to backup systems.
- **Monitoring & Alerting**: Continuous assessment of system health.
- **Degradation**: Offering partial functionality during failures.
- **Self-Healing**: Recovery without human intervention.

Each of these attributes should be intentionally engineered, tested, and maintained.

The Azure Advantage

Azure provides a wide array of services and constructs that support resilient architecture:

- **Availability Zones and Regions**: Geographically isolated locations for redundancy.

- **Azure Front Door and Traffic Manager**: Intelligent routing for global failover.

- **Azure Functions and Durable Functions**: Stateless and stateful serverless computing   with   built-in   retries.

- **Azure Cosmos DB**: Multi-region writes and eventual consistency for geo-resilience.

- **Azure Monitor and Application Insights**: Observability tools for proactive alerting and   tracing.

- **Azure   Site   Recovery**:   Disaster   recovery   orchestration.

These capabilities allow architects and engineers to focus on application logic while Azure handles the infrastructure complexity.

Core Concepts: Reliability vs Resilience

It's important to distinguish between **reliability** and **resilience**. Reliability is the *probability of success*, whereas resilience is the *ability to recover from failure*. A highly reliable system may not be resilient if it cannot recover when something goes wrong.

For example:

Concept	Description	Example
Reliability	System behaves as expected under normal conditions	99.99% uptime
Resilienc e	System recovers gracefully from unexpected failures	Retry logic after transient error

Both must be balanced. Overengineering reliability can result in brittle systems that fail catastrophically when the unexpected occurs.

Resilience by Design

Resilience must be *designed in*, not *bolted on*. This involves several design strategies:

1. **Defensive Coding**: Guard clauses, fallback logic, and exception handling.

2. **Dependency Isolation**: Ensuring one service's failure doesn't cascade.

3. **Timeouts and Retries**: Preventing indefinite waits and transient issue amplification.

4. **Monitoring and Circuit Breakers**: Detecting and halting problematic patterns.

5. **Graceful Degradation**: Providing partial services when full service isn't possible.

Here's a sample retry implementation in C# using Polly:

```csharp
var retryPolicy = Policy
    .Handle<HttpRequestException>()
    .WaitAndRetry(
        retryCount: 3,
        sleepDurationProvider:          attempt          =>
TimeSpan.FromSeconds(Math.Pow(2, attempt)),
        onRetry: (exception, duration, context) =>
        {
            Console.WriteLine($"Retrying          due          to:
{exception.Message}");
        });

await retryPolicy.ExecuteAsync(async () =>
{
    var              response              =              await
httpClient.GetAsync("https://api.contoso.com/data");
    response.EnsureSuccessStatusCode();
});
```

This approach gracefully handles transient failures and implements exponential backoff.

Mindset Shift: Embracing Failure

The shift to resilient systems is as much cultural as it is technical. Teams must:

- Treat   failure   as   normal,   not   exceptional.

- Implement   chaos   engineering   to   proactively   identify   weaknesses.

- Prioritize   observability   and   feedback   loops.

- Automate   remediation   and   reduce   mean   time   to   recovery   (MTTR).

Netflix pioneered this mindset with the Chaos Monkey tool, which randomly disables production systems to test resilience. Azure supports similar principles with tools like Azure Chaos Studio, helping organizations inject faults and validate their preparedness.

When to Start Thinking About Resilience

The answer is *now*. Resilience planning should begin at the earliest stages of system design. Retrofitting resilience is costly, error-prone, and often incomplete. Resilience touches:

- **Infrastructure**: Redundancy, failover, recovery.

- **Application**: Retry logic, fallback handling, observability.

- **Process**: Incident response, root cause analysis, documentation.

Summary

Resilience is a foundational concern for modern cloud-native systems. It affects how systems are designed, built, and operated. Azure offers a rich toolset to help achieve resilience, but the responsibility lies with you—the architect, the engineer, the team—to apply principles thoughtfully and proactively.

In the chapters ahead, we will break down the concrete patterns, platform features, and implementation details that enable you to design for resilience, no matter the complexity or scale of your system.

The Azure Ecosystem and Its Resilience Capabilities

Microsoft Azure provides a comprehensive ecosystem of services designed with resilience, scalability, and global availability in mind. From compute to networking, storage to security, and monitoring to automation, each layer of Azure offers mechanisms and best practices that support the creation of resilient applications. This section explores how Azure's ecosystem enables resilience at every layer of your architecture, and how to effectively utilize these services and features to build systems that gracefully recover from failure.

Global Infrastructure Foundation

At the heart of Azure's resilience capabilities is its **global infrastructure**, comprising:

- **Regions**: Geographically isolated locations containing one or more datacenters.

- **Availability Zones**: Physically separate datacenters within a region, each with independent power, cooling, and networking.

- **Geographies**: Groups of regions that comply with specific data residency and sovereignty requirements.

By architecting across availability zones and regions, applications can tolerate localized failures without downtime. Azure offers native support for zone-redundant and geo-redundant services, making high availability achievable with minimal configuration.

For example, when deploying a resource such as Azure SQL Database, you can enable **zone redundancy** to ensure the service is automatically replicated across multiple availability zones. Similarly, services like Azure Storage can be configured with **GZRS** (Geo-Zone-Redundant Storage) to achieve both intra-region and inter-region replication.

Compute Services and Resilience

Azure provides various compute models, each with resilience features built in or configurable:

Azure App Service

Azure App Service abstracts infrastructure management and provides built-in load balancing, auto-scaling, and regional failover support. Applications hosted on App Service can be deployed across multiple regions using **Traffic Manager** or **Front Door** to route traffic intelligently.

Key features:

- Deployment slots for safe rollouts.

- Auto-heal based on custom rules (e.g., high CPU, HTTP 500 errors).

- Integration with App Insights for diagnostics and monitoring.

Azure Kubernetes Service (AKS)

AKS enables containerized workloads with native Kubernetes orchestration. It offers:

- Node auto-repair and self-healing.

- Horizontal Pod Autoscaling (HPA).

- Multi-zone clusters for high availability.

A sample PodDisruptionBudget in AKS ensures controlled disruptions:

```
apiVersion: policy/v1
kind: PodDisruptionBudget
metadata:
  name: api-pdb
spec:
  minAvailable: 3
```

```
selector:
  matchLabels:
    app: api-service
```

This prevents Azure or user actions from disrupting too many pods simultaneously, protecting uptime.

Azure Functions

For serverless applications, Azure Functions provides event-driven execution with built-in retry policies, isolation per invocation, and support for durable workflows with **Durable Functions**.

```
[FunctionName("RetryActivity")]
public static async Task<string> RunActivity(
    [ActivityTrigger] string name,
    ILogger log)
{
    // Activity function logic here
    return $"Hello {name}!";
}
```

Resilience is further supported through Durable Task Framework's orchestration state management and retry behaviors.

Storage and Data Services

Data is the backbone of most applications, and Azure ensures its durability, availability, and recoverability through robust services:

Azure Storage

Offers multiple redundancy options:

- **LRS**   (Locally   Redundant   Storage)

- **ZRS**   (Zone-Redundant   Storage)

- **GRS**   (Geo-Redundant   Storage)

- **GZRS**   (Geo-Zone-Redundant   Storage)

These options provide trade-offs between cost and resilience. You can also configure **soft delete** for blobs, files, and containers to guard against accidental deletion.

Azure SQL Database

Azure SQL supports **active geo-replication**, **auto-failover groups**, and **point-in-time restore**. These features ensure high availability and disaster recovery capabilities.

Example: Creating a failover group for SQL databases:

```
-- Create failover group
CREATE FAILOVER GROUP myfg
WITH
  (
    PARTNER = 'secondaryserver.database.windows.net',
    DATABASES = ('mydb1', 'mydb2'),
    AUTOMATIC_FAILOVER = ON
  );
```

This enables automatic failover to a secondary region, reducing downtime.

Azure Cosmos DB

Cosmos DB is globally distributed by design. Features include:

- Multi-region writes for high availability.
- Consistency levels (e.g., Eventual, Bounded Staleness).
- SLA-backed availability, latency, throughput, and consistency.

Configuring automatic failover:

```
{
  "failoverPolicies": [
    {
      "regionName": "East US",
      "failoverPriority": 0
    },
    {
      "regionName": "West Europe",
      "failoverPriority": 1
    }
  ]
}
```

This ensures that your application remains operational even if the primary region becomes unavailable.

Networking and Traffic Management

A resilient system must route traffic effectively under failure scenarios. Azure offers several services to achieve this:

Azure Traffic Manager

DNS-based traffic load balancer that routes requests based on:

- Priority (failover)

- Performance (latency-based)

- Geographic rules

Use case: Route primary traffic to East US and failover to West Europe when the primary endpoint is unhealthy.

Azure Front Door

Layer 7 global application delivery network with:

- SSL offloading

- Web Application Firewall (WAF)

- Health probes and automatic failover

- Caching and acceleration

Azure Front Door is ideal for global web applications requiring low latency and intelligent routing.

Azure Load Balancer

Operates at Layer 4 (TCP/UDP) and supports:

- Inbound NAT rules

- Health probes

- Outbound connectivity

Combined with **Availability Sets** or **Virtual Machine Scale Sets (VMSS)**, it provides a resilient front for backend services.

Observability and Automation

Monitoring and automation are essential for detecting, diagnosing, and recovering from failures.

Azure Monitor

Centralized platform for:

- Metrics   collection

- Log   aggregation

- Alerts   and   dashboards

You can configure alerts for custom thresholds and automatically trigger remediation using **Action Groups** or **Azure Logic Apps**.

Application Insights

Provides deep telemetry for applications including:

- Request/response   tracking

- Exception   logging

- Dependency   performance

Configure **Availability Tests** to monitor endpoint uptime and latency from various regions.

Azure Automation

Automates tasks like:

- VM   failover

- Database   failover

- Patching   and   maintenance

PowerShell runbooks can orchestrate complex recovery workflows based on alert triggers.

```
workflow Recover-VM {
  param (
    [string]$VMName
  )

  Start-AzureVM -ServiceName "myService" -Name $VMName
```

```
}
```

This script could be invoked upon VM failure alerts to restore availability.

Identity and Secrets Resilience

Even identity systems must be resilient. Azure Active Directory (Azure AD) provides:

- **Conditional Access** to handle degraded states.
- **Multi-Region Authentication** for SSO services.
- **Privileged Identity Management (PIM)** to control access during incidents.

Azure Key Vault stores secrets, certificates, and keys, with features such as:

- Soft delete and purge protection
- Access policies and role-based access control (RBAC)
- Integration with managed identities for secure access

Governance and Compliance

Governance ensures that resilience practices are followed at scale:

- **Azure Policy**: Enforces standards (e.g., requiring GRS on storage accounts).
- **Azure Blueprints**: Deploys compliant environments consistently.
- **Resource Locks**: Prevents accidental deletion of critical infrastructure.

For example, to prevent deletion of a production database:

```
az lock create --name ProtectSQL --lock-type CanNotDelete --resource-
group      ProdRG      --resource      mydb      --resource-type
"Microsoft.Sql/servers/databases"
```

Service-Level Agreements (SLAs)

Azure publishes SLAs for all major services. Understanding and designing for them is critical to achieving end-to-end resilience. For example:

- Azure App Service: 99.95% (multi-instance)

- Azure SQL Database: 99.99%

- Azure Cosmos DB: 99.999% for reads

To achieve a composite SLA, you must consider the weakest link and design redundancy across dependencies.

Conclusion

The Azure ecosystem offers a powerful, flexible, and integrated set of tools to build resilient systems at every layer—from compute and data to identity and observability. Resilience is not a feature of a single service but the result of orchestrating multiple services with fault-tolerant design patterns and best practices.

By fully understanding Azure's capabilities and strategically applying them, you can architect systems that meet the demands of modern users and businesses—systems that not only recover from failures but continue to deliver value under pressure. The next step is to understand the foundational patterns that enable these capabilities, which we'll cover in the next chapter.

Core Principles of Cloud-Native Design

Designing for the cloud is fundamentally different from traditional on-premises or even basic hosted environments. To build resilient, scalable, and maintainable systems in Azure, we must embrace a new mindset—one rooted in **cloud-native principles**. These principles provide a blueprint for creating applications that fully leverage the elasticity, distribution, and automation capabilities of the cloud. This section explores the core design tenets that guide resilient architectures on Azure.

Principle 1: Embrace Failure as a First-Class Concern

Traditional design often treats failure as an exception; cloud-native design assumes it will happen. Azure services provide built-in capabilities like retries, failovers, and zone redundancy, but application logic must still be built to handle unexpected states.

Resilience begins with designing each component to degrade gracefully or recover automatically. Consider these practices:

- Use **timeouts** and **retry policies** for all remote calls.

- Employ **circuit breakers** to avoid cascading failures.

- Design for **partial availability**, where a subsystem can operate in a degraded mode if another is offline.

- Utilize **queue-based load leveling** to prevent load spikes from overwhelming downstream systems.

An example using Polly for transient fault handling in .NET:

```
var policy = Policy
    .Handle<HttpRequestException>()
    .Or<TaskCanceledException>()
    .CircuitBreaker(handledEventsAllowedBeforeBreaking:        5,
durationOfBreak: TimeSpan.FromSeconds(30));
```

Azure complements this with built-in resilience in services like Azure SQL Database's auto-failover groups or Azure Functions' retry policies.

Principle 2: Design for Horizontal Scalability

Scalability is a cornerstone of resilience. Applications must be able to **scale out**, not just **up**, in response to load and failure events. In the cloud, you do not fix issues by upgrading a bigger server—you do it by deploying more instances.

Techniques to support horizontal scaling:

- Stateless compute tiers (e.g., App Service, Functions, AKS).

- Shared-nothing architecture: avoid shared memory or disk.

- Auto-scaling rules based on performance metrics.

- Distributed caches (e.g., Azure Cache for Redis) to decouple session data from compute.

In AKS, you can define Horizontal Pod Autoscalers (HPA) to scale pods based on CPU or custom metrics:

```
apiVersion: autoscaling/v2
kind: HorizontalPodAutoscaler
metadata:
  name: web-api-hpa  ˙
spec:
  scaleTargetRef:
    apiVersion: apps/v1
    kind: Deployment
    name: web-api
  minReplicas: 2
```

```
maxReplicas: 10
metrics:
- type: Resource
  resource:
    name: cpu
    target:
      type: Utilization
      averageUtilization: 70
```

Principle 3: Build with Disposable and Replaceable Components

Cloud-native systems treat infrastructure as ephemeral. VMs, containers, and even services may be terminated and recreated at any time. Your system must treat all infrastructure as **immutable** and **replaceable**.

Best practices include:

- **Immutable infrastructure** with deployment pipelines (e.g., Bicep, ARM templates, Terraform).

- Use **infrastructure as code (IaC)** to ensure environments are consistent and reproducible.

- Avoid tight coupling between services or to specific instances.

- Replace servers, don't patch them.

Here's an example Azure Bicep snippet for deploying an App Service:

```
resource webApp 'Microsoft.Web/sites@2021-02-01' = {
  name: 'myResilientApp'
  location: resourceGroup().location
  properties: {
    serverFarmId: appServicePlan.id
  }
}
```

Using such templates ensures that deployment environments can be destroyed and recreated reliably.

Principle 4: Automate Everything

Resilience isn't just about design—it's about operations. Automation reduces human error and enables rapid, repeatable responses to failure conditions.

Automate:

- **Deployments** using CI/CD pipelines (e.g., GitHub Actions, Azure DevOps).

- **Scaling rules**, triggered by metrics or schedules.

- **Incident response** through runbooks and alerts.

- **Configuration and secrets management** with Azure Key Vault and Azure App Configuration.

Example GitHub Actions CI/CD snippet for deploying to Azure Web App:

```
jobs:
  deploy:
    runs-on: ubuntu-latest
    steps:
      - uses: actions/checkout@v2
      - uses: azure/webapps-deploy@v2
        with:
          app-name: 'myResilientApp'
          publish-profile: ${{ secrets.AZURE_WEBAPP_PUBLISH_PROFILE
}}
          package: '.'
```

With full automation, recovery from failure becomes a matter of triggering the right pipeline or responding to metrics with preconfigured actions.

Principle 5: Externalize State and Configuration

To make applications stateless and scalable, state must be stored externally. Internal session storage or in-memory data structures tied to a specific instance become a point of failure. Azure provides multiple options:

- **Azure Cache for Redis** for low-latency session state.

- **Azure Blob Storage**, **Azure SQL**, or **Cosmos DB** for durable data.

- **Azure App Configuration** for centralized config values.

- **Azure Key Vault** for secrets, keys, and certificates.

By externalizing configuration and state, you ensure that any application instance can be replaced without loss of function.

Example of reading config from Azure App Configuration in .NET:

```
var builder = new ConfigurationBuilder();
builder.AddAzureAppConfiguration(options =>
{

options.Connect("Endpoint=https://myconfig.azconfig.io;Id=xyz;Secret
=abc")
          .Select("App:*");
});
```

This allows you to roll out configuration changes without redeploying or restarting services.

Principle 6: Observability as a Feature

Monitoring is not an afterthought in cloud-native design—it's an essential feature. Applications must be **observable**, not just monitored. This means having visibility into not just *what happened*, but *why*.

Pillars of observability:

- **Metrics**: CPU, memory, request count, latency.

- **Logs**: Structured logs with correlation IDs.

- **Traces**: Distributed tracing across microservices.

- **Dashboards and Alerts**: Real-time visibility and actionable alerts.

Azure supports all these via Azure Monitor, Application Insights, and Log Analytics.

In a distributed microservices app, enabling telemetry correlation is key:

```
TelemetryClient telemetry = new TelemetryClient();
telemetry.Context.Operation.Id = Activity.Current?.RootId;
telemetry.Context.Operation.ParentId = Activity.Current?.Id;
telemetry.TrackEvent("UserSignupStarted");
```

Without observability, recovery from failure becomes guesswork, not engineering.

Principle 7: Favor Event-Driven and Asynchronous Architectures

Synchronous architectures tightly couple services, reducing resilience. If one service is slow or unavailable, others are blocked. Event-driven architectures introduce decoupling, improving resilience and scalability.

Azure-native event services include:

- **Azure Service Bus** for enterprise-grade messaging.
- **Azure Event Grid** for reactive programming.
- **Azure Event Hubs** for streaming and analytics.

Benefits of asynchronous design:

- Services operate independently.
- Failures are isolated.
- Load can be buffered using queues.
- Systems become more elastic and scalable.

For example, using Azure Service Bus with retries:

```
QueueClient client = new QueueClient(connectionString, queueName);
client.RegisterMessageHandler(
    async (message, token) =>
    {
        await ProcessMessageAsync(message);
        await
client.CompleteAsync(message.SystemProperties.LockToken);
    },
    new MessageHandlerOptions(args => Task.CompletedTask)
    {
        MaxConcurrentCalls = 5,
        AutoComplete = false
    });
```

In the event of a failure, the message can be retried or moved to a **dead-letter queue**, enabling post-mortem analysis or manual intervention.

Principle 8: Secure by Default

Resilience without security is incomplete. A breach or leaked secret can be as damaging as a failure. Cloud-native systems must:

- Use **managed identities** for authentication.
- Enforce **least privilege access** via RBAC and PIM.
- Protect configuration with **Key Vault**.
- Enforce **Zero Trust principles**.

Azure provides:

- Azure AD for federated authentication.
- Key Vault with audit logs and access policies.
- Azure Defender for threat detection.

For instance, assigning a managed identity to access Azure SQL securely:

```
-- Assign user in SQL using the managed identity
CREATE USER [myAppIdentity] FROM EXTERNAL PROVIDER;
ALTER ROLE db_datareader ADD MEMBER [myAppIdentity];
```

This removes the need for storing credentials in code or config.

Conclusion

Cloud-native design is about more than just moving applications to Azure—it's about transforming how you design, build, deploy, and operate systems. By adopting these core principles, you empower your teams to build applications that are inherently resilient, scalable, observable, and secure.

Each principle reinforces the others, and their combined effect creates architectures capable of withstanding failure, adapting to change, and delivering consistent value. Azure offers the tools, but it is up to you to wield them with strategy and discipline.

In the next section, we'll explore why these principles matter by examining real-world failure scenarios and how cloud-native resilience changes the outcome.

Why Resilience Matters: Real-World Failure Scenarios

Resilience in modern software systems is no longer optional—it is a foundational requirement. When downtime equals lost revenue, eroded trust, or compromised safety, designing for failure becomes a core business concern. This section illustrates the importance of resilience by walking through real-world failure scenarios, analyzing what went wrong, and exploring how resilient architecture—especially in Azure—could have mitigated or prevented these incidents. By learning from these examples, architects and developers can internalize the critical role of resilience in modern application design.

Scenario 1: The E-Commerce Holiday Crash

Background:
A major retail company prepared for a Black Friday sale. The application stack consisted of a monolithic API backend hosted on a single App Service instance and an Azure SQL Database on the standard tier. Anticipating higher traffic, they doubled their App Service plan size but did not test under load.

Failure:
Within the first 10 minutes of the sale, the site crashed. The monolith couldn't handle the burst of concurrent users, and the database CPU hit 100%, locking transactions. This caused cascading timeouts across services. The retry logic lacked jitter, causing thundering herds of requests during recovery attempts.

Root Causes:

- No auto-scaling configuration.

- Database bottleneck without read replicas.

- Ineffective retry logic with no backoff strategy.

- No real-time observability or alerts.

Resilient Architecture Response:

1. **Horizontal scaling:** The application should have been decomposed into microservices behind Azure API Management, each auto-scalable with Azure Kubernetes Service (AKS) or Azure App Service scale-out rules.

2. **Read replicas:** Azure SQL Database's Hyperscale tier or Cosmos DB with multi-region reads could reduce read pressure.

3. **Retry policies:** Implement exponential backoff and jitter using libraries like Polly:

```
.WaitAndRetry(
  retryCount: 5,
  sleepDurationProvider: retryAttempt =>
    TimeSpan.FromSeconds(Math.Pow(2, retryAttempt)) +
    TimeSpan.FromMilliseconds(new Random().Next(0, 1000))
```

```
);
```

4. ☐
   Observability: Azure Monitor and Application Insights with alerts would have flagged the CPU spike early.

5. **Caching:** Azure Cache for Redis could offload frequent requests from the database.

Scenario 2: The Global SaaS Outage

Background:
A Software-as-a-Service (SaaS) company hosted its global app in a single Azure region (East US). The application was multi-tenant but lacked geographic failover. One Friday evening, a power fault in the East US data center brought down the region for several hours.

Failure:
All customers experienced full downtime. The company scrambled to reroute traffic but had no automation in place. Deployments to West Europe had never been tested. Recovery took 8 hours.

Root Causes:

- Regional dependency without failover.

- No geo-redundancy for databases or storage.

- Manual disaster recovery plan.

- DNS time-to-live (TTL) set to 24 hours.

Resilient Architecture Response:

1. **Active-passive architecture:** Deploy in both East US and West Europe using Azure Traffic Manager in priority mode:

```
☐{
  "profileStatus": "Enabled",
  "routingMethod": "Priority",
  "endpoints": [
    {"name": "eastUS", "priority": 1},
    {"name": "westEurope", "priority": 2}
  ]
}
```

2. ☐
   Geo-redundant data: Azure Cosmos DB with multi-region writes and automatic failover, or Azure SQL Database with auto-failover groups.

3. **Infrastructure as code:** Use Bicep or ARM templates to replicate the environment across regions automatically.

4. **Disaster Recovery (DR) testing:** Scheduled failover simulations with Azure Chaos Studio or manual exercises.

5. **DNS configuration:** Lower TTL for DNS records to allow rapid propagation during rerouting.

Scenario 3: Microservice Chain Reaction

Background:
An IoT company built a microservices-based telemetry ingestion system using Azure Kubernetes Service (AKS). One microservice parsed device data and posted to another for storage. Services communicated synchronously using REST APIs.

Failure:
A malformed data payload caused the parser service to throw unhandled exceptions, crashing the pod. Kubernetes restarted it, but the service was not isolated—dependent services waited indefinitely on responses. The API gateway overloaded and eventually crashed.

Root Causes:

- Synchronous inter-service communication with tight coupling.

- No circuit breakers or fallback logic.

- No timeout configuration in HTTP clients.

- Health checks marked the app as healthy during crash loops.

Resilient Architecture Response:

1. **Asynchronous communication:** Replace REST with Azure Service Bus or Event Grid. Publish-subscribe model avoids service chaining.

2. **Circuit breakers:** Prevent one service's failure from cascading:

```
Policy
 .Handle<Exception>()
 .CircuitBreaker(3, TimeSpan.FromSeconds(30));
```

3. ☐
    Timeouts: Always define client-side HTTP timeouts (e.g., 5 seconds).

4. **Liveness and readiness probes:** Customize AKS probes to detect crash loops:

```
☐livenessProbe:
  httpGet:
    path: /healthz
    port: 8080
  failureThreshold: 3
  periodSeconds: 10
```

5. ☐
    Queue-based decoupling: Azure Event Hubs or Service Bus enables retry of failed messages without blocking services.

Scenario 4: Secrets and Configuration Leak

Background:
A developer accidentally committed a configuration file containing database credentials and an API key into a public GitHub repository. Within minutes, bots had scanned and used the keys to exfiltrate data and send spam through the system.

Failure:
Sensitive data was exposed. Regulatory fines were levied for data leakage. Business reputation took a hit.

Root Causes:

- Hardcoded secrets in source code.

- No secrets scanning in CI pipelines.

- No Key Vault integration.

- Overly permissive roles for the leaked credentials.

Resilient Architecture Response:

1. **Secrets management:** Store credentials in **Azure Key Vault** with RBAC:

```
☐az keyvault secret set --vault-name MyKeyVault --name "DbPassword"
--value "P@ssw0rd!"
```

2. ☐
   Managed identities: Use system-assigned identities to authenticate services securely.

3. **Credential scanning:** Implement GitHub Actions to scan commits:

```
☐- uses: github/codeql-action/init@v2
 - uses: github/codeql-action/analyze@v2
```

4. ☐
   Key rotation and expiration: Set short-lived secrets with auto-rotation policies.

5. **Audit logs:** Enable Azure Monitor Diagnostic Settings on Key Vault for audit trails.

Scenario 5: Misconfigured Infrastructure as Code

Background:
An infrastructure team used ARM templates to deploy production infrastructure. A new contributor submitted a pull request that modified a network security group (NSG) rule, unintentionally exposing port 22 to the world. This was merged and deployed without peer review.

Failure:
Within hours, malicious bots found the open SSH port, brute-forced a weak password, and deployed crypto-mining software on the VM. Performance degraded and costs spiked.

Root Causes:

- No code review for IaC.
- NSG misconfiguration.
- Lack of just-in-time (JIT) VM access.
- Weak authentication (password over SSH).

Resilient Architecture Response:

1. **IaC governance:** Enforce pull request reviews and policy checks using Azure Policy and GitHub branch protection.

2. **JIT access:** Enable through **Azure Defender for Servers** to restrict SSH/RDP access.

3. **Authentication hardening:** Require SSH key-based login only.

4. **Security scanning:** Use tools like `tflint` or `checkov` for IaC validation.

5. **Monitoring alerts:** Trigger alerts on unusual outbound traffic or CPU usage.

Lessons Learned from Failures

Across these scenarios, we observe recurring themes:

- **Over-reliance on single regions or components.**
- **Lack of automation for recovery.**
- **Synchronous designs causing cascading failures.**
- **Improper handling of configuration and secrets.**
- **Inadequate observability leading to slow diagnosis.**

Resilience is not achieved by a single decision—it's the culmination of dozens of small, intentional practices applied consistently across design, development, deployment, and operations.

Building a Culture of Resilience

To make resilience sustainable, organizations must embed it into their culture:

- Conduct **post-mortems** for every incident, focusing on improvement—not blame.
- Schedule **chaos experiments** using Azure Chaos Studio to validate assumptions.
- Include resilience scenarios in every **design review**.
- Train teams in **site reliability engineering (SRE)** principles.
- Define and monitor **SLOs and SLIs** that align with business impact.

A strong engineering culture recognizes that failures are inevitable, but downtime is not. When resilience becomes a shared goal across development, operations, and security, systems grow stronger over time.

Conclusion

Resilience matters because failure is the default, not the exception, in distributed systems. The real-world scenarios presented in this section reveal the high stakes of unplanned outages and the tangible benefits of resilient architecture. By learning from these failures and applying

Azure-native solutions—such as auto-scaling, geo-redundancy, asynchronous messaging, secrets management, and automated recovery—you can build systems that continue to deliver, even when the unexpected happens.

As we continue into the next chapter, we will explore the foundational architectural patterns that support resilient design, and how to implement them effectively within the Azure ecosystem.

Chapter 2: Foundational Patterns for Resilient Systems

Retry and Circuit Breaker Patterns

The foundation of resilient architecture lies in understanding and correctly implementing fundamental fault-handling patterns. Two of the most critical among these are the **Retry Pattern** and the **Circuit Breaker Pattern**. These patterns help applications tolerate transient failures and prevent cascading outages in distributed systems—scenarios increasingly common in cloud-native architectures.

In this section, we will explore both patterns in detail, outline their use cases, pitfalls, and how to implement them effectively using Azure-native services and code examples in common languages like C# and Python.

The Nature of Transient Failures

Before diving into patterns, it's essential to understand **transient failures**. These are temporary failures that resolve themselves after a short time. Examples include:

- Temporary loss of network connectivity.

- A service being momentarily overwhelmed by traffic.

- A database experiencing a lock timeout.

Such failures don't require escalated remediation—they require retry logic.

However, blindly retrying can exacerbate issues. That's where structured patterns like Retry and Circuit Breaker come into play.

The Retry Pattern

Definition:
The Retry Pattern enables an application to handle transient faults by retrying an operation that has previously failed, on the assumption that the fault is temporary.

When to Use

- Calling external services (e.g., REST APIs, databases).

- Interacting with services like Azure Storage, Cosmos DB, or Service Bus.

- Handling HTTP 429 (Too Many Requests), 503 (Service Unavailable), or timeout errors.

Key Considerations

1. **Retry Count:** How many times to retry before giving up.

2. **Backoff Strategy:** Linear, exponential, or exponential with jitter.

3. **Idempotency:** Ensure retries don't result in unintended side effects.

4. **Error Classification:** Retry only on transient errors, not logic errors (e.g., 400 Bad Request).

Retry Example with Exponential Backoff and Jitter (C# using Polly)

```csharp
var retryPolicy = Policy
    .Handle<HttpRequestException>()
    .Or<TaskCanceledException>()
    .WaitAndRetry(
        retryCount: 5,
        sleepDurationProvider: retryAttempt =>
            TimeSpan.FromSeconds(Math.Pow(2, retryAttempt)) +
            TimeSpan.FromMilliseconds(new Random().Next(0, 1000)),
        onRetry: (exception, timeSpan, retryCount, context) =>
        {
            Console.WriteLine($"Retry        {retryCount}        after
{timeSpan.TotalSeconds}s due to {exception.Message}");
        });

await retryPolicy.ExecuteAsync(async () =>
{
    var              response              =              await
httpClient.GetAsync("https://api.example.com/data");
    response.EnsureSuccessStatusCode();
});
```

Retry in Azure SDKs

Azure SDKs (e.g., for Cosmos DB, Storage) have built-in retry capabilities. You can configure retry options like so:

```csharp
var options = new CosmosClientOptions
```

```
{
    ConnectionMode = ConnectionMode.Gateway,
    MaxRetryAttemptsOnRateLimitedRequests = 5,
    MaxRetryWaitTimeOnRateLimitedRequests = TimeSpan.FromSeconds(10)
};
```

Pitfalls

- **Retry Storms:** Multiple clients retrying simultaneously can create a thundering herd.

- **Retrying Non-Transient Errors:** Blindly retrying on 404 or 500 can be wasteful or harmful.

- **Resource Leaks:** Not properly disposing objects or leaving sockets open.

The Circuit Breaker Pattern

Definition:
The Circuit Breaker Pattern prevents an application from performing an operation that's likely to fail, allowing it to recover from a faulty state or to prevent resource exhaustion.

Inspired by electrical circuits, it has three states:

1. **Closed** – Requests are allowed through.

2. **Open** – Requests fail immediately for a configured period.

3. **Half-Open** – A few requests are allowed through to test if the service has recovered.

When to Use

- To protect services from failing dependencies.

- To prevent cascading failures in microservices.

- To isolate services with poor availability.

Circuit Breaker Example (C# using Polly)
```
var circuitBreaker = Policy
    .Handle<HttpRequestException>()
    .CircuitBreaker(
        handledEventsAllowedBeforeBreaking: 3,
```

```
        durationOfBreak: TimeSpan.FromSeconds(30),
        onBreak: (exception, duration) =>
        {
            Console.WriteLine($"Circuit          opened          for
{duration.TotalSeconds}s due to {exception.Message}");
        },
        onReset: () => Console.WriteLine("Circuit closed, operations
allowed."),
        onHalfOpen:  ()  =>  Console.WriteLine("Circuit  half-open,
testing recovery.")
    );
```

When wrapped around an operation, this pattern avoids further stress on an already struggling service.

Integrating Retry and Circuit Breaker

Combining these patterns can yield the best of both worlds:

```
var resiliencePolicy = Policy.WrapAsync(retryPolicy, circuitBreaker);
```

Retry handles transient errors. Circuit Breaker ensures that persistent issues don't cause infinite retries or bring down dependent services.

Implementing Patterns in Azure Services

Azure provides features to support both retry and circuit breaker patterns at the platform level:

Azure App Service

- Built-in **Auto-Heal** feature allows you to recycle the app on specific failure conditions (e.g.,   response   time,   exceptions).

- Integration with **Application Insights** for request tracking and custom alert rules.

Azure Functions

- Automatically retries failed executions for certain triggers like Queue and Event Hub.

- You   can   configure   retry   policies   with   `FixedDelayRetry`   or `ExponentialBackoffRetry`:

```
[FunctionName("ProcessQueueMessage")]
[ExponentialBackoffRetry(maxRetryCount:     5,       minimumInterval:
"00:00:05", maximumInterval: "00:01:00")]
public  static  void  Run([QueueTrigger("myqueue")]  string  message,
ILogger log)
{
    // Function logic
}
```

Azure Service Bus

Service Bus supports **dead-lettering**, **duplicate detection**, and **retry policies** at the SDK and service levels.

- **Auto-forwarding** from dead-letter queues for secondary processing.

- **MaxDeliveryCount** setting to control how many times a message is retried.

Best Practices

1. **Instrument Everything:** Track retry counts, circuit breaker state, and failure reasons using Application Insights or Log Analytics.

2. **Design for Idempotency:** Especially important when using retries. Ensure operations like order placement, payment, or messaging can tolerate repeated invocations.

3. **Parameterize Configuration:** Keep retry counts, intervals, and failure thresholds configurable via Azure App Configuration.

4. **Test Chaos Scenarios:** Use Azure Chaos Studio to simulate service failures and validate retry/circuit breaker responses.

5. **Avoid Synchronous Chains:** Prefer asynchronous messaging to reduce retry depth and simplify failure recovery.

A Real-World Example

Scenario:
A ride-sharing company implemented a trip assignment service that relied on synchronous

calls to a driver availability API. During peak times, the service would slow down and sometimes fail entirely.

Fix Using Retry + Circuit Breaker:

- Added retry with exponential backoff on the trip service.

- Implemented a circuit breaker to fail fast if 5 consecutive requests failed.

- Enabled Service Bus queue fallback so failed trip assignments could be processed later.

Outcome:
API availability improved by 35% during peak times. Customer complaints dropped significantly.

Conclusion

The Retry and Circuit Breaker patterns are essential to building resilient cloud-native applications. These patterns act as the first line of defense against the unpredictable nature of distributed systems and external dependencies. By applying them thoughtfully, configuring them carefully, and combining them with observability and idempotency, developers can create services that degrade gracefully rather than fail catastrophically.

In the next section, we'll explore **Bulkhead Isolation**, a pattern that ensures failures in one part of the system don't bring down the entire application. This pattern works hand-in-hand with retries and circuit breakers to build layered, defensive systems in Azure.

Bulkhead Isolation

Bulkhead isolation is a key pattern in resilient system design, inspired by naval architecture where ships are compartmentalized into watertight sections (bulkheads). If one compartment is breached, others remain intact, preventing the entire vessel from sinking. Applied to software systems, **bulkhead isolation** means dividing services, components, or operations into isolated pools to prevent failures in one from cascading into others.

This section explores the rationale behind bulkheading, implementation techniques, and how Azure supports it across compute, data, and messaging services. It also covers common pitfalls and how to monitor and test isolated systems effectively.

Why Bulkheads Matter

In monolithic applications or poorly segmented microservices, a failure in one component can quickly escalate. For example, a slow database query in one service might block thread pools, exhaust memory, or overuse a shared API rate limit, eventually causing the entire system to become unresponsive.

Bulkhead isolation protects overall system availability by containing the blast radius of a failure. It enables degraded service rather than total failure.

Consider the following failure scenarios:

- A payment processor's slowness affecting user profile updates.

- A chat system's outage preventing core app usage.

- Overloaded telemetry logging slowing down the core transaction processing path.

With bulkheads, these concerns can be segmented, ensuring that non-critical failures do not affect critical operations.

Dimensions of Isolation

Bulkheading can be applied at several levels:

1. **Service-level   Isolation**
   Microservices are deployed and scaled independently. One service crashing does not affect   others.

2. **Resource-level   Isolation**
   Dedicated thread pools, database connections, and circuit breakers per component.

3. **Data-level   Isolation**
   Separate databases or containers for different functions or tenants.

4. **Network-level   Isolation**
   Isolating traffic using network security groups (NSGs), application gateways, and firewalls.

5. **Tenant-level   Isolation**
   Multi-tenant systems may bulkhead tenants to prevent noisy neighbors from affecting others.

Implementing Bulkhead Isolation in Azure

Azure provides multiple layers and tools for implementing bulkhead isolation effectively.

1. Compute Resource Isolation

Azure   Kubernetes   Service   (AKS)
AKS allows you to isolate workloads at the pod, namespace, or node pool level.

- **Node   Pools**   can   separate   workloads   by   function   or   priority:

    ○ System-critical   services   →   dedicated   node   pool.

    ○ Batch   jobs   or   ML   workloads   →   low-priority   pool.

Example AKS deployment targeting a specific node pool:

```
spec:
  nodeSelector:
    agentpool: critical-services
```

- **Resource Limits** at the pod level ensure one service doesn't starve others:

```
resources:
  requests:
    cpu: "100m"
    memory: "128Mi"
  limits:
    cpu: "250m"
    memory: "256Mi"
```

This protects the cluster from runaway containers.

Azure   App   Service
Different apps can be deployed in separate **App Service Plans**, each with isolated compute. For higher fault tolerance, isolate tiers:

- Frontend   apps   →   Plan   A

- Background   workers   →   Plan   B

- Scheduled   jobs   →   Plan   C

Scaling, resource usage, and faults in one plan won't affect others.

2. Thread and Connection Isolation

For .NET or Java-based services, use separate **thread pools**, **connection pools**, or **task queues** per operation or component.

Example using thread pools in .NET:

```
Task.Run(() => ProcessOrder(), new CancellationTokenSource().Token);
Task.Run(()            =>            SendEmailNotifications(),            new
CancellationTokenSource().Token);
```

Consider setting limits using `ThreadPool.SetMinThreads` and `SetMaxThreads` for critical components to ensure prioritization.

In messaging systems like Azure Service Bus, you can isolate consumers:

- One subscription per component.

- Separate queue per message type.

3. Database and Storage Isolation

Azure SQL Database supports:

- **Elastic Pools** to isolate and cap resources.

- **Geo-replicas** for read-only offloading.

Isolate workloads by schema, user permissions, or entirely separate databases.

Azure Cosmos DB:

- Offers **containers per service**, allowing independent throughput and cost control.

```
{
  "container": "TelemetryData",
  "throughput": 1000
}
```

Different containers → different resource partitions → isolated performance.

Bulkhead Patterns in Messaging and APIs

Messaging systems provide natural boundaries for isolation.

Azure Service Bus:

- Use separate **queues** or **topics** for different bounded contexts.
- Each queue has its own throughput, dead-letter policy, and retry settings.

Azure Event Grid:

- Filter and route events based on topic.
- Allow consumers to fail without affecting other subscribers.

API Management (APIM):

Use **rate limits** and **quotas** per product or consumer group.

```
<rate-limit calls="1000" renewal-period="60" />
<quota calls="10000" renewal-period="3600" />
```

Separate backend APIs per logical domain using APIM policies and route groups.

Tenant and Domain Bulkheading

Multi-tenant systems benefit from tenant isolation:

- **Database per tenant:** Most isolated, highest cost.
- **Schema per tenant:** Isolated structure, shared compute.
- **Row-level isolation:** Shared table, filtered by tenant ID.

Use **Azure SQL Elastic Pools** to balance cost and performance. Configure DTU or vCore limits to prevent noisy tenants.

For **domain isolation**, separate logical functions (e.g., orders, inventory, billing) into bounded contexts:

- Separate codebases and deployments.

- Individual telemetry pipelines.

- Faults in one domain won't ripple across the entire system.

Monitoring and Testing Bulkheads

Without visibility, bulkheading is ineffective.

Azure Monitor and Application Insights:

- Track dependencies and correlate failures.

- Monitor resource usage per service plan, container, or node pool.

Custom Dashboards:

Build dashboards for:

- Request rates per API or queue.

- Container CPU/memory usage.

- Circuit breaker status.

Azure Chaos Studio:

Inject faults to test bulkheads:

- Simulate latency or CPU exhaustion.

- Validate that only the affected service is impacted.

Alerting:

Set thresholds to alert when one component is approaching resource limits, without waiting for downstream effects.

Common Pitfalls

1. **Over-isolation**: Leads to complexity and higher costs. Not every component needs its own database.

2. **Shared dependencies**: Isolating services that still share a single cache or DB nullifies benefits.

3. **Inconsistent configuration**: One misconfigured service can consume all shared compute.

4. **Lack of observability**: Makes it hard to detect bulkhead effectiveness.

5. **No test coverage**: Bulkheading must be validated under fault conditions.

Real-World Example

Scenario:
A fintech startup had a service that processed both critical payments and analytics reporting. The analytics engine ran periodic intensive SQL queries. During month-end reporting, payment transactions began timing out.

Bulkheading Solution:

- Separated analytics to its own Azure Function App and SQL database.

- Deployed payment APIs on an App Service Plan with auto-scale rules.

- Used APIM to throttle analytics endpoints.

- Established dedicated queues for payment and analytics messages.

Results:
Payment reliability improved by 98% during peak load. Analytics could be delayed without affecting critical services.

Conclusion

Bulkhead isolation is essential for containing failures and maintaining system responsiveness. In complex distributed systems, it's not enough to design for average behavior—one component under stress can compromise the entire system. By isolating compute, storage, network, tenants, and domains, you create a robust architecture that can absorb shocks and continue delivering value.

Azure provides the infrastructure and tooling to implement these patterns effectively, from AKS node pools to APIM policies and Cosmos DB throughput controls. With proper observability and ongoing testing, bulkheading transforms reactive failure management into proactive system resilience.

In the next section, we'll explore **Timeout and Backoff Strategies**, another critical mechanism for preventing system overload and recovering from transient issues in a controlled, graceful manner.

Timeout and Backoff Strategies

Timeouts and backoff strategies are foundational to building resilient systems, particularly in distributed environments like Azure. In a tightly coupled system, delays in one service can propagate downstream, amplifying latency, causing retries to stack up, exhausting resources, and ultimately crashing applications. Proper use of **timeouts** and **backoff strategies** ensures that systems fail quickly, recover gracefully, and avoid overwhelming critical resources.

This section examines the mechanics, configuration, and implementation of timeouts and backoff strategies across compute, network, messaging, and storage layers. It also addresses common mistakes and provides concrete patterns you can apply in Azure.

The Purpose of Timeouts

A **timeout** is a predefined duration after which a pending operation is abandoned. Without timeouts, systems can hang indefinitely, consuming threads, memory, or compute resources without ever making forward progress.

Common operations where timeouts are vital:

- HTTP or gRPC service calls.

- Database queries and transactions.

- Messaging queues and topic subscriptions.

- File or blob I/O operations.

- External service API calls (e.g., third-party payments).

When a service depends on others in real time, **timeouts are the boundary between responsiveness and collapse.**

Timeout Strategy Principles

1. **Set Explicit Timeouts:** Never rely on system defaults. Always define the timeout at the point of invocation.

2. **Use Conservative Values:** It's better to timeout early and retry or fail fast than to hold up system resources.

3. **Tailor Timeouts by Operation:** A payment confirmation might warrant a longer timeout than fetching a product description.

4. **Fail Fast Philosophy:** Rapid failure provides quicker recovery and more predictable system behavior.

5. **Instrument Timeouts:** Log every timeout event. They indicate system stress or misconfiguration.

Configuring Timeouts: Language and Azure Examples

HTTP Client in .NET

```
var httpClient = new HttpClient
{
    Timeout = TimeSpan.FromSeconds(5) // Fail after 5 seconds
};
```

HTTP Client in Python

```
response = requests.get("https://api.example.com", timeout=5)
```

SQL Query Timeout

```
SET LOCK_TIMEOUT 5000; -- 5 seconds
```

Azure Cosmos DB

```
var options = new CosmosClientOptions
{
    RequestTimeout = TimeSpan.FromSeconds(2)
};
```

Azure Service Bus

```
var receiver = client.CreateReceiver(queueName, new ServiceBusReceiverOptions
{
    PrefetchCount = 0,
    ReceiveMode = ServiceBusReceiveMode.PeekLock
```

```
});
```

```
var                message                =                await
receiver.ReceiveMessageAsync(TimeSpan.FromSeconds(3));
```

In every scenario, you're defining a window of opportunity. If the operation doesn't complete in that window, it fails fast—freeing your application to retry, fallback, or degrade gracefully.

Understanding Backoff Strategies

Backoff is a delay introduced before retrying a failed operation. Without it, retries can compound system strain, especially during high load or partial outages.

There are three primary backoff strategies:

1. **Fixed   Backoff**
   Wait a static duration (e.g., 2 seconds) between each retry.

2. **Exponential   Backoff**
   Wait time increases exponentially with each retry attempt (e.g., 1s, 2s, 4s, 8s).

3. **Exponential   Backoff   with   Jitter**
   Adds randomness to avoid thundering herds or retry storms across distributed systems.

Example: Exponential Backoff with Jitter (C# with Polly)

```
var policy = Policy
    .Handle<TimeoutException>()
    .WaitAndRetry(
        retryCount: 5,
        sleepDurationProvider: attempt =>
            TimeSpan.FromSeconds(Math.Pow(2, attempt)) +
            TimeSpan.FromMilliseconds(new Random().Next(0, 500)),
        onRetry: (exception, delay, attempt, context) =>
        {
            Console.WriteLine($"Retry          {attempt}          after
{delay.TotalMilliseconds}ms due to {exception.Message}");
        });
```

Example: Exponential Backoff with Jitter (Python)

```python
import time
import random

def retry_with_backoff(func, retries=5):
    for attempt in range(retries):
        try:
            return func()
        except Exception as e:
            wait = (2 ** attempt) + random.uniform(0, 1)
            print(f"Retrying in {wait:.2f} seconds after error: {e}")
            time.sleep(wait)
```

Azure SDK and Service Support for Backoff

Many Azure services have built-in retry and backoff logic, configurable through SDK options:

Azure Storage SDK

```csharp
var options = new BlobClientOptions
{
    Retry =
    {
        Mode = RetryMode.Exponential,
        MaxRetries = 5,
        Delay = TimeSpan.FromSeconds(1),
        MaxDelay = TimeSpan.FromSeconds(10)
    }
};
```

Azure Cosmos DB

```csharp
new CosmosClient("connection-string", new CosmosClientOptions
{
    ConnectionMode = ConnectionMode.Direct,
    MaxRetryAttemptsOnRateLimitedRequests = 5,
    MaxRetryWaitTimeOnRateLimitedRequests = TimeSpan.FromSeconds(10)
});
```

Combining Timeout + Backoff for Maximum Resilience

A timeout without a backoff causes aggressive retry storms. A backoff without a timeout may lead to hangs or unnecessary delays.

Together, they provide an intelligent response to failure:

- Fail   quickly.

- Wait   strategically.

- Retry   cautiously.

This pattern is especially important in **microservice chains**. One service's delay should not block others in a synchronous chain.

Timeout and Backoff in Azure Functions

Azure Functions handles retries natively for some triggers. With Durable Functions, you can define retry policies explicitly:

```
RetryOptions retryOptions = new RetryOptions(
    firstRetryInterval: TimeSpan.FromSeconds(2),
    maxNumberOfAttempts: 5)
{
    BackoffCoefficient = 2.0,
    MaxRetryInterval = TimeSpan.FromSeconds(30)
};
```

You can apply this to an activity function:

```
await context.CallActivityWithRetryAsync("SendEmail", retryOptions,
emailPayload);
```

Best Practices

1. **Tune** **with** **Observability**
   Use Application Insights to monitor how often timeouts or retries occur. Adjust accordingly.

2. **Classify** **Exceptions**
   Retry only on transient errors (timeouts, throttling). Avoid retrying business logic errors (e.g., invalid data).

3. **Set** **Upper** **Boundaries**
Cap the total number of retries and the cumulative delay. Infinite retries lead to infinite pain.

4. **Avoid** **Nested** **Retries**
Don't retry an operation that's already retried by a lower layer. This causes exponential retry storms.

5. **Use** **Circuit** **Breakers**
Combine with circuit breakers (as discussed in Section 2.1) to halt retries when a service is clearly down.

Real-World Scenario

Background:
A stock trading platform used an external exchange API to fetch live quotes. The API had a rate limit and was occasionally slow. When it slowed down, the client retried rapidly, causing even more failures.

Issue:
The lack of backoff and high timeout (30 seconds) meant hundreds of threads blocked waiting. Eventually, the entire app pool crashed.

Fix:

- Timeout reduced to 3 seconds.

- Added exponential backoff with jitter.

- Implemented a circuit breaker.

- Caching layered in front to reduce redundant calls.

Outcome:
System stability improved drastically. Quote API issues were isolated. Timeouts were logged and alerted in real-time.

Conclusion

Timeouts and backoff strategies are critical components of any resilient architecture. They prevent system overload, reduce mean time to recovery (MTTR), and offer graceful degradation under stress. In Azure, both native services and SDKs support configuring these mechanisms to fit your application's needs.

Remember: resilience is not about perfection—it's about survival. When you plan for slowness, delays, and failure using timeout and backoff strategies, you create systems that remain functional, responsive, and dependable even in imperfect conditions.

In the next section, we'll tackle **Idempotency in Distributed Systems**, another essential concept that allows retry mechanisms to operate safely without compromising data integrity.

Idempotency in Distributed Systems

Idempotency is a fundamental concept in building reliable, fault-tolerant distributed systems. It refers to the property of an operation that allows it to be performed multiple times without changing the result beyond the initial application. In cloud-native architectures, where network failures, retries, and asynchronous processing are common, idempotency ensures that systems can handle these scenarios without unintended side effects such as duplicate data, overbilling, or inconsistent state.

This section explores idempotency in depth—what it is, why it's important, and how to implement it in Azure-based systems. We'll examine real-world cases, patterns, and anti-patterns, and how Azure services and code-based strategies can enforce idempotency across APIs, messaging, data layers, and workflows.

Understanding Idempotency

Idempotency means that an operation can be called multiple times with the same input and produce the same result, safely and consistently.

For example:

- Charging a credit card once should deduct the amount only once, even if the request is   sent   twice.

- Creating a user account should not result in multiple identical users.

- Publishing a message should not result in duplicated downstream events.

In distributed systems, operations are frequently retried due to transient failures, timeouts, or network issues. Without idempotency, such retries may cause **side effects**—data duplication, state corruption, or incorrect business logic.

Why Idempotency Is Critical in the Cloud

1. **Retries   Are   Inevitable**
   Services like Azure Functions, Service Bus, and HTTP clients use retry mechanisms

automatically. These retries must be safe.

2. **Network** **Is** **Unreliable**
A request may succeed but the acknowledgment may be lost. The client doesn't know whether to retry or assume success.

3. **Asynchronous** **Messaging**
Messages might be redelivered. Idempotent consumers can process duplicates without harm.

4. **User** **Actions**
Users may hit a browser refresh, resubmit forms, or click buttons multiple times.

5. **Downstream** **Resilience**
Systems calling other services must be idempotent to ensure upstream logic is preserved in face of failures.

Strategies for Idempotency

1. Idempotency Keys

Clients send a unique identifier (idempotency key) with each request. The server stores the key and associates it with the result of the first request. If the same key is received again, the cached result is returned.

HTTP Request with Idempotency Key (e.g., in REST API)

```
POST /orders HTTP/1.1
Idempotency-Key: abc123
Content-Type: application/json

{
  "customerId": "456",
  "items": [ { "productId": "x1", "qty": 2 } ]
}
```

Server Logic:

1. Check if the key exists in the database or cache.

2. If exists, return the previous response.

3. Else, process the request and store the result with the key.

Azure Implementation:

- Use **Azure Cosmos DB**, **Table Storage**, or **Azure Redis Cache** to store idempotency keys.

- Use middleware in Azure API Management (APIM) or App Services to intercept and validate   keys.

2. Natural Idempotency

Some operations are naturally idempotent:

- GET   /users/123

- DELETE   /users/123   (delete   once   or   repeatedly—same   result)

- PUT   /users/123   (replaces   the   resource   with   the   same   content)

Design APIs to favor PUT over POST when possible. PUT is generally idempotent; POST is not.

Idempotency in Messaging Systems

Azure messaging systems like **Service Bus**, **Event Grid**, and **Storage Queues** can redeliver messages due to processing failures or client disconnects. Your consumers must be idempotent to prevent duplicate processing.

1. Azure Service Bus

Enable   **Duplicate**   **Detection**:

```
resource serviceBusNamespace 'Microsoft.ServiceBus/namespaces@2021-
06-01-preview' = {
  name: 'myServiceBus'
  location: resourceGroup().location
  sku: {
    name: 'Standard'
    tier: 'Standard'
  }
  properties: {
    duplicateDetectionHistoryTimeWindow: 'PT10M'
  }
}
```

- Messages with the same `MessageId` within the window are dropped.

- Application Layer: Ensure message processing is idempotent. For example, if a message instructs the system to "ship order 987", check if that order is already shipped before acting.

2. Event Grid and Event Hubs

These services may deliver events more than once. Include a unique identifier (e.g., event ID or correlation ID) in the payload. Track processed event IDs in a fast-access data store to prevent reprocessing.

Idempotency in Workflows and Durable Functions

In **Azure Durable Functions**, idempotency is handled automatically by the orchestrator. If an activity function fails or is retried, it is only executed once in terms of state and outputs.

```
await context.CallActivityAsync("CreateOrder", orderDetails);
```

Even if the function restarts, the activity's output is preserved unless explicitly replayed.

However, side-effecting activity functions (e.g., sending emails or making payments) should still enforce idempotency by checking prior execution status.

Data Layer Idempotency

1. Constraints and Keys
Use **unique constraints** to enforce idempotency at the database level.

```
CREATE        UNIQUE        INDEX        IX_Orders_IdempotencyKey        ON
Orders(IdempotencyKey);
```

-
- Ensure that primary keys are deterministic or client-supplied where possible.

2. Upserts

Use **MERGE, UPSERT,** or **ON CONFLICT DO NOTHING** statements to handle repeated requests safely.

Cosmos DB Example:

```
await            container.UpsertItemAsync(order,            new
PartitionKey(order.CustomerId));
```

PostgreSQL Example:

```
INSERT INTO orders (id, customer_id, total)
VALUES ('abc123', 'cust456', 100)
ON CONFLICT (id) DO NOTHING;
```

Testing and Validating Idempotency

Testing idempotency is critical, especially under failure simulation.

Test Scenarios:

1. Submit the same API request twice – assert only one side effect occurs.

2. Simulate message redelivery – verify message is processed once.

3. Retry failed workflow steps – assert no duplication.

4. Refresh form submission in UI – data consistency remains.

Tools:

- Integration tests with mocks.

- Load tests simulating retries.

- Chaos engineering tools (e.g., Azure Chaos Studio) to induce failures and retries.

Anti-Patterns to Avoid

1. **Using Timestamps or GUIDs as Unique Keys without Coordination**
   If the client does not reuse the same idempotency key, retries will be treated as new requests.

2. **Silent** **Failures**
   If the server fails before storing the result, future retries may incorrectly report success.

3. **Client-Side   Only   Enforcement**
Always enforce idempotency on the server side—clients are unreliable.

4. **No   Result   Caching**
If the result of the first attempt isn't cached, retries will cause repeated processing.

5. **Assuming   Message   Delivery   Guarantees**
Azure queues are *at* *least* *once* delivery. Design accordingly.

Real-World Scenario

Problem:
A SaaS platform allowed users to purchase subscriptions via a REST API. If users clicked the "Buy" button multiple times (due to a slow network), multiple charges occurred.

Fix:

- Implemented idempotency keys on the POST `/purchase` endpoint.

- Stored idempotency keys and responses in Cosmos DB.

- Enforced unique `purchase_id` per user.

Outcome:
Duplicate purchases were eliminated. User trust and payment provider compliance improved.

Conclusion

Idempotency is the cornerstone of safe retries in distributed systems. It enables reliable processing, consistent state management, and graceful degradation during network or system failures. By combining idempotency keys, deduplication techniques, message metadata, and durable storage, developers can build robust systems that resist duplication and remain trustworthy under failure.

In Azure, from API Management and Service Bus to Cosmos DB and Durable Functions, multiple services support and encourage idempotent design. Applying these principles early in the development process avoids some of the most complex and costly failures later on.

With this foundation, we are now ready to explore more advanced design principles for availability and disaster recovery in Chapter 3.

Chapter 3: High Availability and Disaster Recovery Strategies

Availability Zones vs. Regions

When designing resilient cloud-native applications, understanding Azure's global infrastructure and how to use it effectively is crucial. Two of the most foundational constructs in Azure for building highly available systems are **Availability Zones** and **Regions**. These constructs form the basis for geographic redundancy, fault isolation, and disaster recovery planning.

In this section, we will explore the differences, use cases, architectural considerations, service compatibility, and best practices for designing with Availability Zones and Regions. We will also examine failure modes and how to mitigate them using these constructs.

Azure's Global Infrastructure Hierarchy

Azure organizes its infrastructure into the following hierarchy:

- **Geographies**: Geopolitical boundaries, such as the United States or Europe. Used for compliance and data residency.

- **Regions**: A set of data centers within a geography (e.g., East US, West Europe).

- **Availability Zones**: Physically isolated locations within a region, with independent power, cooling, and networking.

- **Data Centers**: The physical buildings hosting servers and other equipment.

Each region contains multiple data centers, and some regions support three or more Availability Zones. These zones are designed to be isolated from failures in one another, offering high availability within the same region.

What Are Availability Zones?

Availability Zones (AZs) are unique physical locations within an Azure region. Each zone consists of one or more datacenters equipped with independent power, cooling, and networking.

Key Characteristics:

- At least three zones per AZ-enabled region.

- Designed for fault isolation.

- Low-latency network connections between zones.

- Provide 99.99% uptime SLA for zone-redundant services.

Use Cases:

- Hosting mission-critical applications with high availability.

- Deploying active-active clusters across zones.

- Protecting against localized hardware or facility failure.

Example: Deploying a Multi-Zone Azure Kubernetes Service (AKS) Cluster

```
az aks create \
  --resource-group myResourceGroup \
  --name myAKSCluster \
  --location eastus2 \
  --enable-cluster-autoscaler \
  --zones 1 2 3 \
  --node-count 3 \
  --node-vm-size Standard_DS2_v2
```

What Are Regions?

Azure Regions are broader geographic areas made up of multiple data centers, often with hundreds of miles between them. Each region is independent and can be used for **disaster recovery**, **compliance**, or **geographic reach**.

Key Characteristics:

- Designed for large-scale geographic failover.
- Suitable for disaster recovery and data residency.
- Typically paired with another region (e.g., East US ↔ West US).

Use Cases:

- Backup and disaster recovery planning.
- Geo-redundant storage and database replication.
- Deploying applications close to end-users around the world.

Region Pairing in Azure: Azure maintains logical **region pairs**. For example:

- East US ↔ West US
- North Europe ↔ West Europe

In these pairs:

- At least one region is updated at a time during planned maintenance.
- Data replication is often enabled between paired regions.
- Higher guarantees of recovery during catastrophic regional outages.

Availability Zones vs. Regions: Comparison

Feature	Availability Zones	Regions
Fault Domain	Intra-region (data center level)	Inter-region (geographic level)
Latency	Low (<2ms)	Higher (depends on region distance)

SLA	99.99% for zone-redundant resources	Depends on service replication
Primary Use	High availability	Disaster recovery, geo-resilience
Data Residency Compliance	Same regional boundary	Cross-region compliance options
Cost	Lower (intra-region egress is free)	Higher (cross-region egress fees)

Designing for Availability with AZs

Patterns:

- **Active-Active across AZs**: Distribute compute nodes (App Service, AKS, VMs) across multiple zones.

- **Zone-redundant storage**: Use ZRS to replicate data across zones.

- **Load balancing**: Use Azure Standard Load Balancer or Application Gateway with zone redundancy.

Best Practices:

- Always use zone-aware SKUs for services (e.g., PremiumV2 App Service Plans).

- Configure **availability sets** or **zone-aware scale sets** for virtual machines.

- For critical databases, use zone-redundant configurations (e.g., SQL Database Business Critical tier).

Designing for Resilience with Regions

Patterns:

- **Active-Passive**: Primary region handles all traffic; secondary region is cold standby or read-only.

- **Active-Active**: Deploy full infrastructure in both regions; use Azure Front Door or Traffic Manager to balance.

- **Cold DR**: Keep only backups or templates in secondary region; bring online during failover.

Service Examples:

Azure SQL Database Auto-Failover Groups

```
CREATE FAILOVER GROUP myfailovergroup

WITH (

  PARTNER = 'myserver-secondary.database.windows.net',

  AUTOMATIC_FAILOVER = ON

);
```

-
- **Azure Storage with GRS or RA-GRS**

- **Azure Site Recovery**: For VM replication and orchestration.

Combined Strategy: AZ + Region

The most resilient architectures use a **tiered strategy**:

- High availability via **Availability Zones** within a region.

- Disaster recovery via **Regions** (cross-region replication and failover).

Example:

- AKS cluster spans three AZs in East US.

- Azure SQL is zone-redundant and configured with an auto-failover group to West US.

- Azure Front Door directs global traffic and provides TLS termination.

Cost Considerations

- **Zone-resilient resources** typically have a small premium (e.g., ZRS vs LRS storage).

- **Cross-region** **egress** is chargeable.

- **Standby regions** incur cost even if not serving traffic, depending on standby strategy.

Tips:

- Leverage Azure Pricing Calculator to estimate DR configurations.

- Use auto-scale and infrastructure-as-code to reduce DR region costs when idle.

Monitoring and Testing

Availability and DR strategies are only effective if monitored and validated.

Monitoring:

- Use Azure Monitor to track zone-specific metrics (e.g., VM health, latency).

- Use Application Insights to track request distribution and regional availability.

- Set up alerts on failover events or region-level service degradation.

Testing:

- Schedule **zone** **failure** **simulations** using Azure Chaos Studio.

- Test **region failover** with Traffic Manager, failover groups, or custom scripts.

- Use **disaster recovery drills** to measure recovery time objective (RTO) and recovery point objective (RPO).

Real-World Scenario

Case: Global Healthcare SaaS Platform

- Primary region: West Europe (AZ-enabled).

- Secondary region: North Europe.

- App Service and Azure SQL deployed with zone redundancy.

- Azure Traffic Manager routes users based on performance.

- Cosmos DB configured with multi-region writes.

Outcome:

- During a regional outage simulation in West Europe, services failed over within minutes.

- No data loss; users experienced a temporary increase in latency only.

- Compliance achieved with GDPR and HIPAA regional requirements.

Conclusion

Availability Zones and Regions are powerful tools in Azure's resilience model. While AZs provide fault isolation and high availability within a single region, Regions enable you to design for disaster recovery and compliance at a global scale. When combined, they allow you to build applications that not only remain online during localized hardware failures but also survive major regional outages.

By leveraging zone-aware services, configuring region-level failover, and automating your DR workflows, you can build systems that meet even the most stringent uptime SLAs and recovery objectives. In the next section, we'll dive into Geo-Redundancy with Azure Services—how to replicate data and infrastructure across regions for seamless disaster recovery.

Geo-Redundancy with Azure Services

Geo-redundancy is a cornerstone of disaster recovery and business continuity planning in cloud architecture. In Azure, geo-redundancy ensures that critical application data and infrastructure remain available, even in the event of a complete regional failure. Unlike local or zonal redundancy that handles data center-level failures, **geo-redundancy spans across Azure regions**, offering protection against natural disasters, large-scale outages, or region-specific service disruptions.

This section explores the core strategies, technologies, and service configurations that enable geo-redundancy in Azure. It covers storage replication options, multi-region database deployments, load distribution mechanisms, and failover orchestration. With a focus on both

data durability and **operational resilience**, we'll dive into how to plan, implement, and validate geo-redundant systems.

What is Geo-Redundancy?

Geo-redundancy refers to the replication of systems and data across geographically separate Azure regions to provide resilience against regional failures. This approach goes beyond high availability (which typically focuses on intra-region uptime) and addresses scenarios where an entire region becomes inaccessible.

Geo-redundant designs typically include:

- Multi-region data replication.

- Global load balancing.

- Automated failover and recovery.

- Cross-region backup and restore.

Azure facilitates geo-redundancy through native support in storage, databases, DNS, networking, and compute services.

Geo-Redundancy in Azure Storage

Azure Storage offers several replication options for durability and availability:

Redundancy Type	Replication Scope	Description
LRS	Single datacenter	Three copies within one facility.
ZRS	Multiple AZs	Three synchronous copies across zones.
GRS	Primary + paired region	LRS + asynchronous copy to another region.

RA-GRS	GRS + Read Access	GRS with read access to secondary.
GZRS	ZRS + geo-replication	Combines ZRS and GRS.
RA-GZRS	GZRS + Read Access	GZRS with read access to secondary.

Example: Configuring RA-GZRS for a storage account using Bicep

```
resource storage 'Microsoft.Storage/storageAccounts@2022-09-01' = {
  name: 'mygeostorage'
  location: 'eastus'
  sku: {
    name: 'Standard_RAGZRS'
  }
  kind: 'StorageV2'
  properties: {
    accessTier: 'Hot'
  }
}
```

With RA-GZRS, the data is synchronously replicated across AZs and asynchronously to a secondary region, enabling both local and global durability.

Geo-Redundancy in Databases

Azure SQL Database

Azure SQL provides **auto-failover groups**, allowing geo-replication of databases across regions.

Key Features:

- Automatic failover on region outage.

- Manual failover for disaster recovery drills.

- DNS-based failover redirection (`<servername>.database.windows.net`).

Setup:

```
CREATE FAILOVER GROUP myfg

WITH (

  PARTNER = 'myserver-secondary.database.windows.net',

  AUTOMATIC_FAILOVER = ON

);
```

Monitoring:

- Track replication lag.

- Monitor failover status with Azure Monitor.

- Include in business continuity plans.

Cosmos DB

Cosmos DB is a globally distributed database with multi-region writes and automatic failover capabilities.

Features:

- Multi-master writes.

- Tunable consistency levels.

- Per-region read/write configuration.

- 99.999% availability SLA.

Configuration Example (C#):

```
CosmosClientOptions options = new CosmosClientOptions

{

    ApplicationRegion = "East US",

    ApplicationPreferredRegions = new List<string> { "East US", "West
Europe" }

};
```

In the event of a regional outage, Cosmos DB routes requests to the next available region, respecting consistency and latency preferences.

Geo-Redundancy for Web Applications

Azure Front Door

Azure Front Door is a global Layer 7 load balancer that enables geo-distributed web application delivery. It intelligently routes traffic based on performance, availability, and health probes.

Use Case:

- Front Door sits in front of apps deployed in multiple regions.
- Users are automatically routed to the fastest or healthiest backend.

Configuration Sample (Azure CLI):

```
az network front-door create \

  --name myFrontDoor \

  --resource-group myRG \

  --backend-address myapp-east.azurewebsites.net \

  --backend-address myapp-west.azurewebsites.net
```

Features:

- TLS   offloading.

- Global   SSL.

- Health-based   routing.

- URL-based   routing   rules.

Azure Traffic Manager

Traffic Manager is a DNS-based global load balancer with routing methods including:

- **Priority**:   Active-passive   failover.

- **Performance**:   Latency-based   routing.

- **Geographic**:   Region-based   traffic   segmentation.

Priority Failover Example: East US is primary, West Europe is secondary. On failure of East US, all traffic shifts to West Europe automatically.

Geo-Redundancy in Compute

Azure Virtual Machines

Use **Azure Site Recovery (ASR)** to replicate VMs from a primary region to a secondary region.

Features:

- Continuous   replication.

- Application-consistent   snapshots.

- Runbooks   for   orchestration.

- Non-disruptive   DR   drills.

Example: Configuring ASR (PowerShell)

```
Set-AzRecoveryServicesAsrReplicationProtectedItem            -
ProtectionDirection "PrimaryToRecovery"
```

Azure App Service

While App Service doesn't support automatic geo-replication, you can deploy identical apps to multiple regions and front them with Azure Front Door or Traffic Manager.

Deployment can be automated via CI/CD pipelines with regional parameters:

```
- task: AzureWebApp@1

  inputs:

    azureSubscription: 'MySub'

    appName: 'myAppEast'

    package: '$(System.DefaultWorkingDirectory)/drop.zip'
```

Cross-Region Backup and Restore

Azure provides backup capabilities that can be replicated across regions:

- **Azure Backup**: Cross-region restore from GRS vaults.
- **Azure SQL Automated Backups**: Stored in paired region.
- **Cosmos DB**: Backups stored in regional blob storage accounts.
- **Blob Storage Snapshots**: Can be replicated manually or with Data Factory.

Example: Azure Backup Vault with Cross-Region Restore

```
resource backupVault 'Microsoft.DataProtection/backupVaults@2021-12-01' = {

  name: 'myBackupVault'

  location: 'eastus'

  properties: {

    crossRegionRestore: true

  }
```

}

Failover Planning and Automation

Manual failover is slow and error-prone. Use automation to ensure quick recovery:

- **Azure Automation**: Runbooks to orchestrate failover sequences.

- **Azure Logic Apps**: Triggered by alerts to perform API-based failovers.

- **Azure Monitor Alerts**: Detect outages and initiate automated workflows.

Example: Logic App triggering SQL Failover

1. Alert detects SQL outage.

2. Logic App calls REST API to initiate failover.

3. DNS alias updates to point to new primary.

Testing Geo-Redundancy

You must **test** geo-redundant architectures regularly to validate assumptions.

- **Chaos Engineering**: Use Azure Chaos Studio to simulate regional failures.

- **DR Drills**: Schedule regular exercises.

- **Simulated Traffic Tests**: Verify performance from various global locations.

Monitor:

- RTO (Recovery Time Objective).

- RPO (Recovery Point Objective).

- DNS failover propagation.

- User impact and observability.

Real-World Case Study

Scenario: Global E-Learning Platform

- Services deployed in East US and North Europe.

- Cosmos DB configured with multi-region writes.

- Azure Front Door used for low-latency global access.

- Azure App Config geo-replicated using GitOps and Azure Pipelines.

- Azure Monitor configured to detect region-specific failures.

Results:

- During a simulated failover of East US, users were automatically routed to North Europe within seconds.

- No data loss occurred.

- SLA compliance was maintained, and business operations continued uninterrupted.

Conclusion

Geo-redundancy is a non-negotiable requirement for systems that must remain operational during large-scale regional failures. Azure's native support for multi-region deployments, coupled with intelligent global traffic routing and automated disaster recovery orchestration, provides a robust foundation for resilient cloud systems.

From geo-replicated databases and storage to cross-region web deployments and DNS routing, the tools and patterns explored in this section allow you to build with confidence. Your users may be global—and your availability strategy should be too.

In the next section, we'll dive into architectural models for building **Active-Active and Active-Passive** systems that take advantage of this geo-redundancy for maximum uptime and fault tolerance.

Building with Active-Active and Active-Passive Models

Resilient cloud systems must be designed with fault domains in mind—ranging from application-level errors to complete regional outages. To effectively address such scenarios, architects commonly employ **Active-Active** and **Active-Passive** deployment models. These patterns ensure that services remain operational even when a primary instance or region is unavailable. Each model has its own trade-offs related to complexity, cost, performance, and failover strategy.

In this section, we'll deeply explore both models, analyze their design characteristics, examine how they apply across compute, data, and networking layers in Azure, and provide examples for implementation. We'll also highlight when to use one over the other, how to monitor them, and how to automate their management.

Active-Active Architecture

Definition:
In an **Active-Active** model, all deployed instances of an application in multiple regions or zones are live, receiving traffic, and processing workloads simultaneously.

Benefits:

- Zero RTO (Recovery Time Objective).

- Load is balanced across regions, improving global performance.

- Enables seamless failover without human intervention.

Challenges:

- Requires global state synchronization.

- Must address consistency and concurrency issues.

- Can be more expensive due to full duplication of workloads.

Use Cases for Active-Active

- **Global SaaS Platforms** with a distributed user base.

- **Real-time APIs** that demand low latency regardless of user location.

- **E-commerce Platforms** with no tolerance for downtime.

- **Financial Services** requiring instantaneous failover.

Designing Active-Active with Azure Services

1. Azure Front Door for Global Load Balancing

Azure Front Door provides:

- Geo-distributed traffic routing.

- Session affinity and health probes.

- SSL termination and WAF protection.

```
az network front-door frontend-endpoint create \

  --resource-group myRG \

  --front-door-name myFrontDoor \

  --name primaryEndpoint \

  --host-name myapp-primary.azurewebsites.net
```

You can configure it to split traffic (e.g., 50/50) between two regions and automatically fail over when one becomes unhealthy.

2. Azure App Services or AKS Across Regions

Deploy the same app to multiple regions:

- East US and West Europe.

- Use GitHub Actions or Azure DevOps to deploy simultaneously.

Ensure **statelessness** at the app tier. Store session data in Azure Cache for Redis (with geo-replication or fallback logic).

3. Cosmos DB with Multi-Region Writes

Use Cosmos DB for distributed data:

- Configure **multi-region writes**.

- Set **consistency level** (Bounded Staleness or Session).

- Enable **automatic** **failover**.

```
var cosmosClient = new CosmosClient(

    "accountEndpoint",

    "authKey",

    new CosmosClientOptions {

        ApplicationPreferredRegions = new List<string> { "East US",
"West Europe" },

        ConsistencyLevel = ConsistencyLevel.Session

    });
```

Active-Passive Architecture

Definition:
In an **Active-Passive** model, the application runs in a **primary region** while a secondary region remains **standby**, ready to take over in the event of a failure.

Benefits:

- Lower operational cost than Active-Active.

- Simpler data synchronization and application logic.

- Easier to manage and test failover procedures.

Challenges:

- RTO is not zero (failover takes time).

- Risk of cold start if the secondary environment isn't frequently tested.

- DNS changes or traffic rerouting may introduce propagation delays.

Use Cases for Active-Passive

- **Line-of-business applications** that tolerate short outages.
- **Internal tools** with lower uptime requirements.
- **Regulatory environments** requiring backup data in a second region.
- **Cost-sensitive architectures** needing DR capability without full duplication.

Designing Active-Passive with Azure Services

1. Azure Traffic Manager

Use **Priority Routing** to send all traffic to the primary region. On failure, Traffic Manager routes to the secondary.

```
{

  "routingMethod": "Priority",

  "endpoints": [

    {

      "name": "primaryRegion",

      "target": "myapp-primary.azurewebsites.net",

      "priority": 1

    },

    {

      "name": "secondaryRegion",

      "target": "myapp-secondary.azurewebsites.net",

      "priority": 2

    }

  ]

}
```

2. Azure SQL Auto-Failover Groups

Enable geo-replication between regions. The application connects using a listener endpoint that updates on failover.

```
ALTER FAILOVER GROUP myfg FORCE_FAILOVER_ALLOW_DATA_LOSS;
```

This triggers a manual failover in the event of a disaster.

3. Azure Site Recovery for VMs

Use ASR to replicate workloads from a primary region to a passive region. Upon disaster, trigger failover manually or automatically.

- Replication is near real-time.

- Supports app-consistent snapshots.

- Integrated with Azure Backup and Azure Automation.

Choosing Between Active-Active and Active-Passive

Criteria	Active-Active	Active-Passive
Cost	High (duplicate resources live)	Lower (standby resources may be inactive)
Complexity	High (multi-region sync, consistency)	Moderate (replication, DNS switching)
RTO	Zero	Minutes (manual or automated failover)
RPO	Zero or near-zero	Variable, depending on replication lag

Suitable For	Real-time apps, global APIs	Business apps, DR plans, non-critical tools
Failover Automation	Built-in, seamless	Requires orchestration or manual action

Recommendation:
Start with Active-Passive for simplicity and cost-efficiency, then move to Active-Active as scale, latency, and uptime demands grow.

Automating Deployment and Failover

Use **Infrastructure-as-Code (IaC)** and **CI/CD pipelines** to deploy to both regions.

Example using Azure DevOps:

```
stages:

- stage: DeployPrimary

  jobs:

  - deployment: WebApp

    environment: EastUS


- stage: DeploySecondary

  jobs:

  - deployment: WebApp

    environment: WestEurope
```

Automate failover with:

- Azure Logic Apps to trigger regional failover.

- Azure Monitor alerts based on health checks.
- DNS or traffic redirection via APIs.

Monitoring and Observability

Active models demand real-time visibility:

- **Azure Monitor**: Track performance, availability per region.
- **Application Insights**: Correlate telemetry across deployments.
- **Health Probes**: Feed status into Front Door or Traffic Manager.
- **Log Analytics**: Aggregate logs from multiple regions.

Set alerts for:

- Backend unavailability.
- Replication lag.
- Health probe failures.
- Failover invocation success/failure.

Testing Your Design

You must test failover scenarios to verify your assumptions.

Tests to run:

- Disable the primary app and observe failover.
- Simulate a zone or region outage using Azure Chaos Studio.
- Test DNS TTL propagation delays.
- Validate data consistency after failover and failback.

Document your **RTO** (how long until system recovers) and **RPO** (maximum tolerated data loss).

Real-World Case Study

Scenario:
A global ticketing platform used an Active-Active setup:

- App deployed in East US and Southeast Asia.

- Cosmos DB with multi-region writes.

- Azure Front Door managed traffic distribution.

- Redis geo-replication handled session caching.

Outcome:

- During a DDoS attack on East US, Front Door rerouted users to Southeast Asia.

- System uptime remained at 100%.

- No user data loss or login interruption.

Conclusion

Active-Active and Active-Passive architectures are vital tools in your resilience design toolkit. Each offers trade-offs, but both help your systems recover from outages—gracefully and predictably. Active-Active maximizes uptime and performance but requires rigorous consistency and state management. Active-Passive offers a balance of protection and simplicity, ideal for many enterprise workloads.

As Azure continues to expand its global infrastructure and support for cross-region services, implementing these models becomes more accessible. The key is choosing the right model for your system's SLA, cost envelope, and business impact, and then rigorously testing it under failure conditions.

In the next section, we'll look at how to **Design for Failover and Failback**, enabling not just recovery but seamless transition back to primary systems once stability is restored.

Designing for Failover and Failback

Failover and failback are essential aspects of any robust disaster recovery and high availability strategy. In Azure and other cloud environments, these processes ensure that systems can not only withstand failures but also **return to normal operations** once the issue has been resolved. Designing for both directions of transition—failover and failback—requires careful planning, automation, observability, and testing.

This section explores the architectural principles, patterns, and tools for implementing failover and failback in Azure-based systems. We'll discuss the different failover types, how to automate decision-making, handle state synchronization, ensure data consistency, and manage DNS, load balancing, and health monitoring. The goal is to enable seamless transitions that minimize downtime, data loss, and user impact.

Understanding Failover and Failback

- **Failover** is the process of switching from a primary system or region to a secondary one when a failure or degradation occurs.

- **Failback** is the process of returning operations from the secondary (or standby) system back to the primary once it is healthy.

Key attributes of a well-designed failover/failback process:

- **Automatic or semi-automatic execution** with minimal human involvement.

- **Data consistency** before, during, and after the transition.

- **Monitoring and health checks** to trigger failover conditions.

- **Auditability and logging** for post-mortem analysis.

Types of Failover

1. **Manual** **Failover**
   Initiated by a human operator after validation and decision-making.

   - Best for non-critical systems or where data integrity is paramount.

   - Common in Active-Passive models.

2. **Automatic** **Failover**
   Triggered by health check failures or monitoring alerts.

- Ideal for Active-Active models or highly available services.

- Requires robust validation to prevent false positives.

3. **Planned** **Failover**
   Used during maintenance, testing, or cost optimization.

- Should simulate real failure conditions to ensure system resilience.

Failover Triggers

The following conditions may trigger failover:

- Application health probe failure.

- VM, container, or App Service crash.

- Regional Azure outage or network isolation.

- Excessive latency or error rates.

- Manual operator decision.

Failover should be **graceful when possible**—allow in-flight requests to complete and preserve critical state.

DNS and Traffic Routing for Failover

Azure Traffic Manager

A DNS-based load balancer with failover and health checks.

```
{

  "routingMethod": "Priority",

  "endpoints": [

    {

      "name": "primary",

      "target": "myapp-primary.azurewebsites.net",
```

```
  "priority": 1

},

{

  "name": "secondary",

  "target": "myapp-secondary.azurewebsites.net",

  "priority": 2

}

]

}
```

Pros:

- Globally   distributed   DNS.
- Supports   automatic   failover   based   on   endpoint   health.

Cons:

- DNS TTL introduces propagation delays (recommend 30 seconds or less).

Azure Front Door

Performs **real-time traffic steering** based on health checks.

- Use   backend   health   probes   to   detect   failure.
- Supports   custom   routing   rules   and   affinity.
- TLS   offloading   and   WAF   integration.

Example: Configure failover to West Europe if East US backend is degraded.

Handling Stateful Failover

Stateless applications can failover with minimal effort, but stateful systems require special consideration.

Data Layer Synchronization

- **Databases**: Use geo-replication (e.g., Azure SQL Auto-Failover Groups, Cosmos DB multi-region   writes).

- **Files and Blobs**: Use RA-GZRS or asynchronously replicate via Data Factory or AzCopy.

- **Caches**: Use Redis with geo-replication or rehydration logic.

Example: SQL Auto-Failover Group Failback

```
-- Once primary is healthy, re-failover to original primary

ALTER FAILOVER GROUP myfg FORCE_FAILOVER_ALLOW_DATA_LOSS;
```

Alternatively, wait for automatic failback if configured.

Application-Level Failover

Your application logic may also need to detect failure and reroute or retry operations against alternate resources.

Retry Logic with Region Awareness

```
try {

    await CallService("https://myservice-eastus.azurewebsites.net");

}

catch (HttpRequestException) {

    await CallService("https://myservice-westus.azurewebsites.net");

}
```

For advanced scenarios, use:

- Azure SDK preferred region settings.
- Global routing libraries.
- Chaos testing to verify fallback mechanisms.

Automation of Failover and Failback

Use Azure-native services to automate transitions:

Azure Monitor and Alerts

- Monitor key metrics (e.g., HTTP errors, latency).
- Trigger alerts that invoke action groups.

Azure Logic Apps or Azure Automation

- Respond to alerts or probe failures.
- Execute failover runbooks.

Example: Logic App to Switch DNS Zone Records

1. Detect failure.
2. Call Azure DNS REST API to update record set.
3. Notify stakeholders.

Azure Site Recovery (ASR)

For VMs and IaaS:

- Set up replication.
- Test failover regularly.
- Configure automation to run post-failover scripts.

Validating Failback Conditions

Failback should only occur once the original primary environment is:

- Fully   operational.

- Updated   with   the   latest   data.

- Re-tested   for   performance   and   availability.

- Cleared   of   root   cause.

Validate using:

- Load   and   stress   testing.

- Data   consistency   checks.

- Canary   deployments.

- Logging   and   health   dashboards.

Use **gradual failback** where appropriate (e.g., shift 10% of traffic back before full cutover).

Documentation and Runbooks

Define runbooks for:

- Manual   failover   procedures.

- Role-based   access   control   for   triggering   actions.

- Failback   validation   steps.

- Post-incident   review.

Use Azure Automation or shared wikis for live operational documentation.

Testing Failover and Failback

You must **test regularly** under real conditions:

- Simulate DNS failures and monitor switchover time.
- Run Azure Chaos Studio experiments on resource groups or services.
- Monitor user impact (latency, error rate) during the transition.
- Validate alerting and automation chains.

Track metrics like:

- Recovery Time Objective (RTO).
- Recovery Point Objective (RPO).
- Failover success rate.
- Customer impact window.

Real-World Scenario

Case: Media Streaming Platform

- Uses Active-Passive model with East US primary and West Europe secondary.
- Cosmos DB with multi-region writes.
- Azure Front Door with weighted routing for failover testing.

During live failover:

- Health probes detected API failure in East US.
- Front Door rerouted traffic to West Europe.
- Logic App updated a status dashboard.
- Operators were notified and began diagnostics.
- After restoration, failback was executed via staged traffic redirection.

Outcome:

- 45-second   disruption.

- Zero   data   loss.

- Seamless   user   experience.

Conclusion

Failover and failback are not just mechanisms—they are strategic enablers of system resilience. Effective design involves planning for both directions of transition, ensuring application and data consistency, and integrating automation and observability throughout the process. Azure offers a wide range of services—from Traffic Manager and Front Door to Auto-Failover Groups and Site Recovery—that allow you to build intelligent, self-healing systems.

By adopting a proactive failover and failback strategy, you transform catastrophic events into recoverable scenarios, achieving true cloud-native resilience. In the next chapter, we'll examine **stateless vs. stateful design on Azure**, and how these architectures influence resilience, scalability, and recovery strategies.

Chapter 4: Stateless and Stateful Design on Azure

Choosing Between Stateless and Stateful Architectures

In cloud-native architecture, one of the most critical and often misunderstood design decisions is choosing between **stateless** and **stateful** components. These two paradigms significantly influence scalability, fault tolerance, performance, and maintainability. In Azure, where elasticity, geo-redundancy, and distributed services are the norm, understanding the role of state in your application is essential to building resilient systems.

This section explores the differences between stateless and stateful designs, their advantages and trade-offs, how Azure supports both, and when to use one over the other. We'll also dive into hybrid models, architectural examples, and implementation patterns that can help you make better design decisions.

What Is Stateless Architecture?

Stateless components do not store any information about previous interactions. Every request is independent and contains all the information required to be processed.

Characteristics:

- Each request is self-contained.
- No reliance on previous requests or sessions.
- Easier to scale horizontally.
- Ideal for distributed, serverless, and containerized systems.

Examples:

- HTTP APIs with all data in the request.
- Azure Functions or Logic Apps triggered by events.
- Stateless microservices behind a load balancer.

Benefits:

- High   scalability.

- Simplified   failover   and   restart   logic.

- Easier   load   balancing.

Drawbacks:

- Requires   external   state   storage   (e.g.,   database,   cache).

- Can introduce additional latency or complexity in managing context externally.

What Is Stateful Architecture?

Stateful components maintain context across requests. The system remembers interactions over time—either within a session, transaction, or a persistent store.

Characteristics:

- State   is   stored   in   memory   or   disk.

- Requests   may   depend   on   previous   context.

- Often   requires   session   affinity   (sticky   sessions).

Examples:

- Web   applications   with   in-memory   user   sessions.

- Long-running   workflows   with   Durable   Functions.

- Stateful   data   processing   in   Azure   Stream   Analytics.

Benefits:

- Easier   to   manage   workflows   and   multi-step   interactions.

- Reduces   external   calls   if   session   data   is   local.

- Better   for   real-time   applications   (e.g.,   gaming,   chat).

Drawbacks:

- Harder to scale out.

- Requires careful state management during failover or scaling.

- May need replication and data synchronization across nodes.

When to Use Stateless Design

Statelessness is preferred in most cloud-native applications. It enables elasticity and resilience by decoupling application logic from context storage.

Ideal Use Cases:

- REST APIs and microservices.

- Serverless functions (Azure Functions).

- Batch processing jobs.

- Event-driven architectures.

Azure Services Optimized for Stateless Workloads:

- **Azure App Service**

- **Azure Functions**

- **Azure Kubernetes Service (AKS)** with ephemeral containers

- **Azure Container Apps**

Design Patterns:

- Store state in Azure Cosmos DB, Azure SQL, or Redis.

- Use JWT tokens or custom headers to pass session context.

- Offload files and blobs to Azure Storage.

When to Use Stateful Design

Stateful designs are appropriate when maintaining context is essential for business logic or performance.

Ideal Use Cases:

- Long-lived transactions (e.g., order processing).
- Session-based applications (e.g., shopping carts).
- Realtime messaging or gaming.
- Durable workflows with checkpoints.

Azure Services for Stateful Workloads:

- **Azure Durable Functions**
- **Azure Service Fabric** (with Reliable Collections)
- **Azure SQL / Cosmos DB** (for persisted state)
- **Azure Redis Cache** (for transient session state)

Design Considerations:

- Ensure state is replicated and backed up.
- Plan for recovery from crashes and restarts.
- Use sticky sessions only when necessary.

Stateful Workflows in Azure Durable Functions

Azure Durable Functions allow you to build **stateful serverless workflows** using an orchestrator function.

Example Orchestration:

```
[FunctionName("OrderWorkflow")]

public static async Task Run(

    [OrchestrationTrigger] IDurableOrchestrationContext context)
```

```
{

    var order = context.GetInput<Order>();

    await context.CallActivityAsync("ValidateOrder", order);

    await context.CallActivityAsync("ReserveInventory", order);

    await context.CallActivityAsync("SendConfirmationEmail", order);

}
```

The orchestrator maintains durable state between function executions, even if the app restarts.

Hybrid Architecture: Combining Stateless and Stateful

In practice, many systems use a **hybrid approach**, with stateless frontends and stateful backends.

Example: E-Commerce Platform

- Stateless APIs for product catalog, search, and checkout.

- Stateful session store for cart management (e.g., Redis).

- Durable backend processes for order fulfillment and delivery tracking.

This pattern maximizes performance while preserving elasticity.

Azure Stack:

- Azure Front Door → App Service (stateless API) → Azure Redis (session) → Azure SQL (persistent state)

- Azure Event Grid triggers background workflows.

Best Practices for Managing State in Azure

1. **Externalize All State**

- Never store critical state in memory unless replicated.
- Use Redis, Azure SQL, Cosmos DB, or Durable Functions.

2. **Avoid Session Affinity When Possible**

   - Sticky sessions make horizontal scaling difficult.
   - Store session data externally and use a common token or key.

3. **Implement Idempotency**

   - Ensure repeated requests don't duplicate state changes.
   - Use idempotency keys or state-based workflows.

4. **Use Durable Patterns for Long-Running Tasks**

   - Implement retries, checkpoints, and compensation logic in Durable Functions or Logic Apps.

5. **Embrace Eventual Consistency**

   - When working across multiple systems, design with the understanding that state propagation may be delayed.

6. **Version and Validate State Models**

   - Schema evolution is critical in stateful systems. Use versioning, migrations, and validation.

Common Anti-Patterns

1. **Tightly Coupled State and Logic**

   - Mixing state with app logic increases complexity and hinders scalability.

2. **Local Memory Sessions**

   - Session data in local memory means losing state during a crash or scale event.

3. **Over-Reliance on Sticky Sessions**

   - May work for small systems but becomes a bottleneck at scale.

4. **Ignoring Failover Scenarios**

   ○ If state isn't replicated or checkpointed, data loss during outages is inevitable.

5. **Assuming State Consistency Without Monitoring**

   ○ Always track synchronization status and use compensating transactions when needed.

Real-World Example

Scenario:
A global travel booking app handled millions of users across regions. Initially, they maintained user sessions in local memory using sticky sessions and stored bookings in a local SQL instance.

Problems:

- Sessions were lost during scaling events.

- Failover to another region required users to log in again.

- Database couldn't replicate fast enough, leading to booking inconsistencies.

Refactored Design:

- Frontend APIs became stateless.

- Azure Redis handled user sessions with a 30-minute TTL.

- Cosmos DB used for distributed booking storage with session consistency.

- Azure Front Door routed users based on performance.

Results:

- Zero session loss during failovers.

- Faster performance globally.

- 40% reduction in operational incidents related to session state.

Conclusion

Choosing between stateless and stateful architectures is not about right or wrong—it's about finding the right balance for your application's context, performance, and resilience requirements. Azure provides first-class support for both models, enabling developers to build systems that scale, recover, and evolve with minimal friction.

Stateless components should be your default, empowering scalability and elasticity. When state is essential, it must be stored externally and managed thoughtfully with resilience in mind. The best architectures mix both strategically—creating services that are responsive, durable, and cloud-native by design.

In the next section, we'll focus on **Session Management in the Cloud**, examining patterns and services that support scalable, resilient user session handling in Azure-based architectures.

Session Management in the Cloud

Managing user sessions is a critical aspect of building responsive and personalized web applications. In the cloud, traditional approaches—like in-memory session storage or sticky sessions—often fall short due to the dynamic and distributed nature of modern architectures. Effective **session management in the cloud** must be designed for scalability, statelessness, resilience, and security.

This section explores the challenges and strategies associated with session management in Azure. We'll look at design patterns, Azure services that support session storage, best practices for implementation, and examples of real-world architectures. We'll also discuss session expiration, recovery, replication, and how to support global access patterns without compromising performance or consistency.

Understanding Sessions in Modern Applications

A **session** is a semi-permanent interactive information interchange between two or more communicating devices, typically between a user and a web application.

Session data might include:

- Authentication   tokens

- User   preferences

- Shopping   cart   items

- In-progress   form   data

- UI state (e.g., selected filters, tabs)

Modern cloud applications—especially stateless ones—need to externalize and manage this session data efficiently to remain scalable and fault-tolerant.

Session Management Challenges in the Cloud

1. **Scalability**

   - Applications scale out dynamically across regions and instances.

   - In-memory sessions don't persist across instances.

2. **Availability**

   - Session data must survive restarts, deployments, or region failovers.

3. **Consistency**

   - Concurrent session access from different devices or regions must not conflict.

4. **Performance**

   - Session data should be fast to read and write, minimizing latency.

5. **Security**

   - Sessions often contain sensitive data and must be encrypted, signed, and expired properly.

Common Session Management Strategies

1. Client-Side Sessions

Session data is stored on the client—often inside cookies or tokens.

Mechanism:

- Use JSON Web Tokens (JWT) or encrypted cookies.

- Validate tokens on each request.

Pros:

- Stateless, easy to scale.
- No server storage needed.

Cons:

- Limited size (~4 KB).
- Exposes data to client (must be encrypted/signed).
- Cannot invalidate tokens without extra logic.

Example: JWT-Based Auth

```
{
  "sub": "user123",
  "exp": 1684185600,
  "role": "admin"
}
```

Backend validates the token using a shared secret or public key.

---

2. Server-Side Sessions

Session data is stored on the server and referenced using a session ID stored in a cookie.

Pros:

- Larger data capacity.
- Easier to invalidate or modify sessions.

Cons:

- Requires shared backend store.

- More complex for global or multi-instance apps.

Best Practice: Store session data in a distributed cache or database.

Azure Solutions for Session Management

Azure Cache for Redis

A popular and high-performance option for storing session state in a distributed and scalable way.

Features:

- Sub-millisecond latency.

- Supports expiration and eviction policies.

- Built-in support in many frameworks (ASP.NET, Node.js, Django).

Architecture:

- Store session data keyed by session ID.

- Use TTL (Time-to-Live) to manage expiry.

Example (ASP.NET Core):

```
services.AddDistributedRedisCache(options =>
{
    options.Configuration =
"myredis.redis.cache.windows.net:6380,password=...";

    options.InstanceName = "myapp:";
});


await _cache.SetStringAsync("session:user123", sessionJson, new
DistributedCacheEntryOptions
{
```

```
AbsoluteExpirationRelativeToNow = TimeSpan.FromMinutes(30)
});
```

Azure Table Storage

For lightweight, semi-structured session data. Offers high availability and low cost.

Pros:

- Durable   storage.
- Easy   to   scale.
- Useful   for   audit   trails   or   rarely   accessed   sessions.

Cons:

- Slower   than   in-memory   solutions.
- Requires   design   for   partition   keys   and   row   keys.

Azure Cosmos DB

For more advanced session scenarios—multi-region replication, complex session objects, and large-scale applications.

Benefits:

- Globally   distributed.
- Millisecond   response   times.
- Fine-grained   consistency   options.

Example:

- Partition   by   userId   or   sessionId.
- TTL   set   at   container   or   document   level.

{

```
"id": "session123",

"userId": "user456",

"cart": [],

"preferences": {},

"ttl": 1800

}
```

Hybrid Model: Client-Side + Server-Side

A robust approach is to use **client-side tokens for authentication** and **server-side storage for user-specific data**.

- JWTs validate user identity.

- Redis stores cart contents, preferences, draft forms.

- TTL on both tokens and session keys for security.

This hybrid model supports statelessness while managing mutable data securely and efficiently.

Session Expiration and Cleanup

Best Practices:

- Always set a TTL on sessions.
- Use sliding expiration for active users.
- Clean up expired sessions via background tasks or built-in Redis eviction.

Redis Configuration Example:

```
maxmemory-policy volatile-lru
```

Ensures least recently used keys with TTL are evicted first.

For Cosmos DB or Table Storage, use TTL indexing and Azure Functions to delete expired items periodically.

Multi-Region and Global Session Management

In globally distributed applications, users may switch between regions due to failover or traffic routing.

Strategies:

1. **Geo-Replicated** **Redis**

   ○ Use **Azure Cache for Redis Enterprise** with Active-Active setup.

   ○ Ensures low-latency access across regions.

2. **Region-Aware** **Session** **Routing**

   ○ Sticky sessions or traffic routing to ensure users land in the same region.

3. **Session** **Sync** **via** **Cosmos** **DB**

   ○ Durable, multi-region writes.

   ○ Great for long-term session storage or post-login state.

4. **Fallback** **Logic**

   ○ If session is not found locally, attempt to retrieve from fallback region.

Monitoring and Observability

- Track session cache hit/miss ratio.

- Monitor latency and error rates.

- Alert on high eviction rates (Redis).

- Use Application Insights to track session lifecycle events.

Example (Log custom session events):

```
telemetry.TrackEvent("SessionStarted", new Dictionary<string, string>
{
    { "userId", "user123" },
    { "region", "East US" }
});
```

Real-World Example

Scenario: Global Retail App

- Stateless APIs deployed in East US, West Europe.
- Azure Front Door routes traffic based on latency.
- Redis cache clusters in each region store session data.
- JWT for identity, Redis for cart/session state.
- Cosmos DB logs persistent session events (e.g., abandoned carts).

During failover:

- JWT ensures user is still authenticated.
- App retrieves cart from backup Redis region or Cosmos DB.

Outcome:

- 99.99% availability.
- No cart loss on region switch.
- Improved page load times due to local caching.

Summary Best Practices

- Use **JWTs** for identity, **Redis** for session state.

- Always set TTLs to manage session lifespan.

- Avoid in-memory or sticky sessions in distributed environments.

- Use **Cosmos DB** for global session durability where needed.

- Monitor session access, expiration, and cache health.

- Validate session design during failover and scaling tests.

Conclusion

Session management in the cloud is more than just storing user data—it's about delivering a fast, seamless, and secure experience across dynamic, elastic infrastructure. Azure provides a rich toolkit to handle sessions efficiently, whether through in-memory caching with Redis, durable storage with Cosmos DB, or secure tokens via Azure AD and JWT.

By externalizing state, designing for failover, and embracing stateless APIs, you ensure your session handling is resilient, scalable, and optimized for the cloud. In the next section, we'll explore **Durable Functions and State Persistence**, focusing on scenarios where application state must survive across time, events, and failures.

Durable Functions and State Persistence

As applications grow more complex and event-driven in the cloud, the need to orchestrate long-running workflows and preserve state between operations becomes increasingly critical. Azure Durable Functions is a powerful framework built on top of Azure Functions that enables **stateful serverless workflows**, allowing developers to write orchestrations using code while Azure handles the state persistence, checkpointing, and event sourcing behind the scenes.

This section explores how Durable Functions works, its key components, common patterns, persistence mechanisms, and how it fits into a resilient and scalable architecture. We will also cover practical design guidance, common pitfalls, and real-world examples that demonstrate how state can be effectively managed in the serverless world.

The Challenge of Orchestrating State in the Cloud

Traditional workflows often require:

- Coordinating multiple activities or services.

- Handling retries, compensation, or timeout logic.

- Persisting intermediate state.

- Maintaining long-running sessions (e.g., approvals, provisioning).

In stateless environments, this becomes difficult. Without external storage and orchestration logic, you risk:

- Duplicate execution.

- Lost progress after failure.

- Complex retry and error-handling logic.

Durable Functions solve this by offering **code-based orchestration** with built-in persistence, retry, and checkpointing, backed by Azure Storage or Durable Task Framework.

Durable Functions Overview

Durable Functions is an extension of Azure Functions that allows you to write **stateful functions** in a **serverless** environment. It maintains workflow state between executions without requiring you to manage any infrastructure or storage manually.

Key Benefits:

- Serverless and autoscaling.

- Orchestration via code.

- Built-in support for retries, checkpoints, and timers.

- Reliable state persistence.

- Event-driven with external triggers.

Core Components

1. **Orchestrator Function**

   o Defines the workflow.

- o Deterministic and replayable.
- o Handles sequencing, parallelism, and error-handling.

2. **Activity** **Function**

- o Executes a single unit of work.
- o Called by the orchestrator.
- o Can be retried, timed out, or compensated.

3. **Client** **Function**

- o Triggers the orchestrator.
- o Initiated via HTTP, queue, blob, or timer.

4. **Durable** **Entity**

- o Represents a stateful object.
- o Supports operations like read, write, delete.
- o Ideal for fine-grained stateful interactions.

Basic Orchestration Example

Order Processing Workflow

```
[FunctionName("OrderOrchestrator")]
public static async Task Run(
    [OrchestrationTrigger] IDurableOrchestrationContext context)
{
    var order = context.GetInput<Order>();
    await context.CallActivityAsync("ValidateOrder", order);
    await context.CallActivityAsync("ChargeCustomer", order);
    await context.CallActivityAsync("SendConfirmation", order);
```

```
}
```

Each activity executes independently. If one fails, only that step is retried. The orchestrator's state is persisted after each action.

Persistence and Checkpointing

Durable Functions uses **Azure Storage Queues, Tables, and Blobs** to persist state:

- After each action or `await`, the orchestrator checkpoints progress.

- If the function app restarts or crashes, the orchestrator replays from the last checkpoint.

- State is deterministic—no reliance on timestamps or randomness.

Storage Costs: Minimal due to compact checkpoint formats.

Reliability: Extremely high due to retry logic, durability guarantees, and distributed design.

Common Orchestration Patterns

1. Function Chaining

Sequential tasks executed in order.

```
await context.CallActivityAsync("StepA", null);

await context.CallActivityAsync("StepB", null);

await context.CallActivityAsync("StepC", null);
```

2. Fan-Out / Fan-In

Parallel execution followed by aggregation.

```
var tasks = new List<Task<int>>();

foreach (var item in items)
```

```
{
    tasks.Add(context.CallActivityAsync<int>("ProcessItem", item));
}

var results = await Task.WhenAll(tasks);
```

3. Async HTTP APIs (External Events)

Wait for external input (e.g., approval).

```
await context.WaitForExternalEvent<string>("ApprovalEvent");
```

Trigger via client function:

```
await       client.RaiseEventAsync(instanceId,       "ApprovalEvent",
"Approved");
```

4. Timers and Delays

Sleep until a future time or timeout.

```
var deadline = context.CurrentUtcDateTime.AddMinutes(10);

await context.CreateTimer(deadline, CancellationToken.None);
```

5. Retry and Compensation

```
await context.CallActivityWithRetryAsync(

    "ChargeCustomer",

    new RetryOptions(TimeSpan.FromSeconds(5), 3),

    input

);
```

If retries fail, you can trigger compensating actions (e.g., refund).

Durable Entities

Entities are **lightweight, stateful objects** managed within Durable Functions. They allow you to model state as **objects** rather than workflows.

Example: Cart Entity

```csharp
[FunctionName("Cart")]

public static Task Run(

    [EntityTrigger] IDurableEntityContext ctx)

{

    switch (ctx.OperationName.ToLowerInvariant())

    {

        case "add":

            var current = ctx.GetState<List<string>>() ?? new
List<string>();

            current.Add(ctx.GetInput<string>());

            ctx.SetState(current);

            break;

        case "get":

            ctx.Return(ctx.GetState<List<string>>());

            break;

    }

    return Task.CompletedTask;

}
```

You can then call it from any orchestrator or client:

```csharp
EntityId id = new EntityId("Cart", "user123");
```

```
await client.SignalEntityAsync(id, "add", "item456");
```

Monitoring and Diagnostics

Durable Functions integrates with **Azure Application Insights** for end-to-end telemetry:

- Visualize orchestrator timelines.
- Track failures and retries.
- Log custom events and state transitions.

Best Practices:

- Log orchestration and activity inputs/outputs.
- Tag instance IDs for correlation.
- Set custom metrics (e.g., execution time, retry count).

Real-World Scenarios

1. User Signup Flows

- Validate email
- Create user in identity store
- Send welcome message
- Track progress and retry on failure

2. Data Processing Pipelines

- Extract, Transform, Load (ETL) from multiple sources
- Handle partial failures gracefully
- Fan-out/fan-in for parallel processing

3. Approval Workflows

- Submit   request
- Wait   for   manager   approval
- Timeout   after   48   hours
- Notify   user   of   outcome

4. Scheduled Maintenance

- Schedule   a   future   job   (e.g.,   subscription   cancellation)
- Send   notifications   before   executing
- Run   logic   after   a   delay

Resilience Considerations

- Always   use   idempotent   activity   functions.
- Implement   retry   and   error-handling   inside   orchestrators.
- Validate   external   event   inputs.
- Test   for   failover   and   restarts   (orchestrators   should   replay   correctly).
- Monitor   for   stuck   or   long-running   instances.

Concurrency: Durable Functions ensures single-threaded execution for orchestrators and entities—this avoids race conditions but may require design considerations in high-throughput systems.

Scaling: Scaling is driven by the underlying function app—use Premium Plans or Dedicated App Service for high-scale workloads.

Conclusion

Azure Durable Functions is a robust, developer-friendly platform for building stateful, resilient, and scalable workflows in the cloud. By abstracting away the complexity of orchestration, state management, retries, and timeouts, it allows developers to focus on business logic while ensuring fault tolerance and operational consistency.

Whether you're building long-running business workflows, human-in-the-loop approvals, or IoT control loops, Durable Functions provide a powerful, cost-effective, and reliable foundation. In the next section, we'll explore how to enhance these patterns using **Azure Cache and Redis** to deliver low-latency, high-throughput state management for front-end and backend systems alike.

Leveraging Azure Cache and Redis for Performance

In cloud-native applications, performance, scalability, and responsiveness are critical to both user experience and operational efficiency. One of the most powerful techniques for enhancing these characteristics is **caching**—the practice of storing frequently accessed data in a high-speed data store to avoid repeated computation or slow data source access. On Azure, the most common and highly optimized caching solution is **Azure Cache for Redis**.

This section explores how to effectively use Azure Cache and Redis to boost performance, offload backend systems, support stateful patterns, and increase resilience. We'll cover caching patterns, implementation techniques, data consistency considerations, and architectural use cases. By the end, you'll understand how to integrate caching into your applications for better performance and availability without compromising correctness.

Why Caching Matters

Modern applications often perform repetitive operations:

- Fetching   product   catalogs

- Validating   tokens

- Querying   user   profiles

- Rendering   dashboards

Every one of these operations consumes compute, incurs latency, or places load on databases. Caching can reduce:

- Round-trips   to   slower   storage   (e.g.,   Azure   SQL,   Cosmos   DB)

- API   response   times   from   seconds   to   milliseconds

- Application   costs   due   to   reduced   consumption   of   compute   or   IOPS

Benefits:

- Reduced   latency

- Improved   scalability

- Lower   backend   load

- Enhanced   resilience   (through   local   failover   data)

Azure Cache for Redis Overview

Azure Cache for Redis is a fully managed in-memory cache built on the open-source Redis engine. It supports advanced features like pub/sub messaging, sorted sets, streams, geospatial data, and more.

Tiers:

- **Basic**:   Single-node   cache,   good   for   development.

- **Standard**:   Replicated,   primary/replica   architecture   with   automatic   failover.

- **Premium**:   Includes   clustering,   persistence,   geo-replication,   VNet   integration.

- **Enterprise**:   Active-active   caching,   Redis   modules   support,   higher   SLA.

Core Caching Patterns

1. Read-Through Cache

On a cache miss, the application fetches the value from the source (e.g., database), stores it in the cache, and returns it.

```
var data = await cache.GetStringAsync("user:123");

if (data == null)

{

    data = await database.GetUserAsync("123");

    await cache.SetStringAsync("user:123", data, options);
```

}

Use Cases:

- Product   catalog
- User   profiles
- Configuration   values

Pros:

- Simplified   application   logic
- Only   load   data   when   needed

---

2. Write-Through Cache

Data is written to both the cache and the underlying data source simultaneously.

```
await cache.SetStringAsync("product:456", jsonData);
await database.UpdateProductAsync("456", data);
```

Use Cases:

- Low-latency   applications   that   require   consistency
- Dashboards

Pros:

- Always   fresh   cache
- Reduced   read   latency

Cons:

- Risk   of   write   failure   to   one   system   (need   atomic   handling)

3. Cache Aside (Lazy Loading)

Application directly manages cache reads/writes. This is the most common approach.

```
string cacheKey = $"session:{userId}";

var sessionData = await redisCache.GetStringAsync(cacheKey);


if (sessionData == null)

{

    sessionData = await GetSessionFromDbAsync(userId);

    await    redisCache.SetStringAsync(cacheKey,    sessionData,    new
DistributedCacheEntryOptions

    {

        AbsoluteExpirationRelativeToNow = TimeSpan.FromMinutes(30)

    });

}
```

Use Cases:

- Any   application   that   uses   session   or   profile   data
- Reducing   duplicate   external   API   calls

Pros:

- Simple   to   implement
- Full   control   over   cache   timing

4. Write-Behind (Asynchronous Write)

Write to cache first, then update the backend system asynchronously.

Use Cases:

- High-throughput   logging

- Telemetry

- Event   buffering

Requires: Message queue or background processor to ensure backend sync.

---

5. Expiration and Eviction Policies

Every cached item should have a defined **TTL (Time-to-Live)**. Redis supports:

- **Absolute**   **expiration**

- **Sliding**   **expiration**

- **Eviction policies** like LRU (Least Recently Used), LFU (Least Frequently Used)

```
maxmemory 512mb

maxmemory-policy volatile-lru
```

This helps control memory usage and prevent stale data.

Integrating Redis with Azure Applications

ASP.NET Core Example

```
services.AddStackExchangeRedisCache(options =>

{

    options.Configuration                                          =
"myredis.redis.cache.windows.net:6380,password=...";

    options.InstanceName = "MyApp:";

});
```

Set and get session or configuration data:

```
await cache.SetStringAsync("key", "value");

string value = await cache.GetStringAsync("key");
```

Node.js Example with ioredis

```
const Redis = require('ioredis');

const redis = new Redis("rediss://:password@hostname:6380");


await redis.set("user:123", JSON.stringify(profile), 'EX', 1800);

const user = await redis.get("user:123");
```

Redis for Resilience and High Availability

Geo-Replication

Premium and Enterprise tiers support **geo-redundancy** between Azure regions.

- Use **active-active** cache topology in Enterprise tier.
- Ensures regional failover resilience.
- Data is automatically replicated.

```
az redis geo-replicate --name myRedis \

  --source-location eastus \

  --target-location westus
```

Persistence

Premium tiers support **RDB snapshots** and **AOF (Append Only File)** logs for durability.

- Snapshots every N minutes.

- Restore cache after restart or crash.

- Good for preserving state in stateful applications.

Advanced Redis Features

Pub/Sub Messaging

Useful for event propagation between microservices or instances.

```
PUBLISH newOrder "OrderID:12345"

SUBSCRIBE newOrder
```

Use Cases:

- Notifications

- Real-time chat

- Distributed triggers

Redis Streams

Log-based messaging for queue-style operations.

```
XADD mystream * message "Order Placed"
XREAD COUNT 1 STREAMS mystream $
```

Ideal for:

- Event sourcing

- Durable message queues

- Analytics pipelines

Cache Invalidation Strategies

1. **Time-Based**   **Expiry**

    o   Most   common   and   easy   to   implement.

2. **Explicit**   **Invalidation**

    o   Delete   keys   on   update   or   delete.

```
await redisCache.RemoveAsync("product:456");
```

3. **Versioned**   **Keys**

    o   Append a version number to keys. Update version to invalidate the whole
        group.

```
string cacheKey = $"user:v1:{userId}";
```

4. **Event-Driven**   **Invalidation**

    o   Invalidate based on events from a queue or database change feed (e.g.,
        Cosmos   DB   Change   Feed).

Real-World Case Study

Scenario:
 A high-traffic news platform was experiencing performance bottlenecks due to frequent reads
from Azure SQL for article metadata.

Implementation:

- Moved   metadata   to   Redis   cache   using   cache-aside   pattern.

- Cached   each   article   with   a   10-minute   TTL.

- Used   Redis   streams   to   notify   other   services   of   updates.

- Introduced   automatic   fallback   to   Cosmos   DB   if   Redis   was   unreachable.

Results:

- Reduced SQL read traffic by 80%.
- Page load times improved from 900ms to 140ms.
- Cache hit ratio averaged 94% during peak traffic.

Monitoring and Metrics

Use **Azure Monitor** and **Redis Metrics**:

- Cache hit ratio
- Evictions
- Memory usage
- CPU and latency
- Network throughput

Configure alerts to detect performance degradation or data loss risks.

Best Practices Summary

- Always use expiration (TTL) on keys.
- Prefer cache-aside for flexibility.
- Monitor hit ratios and eviction rates.
- Secure Redis with firewall rules and TLS.
- Use clustering for large-scale apps.
- Consider persistence for critical data.
- Avoid over-caching dynamic data.

Conclusion

Azure Cache for Redis is a cornerstone of high-performance, resilient applications. When used effectively, it transforms application responsiveness, lowers backend strain, and introduces powerful architectural flexibility. Whether caching sessions, configuration, product data, or orchestrating pub/sub messaging, Redis offers a mature, scalable, and feature-rich platform to meet the needs of cloud-native systems.

By designing your applications to incorporate caching thoughtfully—with well-managed TTLs, consistency strategies, and fallback mechanisms—you unlock significant gains in both speed and reliability. In the next chapter, we'll move into **Resilience in Data Architectures**, exploring how to build highly available, partitioned, and recoverable data layers in Azure.

Chapter 5: Resilience in Data Architectures

Azure SQL and Cosmos DB Resilience Features

Data is the backbone of any application. Whether it's user information, transactional records, product catalogs, or telemetry, a system's ability to withstand faults is only as strong as the resilience of its data layer. Azure provides two powerful database platforms—**Azure SQL Database** and **Azure Cosmos DB**—each offering a range of features that support high availability, disaster recovery, scalability, and consistency.

This section explores the native resilience features of both Azure SQL and Cosmos DB. We'll examine architectural patterns, configurations, and operational practices to ensure that your data remains consistent, durable, and highly available even under adverse conditions. We'll also highlight best practices and provide architectural examples relevant to modern cloud-based systems.

Azure SQL Database: Overview and Availability Tiers

Azure SQL Database is a fully managed relational database-as-a-service (DBaaS) built on SQL Server. It offers built-in intelligence, automated backups, tuning, scaling, and resilience features across different service tiers.

Service Tiers:

- **General Purpose** – Balanced compute and storage, suitable for most workloads.

- **Business Critical** – High availability through Always On availability groups.

- **Hyperscale** – Highly scalable storage and compute, suitable for large databases.

Each tier offers different levels of availability, performance, and recovery options.

Resilience Features in Azure SQL

1. High Availability (HA)

- **Zone-Redundant Deployments (Business Critical tier):**
    - Replicas are spread across Availability Zones.

- o Provides automatic failover with minimal downtime.

- o SLA: 99.99%.

- **Automatic Failover Groups:**

  - o Supports geo-replication across regions.

  - o Failover is initiated automatically on outage or manually for testing.

```
CREATE FAILOVER GROUP MyGroup

WITH (

    PARTNER = 'myserver-secondary.database.windows.net',

    AUTOMATIC_FAILOVER = ON

);
```

- **Multiple Replicas:**

  - o Business Critical tier uses 3–4 replicas (1 primary, 2-3 secondaries).

  - o Automatic replica failover occurs if the primary becomes unavailable.

---

2. Geo-Replication

Azure SQL supports **active geo-replication**, which creates readable secondaries in up to four regions.

Benefits:

- Improved read performance for global apps.

- Fast disaster recovery.

- Supports planned failovers and DR testing.

Failover Time: ~30 seconds to a few minutes depending on data volume and region proximity.

```
ALTER  DATABASE  mydb  ADD  SECONDARY  ON  SERVER  mysecondary  WITH
(ALLOW_CONNECTIONS = ALL);
```

3. Automated Backups and Point-in-Time Restore

Azure SQL automatically backs up your database every 5–10 minutes and retains backups for:

- 7–35 days (configurable)
- Up to 10 years with **long-term retention (LTR)**

Point-in-Time Restore (PITR):

- Restore to any second within the backup retention window.
- Useful for accidental deletes or data corruption.

```
az sql db restore --dest-name mydb-restore \
  --name mydb --time "2025-01-01T10:00:00Z"
```

4. Connection Resiliency

Azure SQL's client libraries (like `Microsoft.Data.SqlClient` or Entity Framework) support built-in retry logic for transient faults.

Best Practices:

- Use `ExecutionStrategy` in EF Core.
- Set up connection retry policies.
- Monitor for frequent retries (may indicate upstream issues).

5. Monitoring and Diagnostics

Tools:

- **Query** **Performance** **Insight**

- **SQL** **Analytics** **(Log** **Analytics** **workspace)**

- **Intelligent** **Insights** for performance tuning and anomaly detection.

Metrics to monitor:

- Replica lag

- DTU utilization

- Deadlocks

- Error 40613 (failover in progress)

Azure Cosmos DB: Overview and Multi-Region Features

Cosmos DB is a globally distributed NoSQL database designed for high availability, horizontal scalability, and low-latency access to data across the globe. It supports multiple APIs including Core (SQL), MongoDB, Cassandra, Gremlin, and Table.

Key Attributes:

- 99.999% availability SLA for multi-region writes.

- Single-digit millisecond reads and writes.

- Multi-region replication with tunable consistency.

Resilience Features in Cosmos DB

1. Multi-Region Deployment

Cosmos DB can be configured to replicate data across any number of Azure regions.

Write Regions:

- Supports **multi-master** **(multi-region** **write)** deployments.

- Conflict resolution is built-in (last writer wins, custom, or user-defined functions).

Read Regions:

- Automatically routes reads to the nearest region.
- Offers faster access for global users.

```
var client = new CosmosClient(accountEndpoint, accountKey, new
CosmosClientOptions

{

    ApplicationPreferredRegions = new List<string> { "East US", "West
Europe" },

    ConsistencyLevel = ConsistencyLevel.Session

});
```

---

2. Consistency Levels

Cosmos DB offers five levels of consistency:

Level	Availability	Latency	Consistency
Strong	Low	High	Total order
Bounded Staleness	Medium	Medium	Predictable lag
Session	High	Low	Per-session
Consistent Prefix	High	Low	Ordered reads

Eventual   Highest   Lowest   No ordering guarantee

Session consistency is the default and provides a balance for most workloads.

---

3. Automatic Failover

With multi-region deployments, Cosmos DB automatically fails over to another region in case of outages.

- **Manual** or **Automatic** failover configuration.
- Update priority list for region order.
- No manual intervention required once configured.

```
az cosmosdb failover-priority-change --name mydb \

  --resource-group myrg \

  --failover-policies WestEurope=0 EastUS=1
```

---

4. Partitioning and Throughput

- **Partitioning** enables horizontal scaling across containers.
- Define partition key wisely to avoid hot partitions.
- Supports **autoscale throughput** (400 RU/s – 1M RU/s).

```json
{

  "id": "order123",

  "userId": "user456",

  "partitionKey": "userId"

}
```

Autoscale adapts to workload fluctuations while ensuring cost-efficiency and availability.

---

5. Backup and Restore

While Cosmos DB does not provide traditional on-demand backup/restore in the portal (as of current capabilities), it does support:

- **Automatic** **backups** **every** **4** **hours**.
- **Retention** **up** **to** **30** **days**.
- **Point-in-time** **restore** (Preview).
- **Change** **Feed** for real-time data tracking and recovery.

Use **Azure Data Factory**, **Functions**, or **Custom Pipelines** for exporting backups or replicating data.

Monitoring and Diagnostics in Cosmos DB

- **Azure** **Monitor** **integration** for metrics and logs.
- **Diagnostic** **settings** export to Log Analytics or Event Hubs.
- Use **Cosmos** **DB** **Profiler** for local development.

Key metrics:

- RU/s consumption
- Request latency
- Throttled requests
- Data replication lag

Best Practices for Resilient Data Architectures

1. **Use Geo-Redundancy**
   - SQL: Auto-failover groups.
   - Cosmos: Multi-region writes and read regions.

2. **Monitor for Failures**
   - Use Application Insights, Alerts, and Health Checks.

3. **Design for Partitioning and Throughput**
   - Choose appropriate partition keys in Cosmos DB.
   - Monitor hot partitions.

4. **Implement Retry Logic**
   - SQL: Use transient fault handling libraries.
   - Cosmos: Use `RetryOptions` in the SDK.

5. **Test DR Scenarios Regularly**
   - Perform failover and failback testing.
   - Validate consistency and availability after region outage.

Real-World Case Study

Scenario: A ride-sharing app stored location data and user sessions in Cosmos DB and used Azure SQL for transactional metadata (billing, invoices).

Architecture:

- Cosmos DB with multi-region writes in East US and West Europe.
- Azure SQL with auto-failover group to Central US.
- Application APIs used cache-aside with Redis for recent trip data.
- Cosmos DB Change Feed processed via Azure Functions for analytics.

Resilience Outcomes:

- During a planned outage in East US, Cosmos DB redirected traffic seamlessly.

- Auto-failover group kept SQL online without noticeable impact.

- RTO was under 60 seconds; no data loss occurred.

Conclusion

Both Azure SQL and Cosmos DB are architected to deliver high availability and resilience. Azure SQL offers strong consistency, automated backups, and reliable HA/DR configurations for relational workloads. Cosmos DB, on the other hand, provides unmatched flexibility and global distribution for NoSQL workloads with advanced multi-region capabilities and tunable consistency.

Choosing the right database and configuring its resilience features thoughtfully ensures that your applications can withstand failures, maintain service continuity, and deliver a seamless experience to users worldwide. In the next section, we will explore **Replication and Partitioning Strategies** to further enhance performance and fault tolerance in distributed data systems.

Replication and Partitioning Strategies

Replication and partitioning are foundational strategies for designing scalable, resilient, and high-performing data architectures in the cloud. In Azure, these techniques empower applications to distribute workload, minimize latency, prevent bottlenecks, and survive component or region failures. Replication ensures high availability and data redundancy, while partitioning—also known as sharding—distributes data across storage units to support massive scale-out.

This section explores replication and partitioning strategies in both Azure SQL and Cosmos DB, providing patterns, implementation guidance, and best practices to help you design resilient data systems. We'll examine logical versus physical partitioning, synchronous versus asynchronous replication, and how to combine these patterns to meet high-throughput, low-latency, and disaster recovery goals.

Understanding Replication

Replication is the process of copying and maintaining database objects in multiple databases across different locations. It improves fault tolerance and enables read scalability, especially in global applications.

Benefits of Replication

- **High availability**: If the primary replica fails, another replica can take over.

- **Disaster recovery**: Geographic replication protects against regional outages.

- **Read scaling**: Read requests can be served from multiple replicas.

- **Low latency**: Users are directed to the nearest replica for faster access.

Replication in Azure SQL

Azure SQL Database offers **active geo-replication** and **auto-failover groups** as core mechanisms for data replication.

1. Active Geo-Replication

- Supports up to four readable secondary replicas.

- Uses **asynchronous** **replication**.

- Designed for applications that need fast, geographically distributed reads.

```
-- Add a secondary replica

ALTER DATABASE MyDatabase ADD SECONDARY ON SERVER MySecondary WITH
(ALLOW_CONNECTIONS = ALL);
```

- Failover is manual and must be handled by the client or administrator.

- Each secondary can serve read-only traffic.

2. Auto-Failover Groups

- Extends active geo-replication by automating failover.

- Includes both primary and secondary servers.

- Provides a DNS-based listener that automatically redirects connections.

```
-- Create failover group

CREATE FAILOVER GROUP myFailoverGroup
```

```
WITH (

    PARTNER = 'mySecondaryServer.database.windows.net',

    AUTOMATIC_FAILOVER = ON

);
```

Replication latency is usually under a few seconds but not guaranteed to be zero.

Replication in Cosmos DB

Azure Cosmos DB offers **multi-region replication** natively. Each region acts as a replica, and data is replicated **asynchronously** across them.

Multi-Region Replication

- Configure replication through the Azure portal or CLI.
- Choose which regions can accept reads and/or writes.
- Use **automatic failover** or set manual policies.

```
az cosmosdb update \

  --name myCosmosDb \

  --resource-group myResourceGroup \

  --locations regionName=EastUS failoverPriority=0 \

  --locations regionName=WestEurope failoverPriority=1
```

Write Region Replication

- **Multi-region writes** provide active-active configurations.
- Ideal for globally distributed apps with low-latency write requirements.
- Uses conflict resolution strategies: Last Write Wins (LWW), custom logic, or user-defined functions.

Replication Considerations

- **Consistency**: Azure SQL provides strong consistency for primary replicas, eventual for secondaries. Cosmos DB offers five consistency levels.

- **Latency**: Higher with geo-replication, especially for writes in asynchronous setups.

- **Conflict resolution**: Needed for active-active scenarios, especially in Cosmos DB.

Understanding Partitioning

Partitioning is a strategy to divide data into smaller, more manageable pieces (partitions) across multiple servers, disks, or compute nodes. This enables horizontal scalability and improved performance.

Types of Partitioning

1. **Horizontal Partitioning (Sharding)**

   - Distributes rows across partitions based on a key.

   - Common in NoSQL databases like Cosmos DB.

2. **Vertical Partitioning**

   - Separates columns into different tables or databases.

   - Useful when dealing with large and infrequently accessed fields (e.g., logs, metadata).

3. **Functional Partitioning**

   - Different microservices or business domains use separate databases.

   - Supports separation of concerns and domain boundaries.

Partitioning in Azure SQL

Azure SQL does not offer automatic partitioning, but supports **partitioned tables** and **elastic database sharding**.

1. Partitioned Tables

Split large tables into chunks using partition functions.

```
CREATE PARTITION FUNCTION pfRange (int)
AS RANGE LEFT FOR VALUES (10000, 20000, 30000);
```

Use Cases:

- Time-series data.
- Archiving and purging strategies.
- Optimizing query performance via partition elimination.

2. Elastic Database Sharding

- Application logic determines the shard based on a shard key.
- Use **Elastic Database Client Library** or build custom routing logic.

Common patterns:

- User ID or Tenant ID as shard key.
- Metadata service maps keys to databases.

Challenges:

- Requires custom management of routing, migrations, and cross-shard queries.

Partitioning in Cosmos DB

Cosmos DB is a **natively partitioned** database. Every container must define a partition key that determines how data is distributed.

Choosing a Partition Key

Good keys have:

- High cardinality (many unique values).
- Even distribution of workload.
- Low cross-partition query requirements.

Example Document:

```
{
  "id": "order789",
  "userId": "user123",
  "partitionKey": "userId"
}
```

Best Practice: Avoid using values with few unique values (e.g., "country") as partition keys. This leads to **hot partitions** and throttling.

Monitoring Partitions

Use Azure Monitor to track:

- RU consumption per partition
- Hot partitions
- Partition size growth

Combining Replication and Partitioning

In highly scalable and resilient architectures, both techniques are combined:

Example: Global SaaS App

- Cosmos DB with userId-based partitioning.
- Replicated to East US, Europe, and Asia.
- Azure SQL for billing with partitioned monthly data.

- SQL failover group configured for geo-redundancy.
- Redis cache in each region reduces backend queries.

Data Movement and Migration Tools

1. **Azure Data Factory**
   - Move data across databases, regions, and storage accounts.
   - Supports incremental copies and transformations.
2. **Cosmos DB Data Migration Tool**
   - Import/export data from SQL, MongoDB, JSON, CSV.
3. **Elastic Jobs for SQL**
   - Automate cross-database management operations.

Best Practices

- **For Replication:**
  - Use automatic failover where possible.
  - Monitor replica lag and availability.
  - Design clients to retry reads/writes gracefully.
- **For Partitioning:**
  - Choose a partition key that aligns with your query patterns.
  - Avoid hot spots by testing cardinality and distribution.
  - Monitor RU consumption and adjust as needed.
- **For Both:**
  - Architect for elasticity: allow your system to grow or contract with demand.

- o Design for failure: assume one partition or replica can go offline.

- o Separate read and write paths for optimization.

Real-World Example

Scenario: A streaming analytics platform processes logs from IoT devices worldwide.

- Cosmos DB stores telemetry with `deviceId` as partition key.

- Data replicated to 3 regions for availability.

- Read-heavy dashboards served from nearest region.

- Azure SQL used for account metadata, with geo-replication and sharded by tenant.

- Redis used for frequently accessed dashboards.

Outcome:

- Achieved 99.999% data availability.

- Zero-impact failover during regional outage.

- 60% lower latency for end users across regions.

Conclusion

Replication and partitioning are core techniques for building resilient and scalable data architectures in Azure. Replication ensures availability and fault tolerance, while partitioning unlocks horizontal scalability and performance optimization. Mastering both strategies enables you to support global user bases, withstand failures, and deliver low-latency experiences without compromising data integrity or throughput.

In the next section, we'll explore **Backup, Restore, and Data Retention Best Practices**, ensuring your data is not only always available but also recoverable, auditable, and compliant with regulatory requirements.

Backup, Restore, and Data Retention Best Practices

In any resilient data architecture, ensuring the **availability of backups**, the ability to **restore data quickly,** and maintaining **compliance with retention policies** is essential. No matter how robust a system is, data loss can occur—due to software bugs, operator errors, security incidents, or infrastructure failure. In such cases, backups are often the last line of defense. Azure provides a comprehensive set of tools and configurations across its data services to enable efficient and reliable data protection strategies.

This section focuses on backup strategies, restore operations, and data retention policies for Azure SQL, Cosmos DB, and other critical Azure storage services. We'll cover automation, encryption, security, versioning, and compliance considerations. Real-world use cases, best practices, and patterns will guide you in designing a backup and recovery architecture that supports both operational recovery and long-term retention.

Objectives of Backup and Retention

An effective backup strategy must address the following:

- **Recovery Time Objective (RTO):** How quickly you can restore service.

- **Recovery Point Objective (RPO):** How much data loss is acceptable.

- **Retention:** How long backups are stored (operational, legal, archival).

- **Security:** How backups are encrypted and protected.

- **Auditability:** Ability to prove compliance and conduct forensic analysis.

Azure SQL Database Backup

Azure SQL offers **automatic backups** for every database.

Key Features

- **Point-in-Time Restore (PITR):**

  o Restore to any second within the retention window.

  o Supports operational recovery (e.g., data corruption or accidental deletion).

- **Long-Term Retention (LTR):**

  o Keep backups for up to 10 years.

    ◦ Designed for compliance with legal or industry standards.

Configuration

- PITR is enabled by default:
  ◦ Retention: 7–35 days (General Purpose/Business Critical)
  ◦ 1–35 days (Hyperscale)

```
az sql db restore --dest-name db-restore \
  --name mydb --time "2024-12-01T13:00:00Z"
```

- LTR configuration (via portal or CLI):

```
az sql db ltr-policy set \
  --resource-group myrg \
  --server myserver \
  --database mydb \
  --weekly-retention P12W \
  --monthly-retention P6M \
  --yearly-retention P5Y
```

- Backups stored in RA-GRS storage, automatically geo-redundant.

Azure Cosmos DB Backup

Cosmos DB provides **automatic, continuous backups** with optional long-term retention.

Backup Characteristics

- **Continuous**   **mode**:
  - Every write operation is backed up.
  - Restore to any point in the retention window (7–30 days).
- **Periodic**   **mode**:
  - Backups every 4 hours.
  - Retention configurable up to 30 days.

Point-in-Time Restore

- PITR is enabled per account.
- Supports database and container-level restore.

```
az cosmosdb restore \
  --account-name mycosmosdb \
  --resource-group myrg \
  --restore-timestamp "2024-12-01T12:00:00Z" \
  --target-account-name mycosmosdb-restore
```

- Restore is done to a new account.
- You must redirect applications or data pipelines to the new account.

Azure Blob Storage Backup and Versioning

Blob Storage often contains critical unstructured data—documents, media, application assets. Azure provides several options for backup and data protection.

Versioning

- Automatically maintains previous versions of a blob.

- Allows recovery from accidental overwrite or delete.

```
az storage blob service-properties update \
  --account-name mystorage \
  --enable-versioning true
```

Soft Delete

- Retains deleted blobs for a specified period.

```
az storage blob service-properties delete-policy update \
  --account-name mystorage \
  --days-retained 30 \
  --enable true
```

Immutable Blob Policies (WORM)

- Prevent deletion or modification for a defined time.
- Useful for regulatory compliance.

```
az storage container immutability-policy create \
  --account-name mystorage \
  --container-name compliance \
  --period 365
```

Automation and Backup Scheduling

Azure supports automation through:

- **Azure Backup Vault** for VMs, Azure Files, and SQL Server in Azure VMs.

- **Azure Automation Runbooks** for custom backup orchestration.

- **Azure Logic Apps** for triggering backups on events or schedules.

- **Azure Data Factory** for cross-region data exports.

Example Runbook Pseudocode (Azure Automation):

```
Start-AzSqlDatabaseExport `

  -ResourceGroupName "myrg" `

  -ServerName "myserver" `

  -DatabaseName "mydb" `

  -StorageKeyType "StorageAccessKey" `

  -StorageKey $accessKey `

  -StorageUri
"https://mystorage.blob.core.windows.net/backups/mydb.bacpac"
```

Retention Policy Design

Considerations:

- Match retention periods with business, legal, or compliance requirements.

- Use tiered retention (e.g., daily for 30 days, monthly for 1 year).

- Evaluate costs—long-term retention consumes storage.

- Use lifecycle policies to move data between hot, cool, and archive tiers.

Security and Encryption

All backups in Azure are encrypted at rest using **Azure-managed keys** by default. You can also use **customer-managed keys (CMKs)** for more control.

- Blob Storage: SSE (Storage Service Encryption) and Azure Key Vault integration.

- SQL: TDE (Transparent Data Encryption) and optional CMKs.

- Cosmos DB: Encrypted with Microsoft-managed keys or user-assigned keys.

Secure Backup Best Practices:

- Restrict access to backup storage accounts.

- Enable firewall and VNet integration.

- Use private endpoints for secure data movement.

- Log all backup and restore operations (Azure Activity Logs).

Backup and Restore for Azure Kubernetes (AKS)

For stateful applications running in Kubernetes:

- Use **Velero** for backup and restore of Kubernetes objects and PVs.

- Integrate with Azure Blob Storage for durable backups.

- Schedule cluster backups or create snapshots of persistent volumes.

Testing and Validation

A backup is only as good as its ability to restore. Periodic validation is essential.

Testing Tips:

- Perform **quarterly** **restore** **drills**.

- Use sandbox environments to validate backup integrity.

- Automate test restores via CI/CD or scheduled jobs.

- Monitor restore duration (for RTO validation).

Real-World Case Study

Scenario: A healthcare SaaS provider stores sensitive patient data in Azure SQL and document attachments in Blob Storage. The system must comply with HIPAA and regional data retention policies.

Implementation:

- Azure SQL with 35-day PITR and 5-year LTR configured.
- Blob Storage with versioning, soft delete, and WORM policies.
- Cosmos DB with continuous backup and 30-day retention.
- Backup operations logged and reviewed quarterly.
- Restore tests automated with Azure DevOps pipelines.

Results:

- Passed HIPAA audit with zero findings.
- Successfully restored a deleted patient record within 15 minutes.
- Achieved RTO < 1 hour, RPO < 10 minutes.

Best Practices Summary

- Enable PITR and LTR on all critical databases.
- Use versioning and soft delete for Blob Storage.
- Test your restore processes regularly.
- Store backups in geo-redundant storage.
- Automate backup policies using Infrastructure-as-Code.
- Secure backup access and log all operations.
- Document and monitor RTO and RPO targets.

Conclusion

Backup, restore, and retention policies form the foundation of data resilience. Azure provides a robust set of native tools to automate, secure, and scale your backup strategies—ensuring data is protected against loss, tampering, or disaster. By aligning your approach with operational and compliance needs, and validating it through regular testing, you can ensure rapid recovery and business continuity under any circumstance.

In the next section, we'll explore **Handling Eventual Consistency**, a key concept in distributed systems that plays a vital role in designing globally resilient and highly available architectures.

Handling Eventual Consistency

In distributed systems—especially cloud-native, geo-distributed architectures—**eventual consistency** is a fundamental concept. It acknowledges the trade-off between immediate consistency, availability, and partition tolerance, famously encapsulated by the **CAP theorem**. While strong consistency is ideal, it is not always practical or necessary in modern systems that prioritize global availability, low latency, and scalability. Eventual consistency offers a more flexible, resilient alternative.

In this section, we will explore the principles of eventual consistency, how it manifests in Azure services like Cosmos DB, Azure Storage, and messaging systems, and how to design applications that remain **correct, reliable, and user-friendly** despite the temporary inconsistencies that may arise. We'll also discuss techniques like conflict resolution, convergence patterns, compensating transactions, and testing strategies to help you manage consistency in real-world cloud solutions.

What is Eventual Consistency?

Eventual consistency is a **consistency model** in which updates to a distributed system are guaranteed to propagate to all replicas eventually, but not necessarily immediately.

Key Points:

- All updates will eventually be visible to all nodes.

- There is a window where different nodes may return different responses.

- Data convergence is guaranteed, but timeliness is not.

Example:
A product inventory update is made in the East US region. A read in West Europe may still return the old stock value for a few seconds until replication catches up.

Why Eventual Consistency is Needed

1. **Geographic**   **Distribution**

   o Replicating data across regions introduces latency and network unpredictability.

   o Synchronous replication can slow performance or reduce availability.

2. **High**   **Availability**

   o Eventual consistency enables systems to remain operational even when partitions occur.

3. **Scalability**

   o Systems designed around eventual consistency can better scale horizontally.

4. **Latency**   **Reduction**

   o Local reads are faster without the need to coordinate with remote writes.

Eventual Consistency in Azure Cosmos DB

Azure Cosmos DB offers **five consistency levels**, providing a spectrum from strong to eventual consistency:

Level	Consistency	Availability	Latency
Strong	Linearizability	Low	High
Bounded Staleness	Tunable lag	Medium	Medium
Session	Per-session	High	Low

Consistent Prefix	Order-preserved	High	Low
Eventual	No guarantees	Highest	Lowest

The **Eventual** level allows highest availability and lowest latency but provides no ordering or staleness guarantees.

Best Use Cases for Eventual Consistency:

- Social feeds and timelines

- Product recommendations

- User activity logs

- Analytics pipelines

Designing for Eventual Consistency

To work effectively with eventually consistent systems, applications must be designed to tolerate and **resolve temporary inconsistencies**.

1. Read/Write Model Adjustments

- Design for **stale reads**: show a "last updated" timestamp.

- Use **retry and backoff** for reads immediately following writes.

- Cache data carefully to avoid amplifying inconsistency.

```
var result = await container.ReadItemAsync<Order>("order123", new
PartitionKey("user456"));

// If result is null, consider retrying after a short delay.
```

2. Client-Side Logic

- Display optimistic UI updates with fallback correction.
- Defer critical decisions until consistency is guaranteed.

3. Convergence Patterns

Ensure that updates eventually lead to the same result:

- **Idempotent writes**: Multiple identical updates produce the same state.
- **Commutative operations**: Order of updates doesn't affect the outcome.

Conflict Resolution

In multi-region writes, **conflict resolution** is necessary when concurrent updates occur.

Cosmos DB Conflict Resolution Strategies:

1. **Last Write Wins (LWW)**
   - Default strategy.
   - Uses a timestamp to resolve conflicts.
2. **Custom Conflict Resolution**
   - Define a stored procedure that merges document versions.
   - Full control over merge logic.
3. **Manual Resolution**
   - Application reviews conflicts and resolves them (logged in conflict feed).

Example Custom Resolver:

```
function resolveConflict(conflict, current) {
    if (conflict.status === "priority") return conflict;
    return current;
}
```

Conflict resolution logic must be:

- Deterministic

- Fast

- Stateless   (if   possible)

Compensating Transactions

Since distributed systems may not guarantee atomicity across services, compensating actions are used to "undo" or correct operations.

Use   Case:
 If a payment succeeded but the product allocation failed due to stale inventory count, a compensating transaction should refund the payment.

Implementation Patterns:

- Saga   pattern   (using   Durable   Functions)

- Outbox   pattern   for   reliable   messaging

- Explicit   rollback   APIs

Messaging Systems and Eventual Consistency

Azure messaging services like **Service Bus**, **Event Grid**, and **Event Hubs** operate in an eventually consistent manner.

- Message   delivery   is   at-least-once   by   default.

- Delivery   order   is   not   guaranteed   across   partitions.

- Event   handlers   may   process   events   out   of   sequence   or   with   delay.

Design Recommendations:

- Events   should   be   idempotent.

- Event handlers should store processing checkpoints.

- Use message deduplication where supported (e.g., Service Bus with duplicate detection).

Testing Eventual Consistency

Eventual consistency is not a bug; it's a feature. However, you must validate how your application behaves during inconsistency windows.

Testing Scenarios:

- **Stale reads**: Simulate delayed replication and check UI behavior.

- **Race conditions**: Simulate concurrent updates in different regions.

- **Conflict resolution**: Force conflicting writes and verify resolution logic.

Chaos Engineering tools like **Azure Chaos Studio** can introduce faults to validate resilience under replication lag or service partitioning.

Monitoring and Observability

Track consistency-related metrics:

- **Replication lag** (Cosmos DB diagnostics)

- **Conflict frequency**

- **Retry count**

- **Client latency spikes**

- **Custom logs for data divergence**

Use **Azure Monitor**, **Application Insights**, and **custom telemetry** to trace inconsistencies across systems.

Real-World Scenario

Scenario: A global photo-sharing app lets users like and comment on images. Data is stored in Cosmos DB with multi-region writes enabled.

Consistency Setup:

- Session consistency for user metadata.

- Eventual consistency for photo interactions and comments.

Challenges Encountered:

- Duplicate likes due to replays.

- Comment order mismatch between users in different regions.

Solution:

- Made like operations idempotent.

- Displayed "processing" states in UI for recent comments.

- Introduced conflict resolver to merge identical comments by same user.

Outcome:

- Improved perceived performance.

- System remained available during regional outages.

- Users experienced minimal inconsistency impact.

Best Practices Summary

- Use **eventual consistency** where strong consistency is not critical.

- Clearly communicate potential inconsistency to users.

- Use **timestamps**, **versioning**, or **vector clocks** for tracking state changes.

- Apply **conflict resolution** strategies suitable to your domain.

- Design for **idempotency**, **commutativity**, and **statelessness**.

- Implement **retry and convergence** logic for stale reads.

- Monitor and test for consistency anomalies proactively.

Conclusion

Eventual consistency is a natural byproduct of scalable, highly available distributed systems. When understood and embraced properly, it enables resilient, low-latency, and globally distributed applications to function reliably—even in the face of outages and network delays. Azure provides the tools and patterns necessary to work with eventual consistency while maintaining correctness and user experience.

In the next chapter, we'll move into **Messaging and Event-Driven Patterns**, which complement distributed data systems and help decouple services, buffer workloads, and improve fault isolation across microservices.

Chapter 6: Messaging and Event-Driven Patterns

Decoupling with Azure Service Bus and Event Grid

In distributed and microservice-based systems, **tight coupling between components** significantly limits scalability, fault tolerance, and agility. A change in one component can ripple through the system, forcing synchronized deployments and introducing fragility. One of the most effective ways to achieve **loose coupling** and **resilience** is by introducing **messaging** as a communication pattern.

Azure provides multiple messaging services, with **Azure Service Bus** and **Azure Event Grid** being the primary tools for building event-driven and decoupled systems. Each service serves different roles in the architecture, and understanding their use cases, patterns, and integration points is essential for building scalable, fault-isolated systems.

This section covers how to use these services to decouple components, buffer workload spikes, improve fault tolerance, and enable asynchronous communication across microservices or serverless components.

Why Decoupling Matters

Coupling increases complexity and brittleness in systems. In tightly coupled systems:

- A failure in one service can cascade to others.
- Services must be online and responsive at the same time.
- Deployments must be coordinated.
- Scaling one service often requires scaling others.

By **decoupling producers from consumers** using messaging:

- Services operate independently.
- Failures are isolated.
- Asynchronous communication improves responsiveness.
- Scaling is granular and demand-driven.

Azure Service Bus Overview

Azure Service Bus is a fully managed enterprise message broker. It supports advanced messaging features like:

- **Queues** **and** **topics**
- **Sessions** **and** **message** **ordering**
- **Dead-letter** **queues**
- **Scheduled** **delivery** **and** **retries**

Best Use Cases:

- Business transactions (e.g., order processing).
- Commands between services.
- Asynchronous workflows with ordered . steps.

Queues vs. Topics

Feature	Queue	Topic
Pattern	Point-to-point	Publish-subscribe
Consumers	One	Many
Scalability	Scales with receiver count	Scales with subscribers

Example: Decoupling Order Processing with Service Bus

An e-commerce application processes orders asynchronously to avoid blocking the frontend.

Architecture:

- Frontend posts a message to `orders` queue.

- Order processor backend picks it up and handles payment, shipping, etc.

- Failures are retried or moved to dead-letter queue (DLQ).

Code Sample (Sender - C#):

```csharp
ServiceBusSender sender = client.CreateSender("orders");


var message = new ServiceBusMessage(orderJson)
{
    MessageId = orderId,
    ContentType = "application/json"
};


await sender.SendMessageAsync(message);
```

Code Sample (Receiver - C#):

```csharp
ServiceBusProcessor processor = client.CreateProcessor("orders");


processor.ProcessMessageAsync += async args =>
{
    var body = args.Message.Body.ToString();
    // Process order
    await args.CompleteMessageAsync(args.Message);
};
```

Azure Event Grid Overview

Azure Event Grid enables reactive, event-based architectures. It routes discrete events from publishers (like Blob Storage, Cosmos DB, custom apps) to subscribers.

Key Features:

- Push-based delivery.

- Near-real-time event routing.

- Support for multiple event handlers.

- Built-in integration with Azure services.

Best Use Cases:

- Event-driven automation (e.g., image upload triggers thumbnail generation).

- Data pipelines (e.g., file drop triggers processing).

- Notifications and integrations (e.g., audit log to SIEM).

Example: Serverless Processing with Event Grid

Use Event Grid to automatically trigger image resizing when a blob is uploaded.

Flow:

1. User uploads image to Blob Storage.

2. Event Grid publishes a BlobCreated event.

3. Azure Function is triggered to process the image.

Event Subscription:

```
az eventgrid event-subscription create \
  --name imageProcessor \
```

```
  --source-resource-id
"/subscriptions/xxx/resourceGroups/rg/providers/Microsoft.Storage/st
orageAccounts/mystorage" \

  --endpoint-type azurefunction \

  --endpoint
"/subscriptions/xxx/resourceGroups/rg/providers/Microsoft.Web/sites/
myfunc/functions/ResizeImage"
```

Function Trigger (JavaScript):

```javascript
module.exports = async function (context, eventGridEvent) {

    const blobUrl = eventGridEvent.data.url;

    // Resize image logic

};
```

Decoupling Patterns

1. Producer-Consumer (Queue-Based)

- Producer places messages on queue.
- One or more consumers process messages independently.
- Use when you need durability, retries, and ordered processing.

2. Publish-Subscribe (Topic/Event-Based)

- One publisher emits events.
- Multiple subscribers handle them in isolation.
- Ideal for broadcasting notifications, multi-team integrations.

3. Event-Carried State Transfer

- Events carry enough data to make processing self-contained.
- Consumers don't query external systems to enrich the message.

4. Command/Event Separation

- Use commands for imperative actions (via Service Bus).
- Use events to signal something happened (via Event Grid).

Ensuring Reliability

1. **Dead Letter Queues (DLQ)**

Messages that cannot be processed (e.g., after retries) are moved to a DLQ.

```
// Check dead-letter reason
var deadLetterMessage = await receiver.ReceiveMessageAsync();
Console.WriteLine(deadLetterMessage.DeadLetterReason);
```

2. **Duplicate Detection**

Service Bus allows setting a **message ID** with a **deduplication window** to avoid processing duplicates.

```
new ServiceBusMessage(orderJson)
{
    MessageId = orderId
}
```

3. **Retry Policies**

Use exponential backoff retry logic in consumers to reduce transient failures.

Monitoring and Observability

- Enable **Diagnostic Settings** to stream logs to Azure Monitor.

- Use **Application Insights** to track message delivery and handler execution.

- Monitor metrics like:

  - Message count

  - Delivery latency

  - DLQ rate

  - Subscriber success/failure rate

Alerting Example:

```
az monitor metrics alert create \

  --name DLQAlert \

  --resource myservicebus \

  --metric "DeadletteredMessages" \

  --threshold 10 \

  --condition "GreaterThan" \

  --aggregation "Total"
```

Real-World Example

Scenario: A financial tech startup uses event-driven architecture to decouple transaction handling from fraud detection and notifications.

Services Used:

- Service Bus queue for incoming payment processing.

- Topic with subscriptions for:

  - Audit logging (Storage Queue)

  - Real-time fraud detection (Azure Function)

  - User notifications (Event Grid to SignalR)

Benefits Realized:

- Failure in fraud detection did not delay payment processing.
- Teams could deploy independently.
- User latency reduced by 40%.

Best Practices Summary

- Use **Service Bus** for reliable, ordered, and transactional messaging.
- Use **Event Grid** for reactive, fan-out, and loosely-coupled event processing.
- Avoid tight coupling between producers and consumers.
- Design for failure with dead-letter handling and retry logic.
- Monitor and alert on messaging system health and throughput.
- Clearly define message contracts and schemas.
- Apply idempotency in consumers to avoid side effects from replays.

Conclusion

Decoupling through messaging is a cornerstone of resilient cloud architectures. By leveraging Azure Service Bus and Event Grid, developers can build systems that are scalable, responsive, and fault-tolerant. These messaging platforms abstract the complexity of communication, enabling components to operate independently while maintaining eventual coordination.

As we continue through the messaging landscape, the next section will focus on **Message Delivery Guarantees**—covering exactly-once, at-least-once, and at-most-once semantics—and how to architect for reliability and correctness in asynchronous systems.

Message Delivery Guarantees

In distributed systems, messaging guarantees define the reliability and semantics of how messages are transmitted and received between components. When designing event-driven architectures, understanding these **message delivery guarantees** is crucial to ensuring the correctness, resilience, and idempotency of business logic.

Azure's messaging ecosystem—comprising **Service Bus**, **Event Grid**, **Event Hubs**, and others—supports varying degrees of message delivery guarantees: **at-most-once**, **at-least-once**, and **exactly-once**. Each of these semantics has implications on system design, data integrity, fault handling, and duplication strategies.

This section explores each delivery guarantee in detail, illustrates how they apply in Azure messaging services, and offers architectural patterns and mitigation strategies to handle their trade-offs. We also discuss how to apply these guarantees in real-world applications to ensure system correctness and user experience continuity.

The Three Core Delivery Guarantees

1. At-Most-Once Delivery

- A message is **delivered** **zero** **or** **one** **time**.
- No retries are attempted in case of failure.
- There is **no** **duplication**, but there is a risk of **message** **loss**.

Pros:

- Simple logic.
- No duplicates.

Cons:

- Not reliable in failure scenarios.
- Risk of permanent data loss.

Use Cases:

- Non-critical   telemetry.

- Idempotent   or   time-insensitive   logs.

- Metrics   where   occasional   loss   is   acceptable.

---

2. At-Least-Once Delivery

- A message is **guaranteed to be delivered**, but it may be **delivered more than once**.

- Retries are used to ensure delivery in the face of transient failures.

- Applications must implement **idempotency** to avoid duplicate processing.

Pros:

- Durable   and   reliable   delivery.

- Works   well   across   flaky   networks   or   transient   failures.

Cons:

- Duplicates   may   require   complex   handling.

- Downstream   services   must   be   idempotent.

Use Cases:

- Payments,   orders,   transactions.

- Notifications,   workflow   triggers.

- Event   sourcing.

---

3. Exactly-Once Delivery

- A message is **guaranteed to be delivered once and only once**.

- Requires   coordination   and   transactional   state.

- Harder to achieve in distributed systems without native support.

Pros:

- Strong correctness guarantees.
- Simplifies business logic (no deduplication needed).

Cons:

- Complex and costly to implement.
- Often limited to specific systems or transaction scopes.

Use Cases:

- Financial systems with strict auditing.
- Inventory and stock level management.
- Compliance-bound workflows.

Delivery Guarantees in Azure Messaging Services

Service	At-Most-Once	At-Least-Once	Exactly-Once
Azure Service Bus	✗	✓ (default)	✓ (with sessions/transactions)
Azure Event Grid	✓ (default)	✓ (with retry)	✗
Azure Event Hubs	✓	✓	✗

Azure Service Bus: Guarantee Details

Service Bus provides **at-least-once delivery** by default. It supports **sessions**, **transactions**, and **duplicate detection** which can be used to approximate exactly-once semantics.

Duplicate Detection

If enabled, Service Bus can automatically discard messages with the same `MessageId` within a deduplication window (up to 7 days).

```
var message = new ServiceBusMessage(payload)

{

    MessageId = "txn-1234"

};
```

Enable duplicate detection on the queue or topic:

```
az servicebus queue create \

  --name myqueue \

  --resource-group myrg \

  --namespace-name myns \

  --enable-duplicate-detection true \

  --duplicate-detection-history-time-window "PT10M"
```

Sessions for Ordering + Exactly-Once Semantics

- Sessions ensure messages with the same `SessionId` are processed in order.
- Combined with **transactions**, they approximate exactly-once processing for session-bound workflows.

```
var message = new ServiceBusMessage(orderJson)

{

    SessionId = "order-5678"

};
```

Azure Event Grid: Guarantee Details

Event Grid offers **at-most-once delivery** by default but can be configured to support **at-least-once** using retry logic.

Retry Logic

- Retries automatically occur for up to 24 hours.

- Retry intervals use exponential backoff.

- Events not acknowledged with HTTP 2xx are redelivered.

Idempotent Subscriber Logic Example:

```
module.exports = async function (context, event) {

    const eventId = event.id;


    // Check if already processed

    const exists = await checkEventProcessed(eventId);

    if (!exists) {

        await processEvent(event);

        await markEventProcessed(eventId);

    }

};
```

Dead-Lettering in Event Grid

If delivery to a destination fails after retry, events can be routed to a dead-letter destination such as Blob Storage for inspection and reprocessing.

Azure Event Hubs: Guarantee Details

Event Hubs is designed for **high-throughput telemetry ingestion** and operates with **at-most-once** or **at-least-once** semantics depending on consumer implementation.

- **Producers** send messages with no built-in retries.

- **Consumers** are responsible for checkpointing and deduplication.

Best Practice:

- Use **Azure Event Processor Host** or **Azure Functions with Event Hub trigger**.

- Store checkpoints in **Azure** **Blob** **Storage**.

Designing for At-Least-Once

To safely use at-least-once delivery:

1. **Implement** **Idempotency**

Ensure that processing the same message multiple times has no side effect.

- Use unique transaction IDs.

- Lock resources before processing.

- Store processed message IDs in a cache or DB.

2. **Track** **Message** **State**

Maintain a durable log of processed message IDs (e.g., Cosmos DB, Redis).

3. **Use** **Durable** **Queues** **and** **DLQs**

Capture unprocessed messages in a **dead-letter queue** for manual or automated retry.

Designing for Exactly-Once

1. **Use** **Service** **Bus** **Transactions**

Wrap operations in a transaction that includes message completion and database writes.

```
await using var ts = await receiver.CreateTransactionAsync();


await ProcessMessage(message);

await receiver.CompleteMessageAsync(message, ts);

await ts.CommitAsync();
```

2. **Enable** **Duplicate** **Detection**

Use `MessageId` to discard replays during the deduplication window.

3. **Session** **Binding**

Group related messages by session and process them in order to maintain consistency.

Real-World Example: Payment Processing System

Scenario:

- A fintech application processes customer payments using Azure Service Bus.

- Each payment is sent with a unique transaction ID.

Architecture:

- Service Bus queue with duplicate detection enabled (10 min window).

- Consumer checks if payment has already been processed using a `ProcessedTransactions` table.

- If not, it proceeds with processing and logs the ID.

Outcome:

- Duplicate payments prevented during transient retry storms.

- Zero downtime during network blips due to retry resilience.
- Transactions committed exactly once using Service Bus transactions.

Monitoring and Troubleshooting

Key metrics to monitor:

- Delivery attempts
- DLQ message count
- Duplicate message detection rate
- Session state size (for Service Bus)

Use **Application Insights** or **Azure Monitor** to:

- Log message processing start and completion.
- Track retries, exceptions, and deduplication events.
- Alert on DLQ spikes or consumer lag.

Best Practices Summary

- Favor **at-least-once** for critical workflows; ensure **idempotency** in consumers.
- Use **duplicate detection** and **message IDs** in Service Bus for deduplication.
- For **exactly-once**, combine Service Bus **sessions** with **transactions**.
- Use **dead-letter queues** to capture and inspect undelivered or failed messages.
- Log all message processing attempts with **correlation IDs**.
- Monitor delivery latency and failure patterns to identify issues early.
- Test your system with **message duplication and delay scenarios**.

Conclusion

Message delivery guarantees are not just theoretical models—they directly impact the correctness, user experience, and fault tolerance of your applications. Azure offers tools across its messaging stack to support different levels of guarantees, enabling developers to design systems that are both resilient and performant. Understanding how to work within these semantics—especially implementing idempotent logic and using features like deduplication and transactions—is critical to success in distributed event-driven architectures.

In the next section, we'll examine **Handling Poison Messages**, where we discuss strategies to identify, isolate, and remediate malformed or unprocessable messages that could otherwise halt or degrade message-driven systems.

Handling Poison Messages

In any event-driven or message-based architecture, **poison messages** are an inevitable reality. These are messages that, for one reason or another, consistently fail processing—even after multiple retries—due to malformed content, missing data, unhandled logic errors, or incompatibilities in the consuming application. If not managed properly, poison messages can block message queues, cause cascading failures, and bring down entire subsystems.

This section dives deep into how to detect, handle, and remediate poison messages within Azure-based systems, particularly using **Azure Service Bus**, **Event Grid**, and **Event Hubs**. We'll explore dead-letter queues (DLQs), logging and monitoring strategies, automated remediation techniques, and best practices for ensuring system resilience when encountering such messages.

What Are Poison Messages?

A **poison message** is a message that cannot be processed by a consumer despite multiple retry attempts. These messages are different from transient failures because they are persistent and result in repeated failure.

Common Causes:

- Malformed payloads (e.g., invalid JSON).
- Business rule violations (e.g., invalid order amount).
- Missing or incorrect metadata.
- Version mismatches between producer and consumer.
- Bugs in the processing logic.

Symptoms of Poison Messages

- Message stuck in queue with repeated delivery attempts.
- High failure rate in telemetry logs.
- Dead-letter queue growth.
- Throttling or backpressure in message consumers.
- Slow processing of subsequent valid messages.

Azure Service Bus: Built-in Poison Message Handling

Azure Service Bus includes **automatic dead-lettering** for poison messages. After a predefined number of delivery attempts (default is 10), the message is moved to a **dead-letter queue (DLQ)**.

Dead-letter Queue Features

- Each queue or subscription has its own DLQ.
- DLQs are append-only, separate from main queues.
- DLQ messages retain full metadata and failure reason.

Dead-letter queue name format:

```
<entity path>/$DeadLetterQueue
```

DLQ Access Example:

```
var receiver = client.CreateReceiver("myqueue", new ServiceBusReceiverOptions
{
    SubQueue = SubQueue.DeadLetter
});
```

```
var message = await receiver.ReceiveMessageAsync();

Console.WriteLine(message.DeadLetterReason);

Console.WriteLine(message.DeadLetterErrorDescription);
```

Manual Inspection and Reprocessing

Poison messages can be inspected manually via tools such as:

- Azure Service Bus Explorer
- Azure Portal > Service Bus > Dead-letter messages
- Custom dashboards or logs

Reprocessing Strategy:

1. Fix the root cause (e.g., code bug, data inconsistency).

2. Reprocess messages using a script or requeue tool.

3. Archive or discard non-recoverable messages.

Example Script (Azure CLI):

```
az servicebus queue message transfer \
    --resource-group myrg \
    --namespace-name myns \
    --queue-name myqueue \
    --from-subqueue DeadLetter \
    --to-subqueue Main
```

Custom Dead-lettering Logic

Instead of relying solely on automatic DLQ handling, you can implement custom poison message detection.

Strategy:

- Wrap your message handler with try-catch.
- Log and flag repeated failures.
- Move message to a "quarantine" queue or blob storage.

```
try

{

    await ProcessMessageAsync(message);

    await args.CompleteMessageAsync(message);

}

catch (Exception ex)

{

    if (args.DeliveryCount > 5)

    {

        await                    args.DeadLetterMessageAsync(message,
"ProcessingFailed", ex.Message);

    }

    else

    {

        throw;

    }

}
```

Azure Event Grid and Poison Messages

Event Grid uses push-based delivery, where the destination (e.g., Azure Function, webhook) must return a **2xx HTTP status code** to confirm success.

If the destination fails repeatedly:

- Event Grid **retries with exponential backoff** for up to 24 hours.

- After exhaustion, events are **dead-lettered** if a DLQ is configured.

Configuring Dead-letter Destination

```
az eventgrid event-subscription create \

  --name mysub \

  --source-resource-id
/subscriptions/xxx/resourceGroups/myrg/providers/Microsoft.Storage/s
torageAccounts/mystorage \

  --endpoint <webhook-url> \

  --deadletter-destination \

    blob-container=mycontainer \

    storage-account-
id=/subscriptions/xxx/resourceGroups/myrg/providers/Microsoft.Storag
e/storageAccounts/mystorage
```

Dead-lettered events are stored as blobs and can be reviewed and retried.

Azure Event Hubs and Poison Message Handling

Event Hubs is primarily a data ingestion pipeline (e.g., telemetry, logs). It does not provide a DLQ, but poison message handling can be built into the **consumer logic**.

Approach:

- Validate event schema and content in the consumer.

- Log poison messages to a secondary store (e.g., Blob, Cosmos DB).

- Tag events with processing status or error codes.

Example:

```
try
{
    var data = JsonConvert.DeserializeObject<MyEvent>(eventBody);
    await ProcessData(data);
}
catch (JsonException je)
{
    await SaveToBlobAsync(eventBody, "poison");
}
```

Poison Message Patterns and Strategies

1. Quarantine Queue Pattern

Move unprocessable messages to a special queue or topic for inspection and recovery.

- Allows decoupling recovery logic from main processing.
- Enables alerts and dashboards for manual triage.

2. Retry with Backoff

Add retry logic with delay to handle transient errors.

- Avoid immediate repeated attempts.
- Combine with DLQ for ultimate fallback.

3. Poison Message Auditing

Log metadata about failed messages:

- Message   ID
- Timestamp
- Error   stack
- Source   system
- Processing   attempts

Store in:

- Application   Insights
- Log   Analytics
- Azure   Storage   or   Cosmos   DB

4. Schema Validation

Use schemas (e.g., JSON Schema) to validate messages early and catch structural issues.

- Helps   detect   malformed   messages   before   processing.
- Improves   confidence   in   automation   pipelines.

Monitoring and Alerting

Establish proactive alerts and dashboards:

- Track   **dead-letter**   **count**   using   Azure   Monitor   metrics.
- Alert   on   spikes   in   DLQ   or   processing   failure   rate.
- Use   **Application** **Insights**   to   trace   exceptions   with   correlation   IDs.
- Visualize   DLQ   trends   and   resolution   progress   over   time.

Azure Monitor Alert Example:

```
az monitor metrics alert create \

  --name PoisonMessageAlert \

  --resource myservicebus \

  --metric "DeadletteredMessages" \

  --condition "GreaterThan" 10 \

  --aggregation "Total"
```

Real-World Case Study

Scenario: A ride-sharing company experienced booking failures due to region-specific data anomalies from legacy systems. These anomalies resulted in malformed JSON payloads reaching the queue.

Architecture:

- Azure Service Bus queue with DLQ enabled.

- Poison messages routed to DLQ after 5 retries.

- Azure Function periodically read from DLQ and logged metadata to Cosmos DB.

- Developers triaged messages and built fixes for known issues.

- Once fixed, messages were replayed from Cosmos DB into the main queue.

Outcomes:

- Reduced downtime caused by faulty messages.

- 90% of poison messages recovered automatically.

- Mean time to recovery (MTTR) improved by 65%.

Best Practices Summary

- **Enable dead-lettering** on all messaging services where supported.

- Implement **idempotent and resilient consumers** with structured error handling.

- Use **quarantine queues** or blob storage for poison message triage.

- Monitor and alert on DLQ growth and processing errors.

- **Log all poison messages** with detailed metadata for investigation.

- Validate message structure early to catch malformed data.

- Regularly analyze DLQ contents to find systemic issues.

- Build **replay tools** to recover valid messages after fixing logic errors.

Conclusion

Poison messages are a natural byproduct of complex, distributed systems. The key to resilience lies not in avoiding them entirely, but in anticipating, detecting, and recovering from them efficiently. Azure's messaging services provide strong built-in support for handling poison messages, and with the right patterns—like dead-lettering, schema validation, and reprocessing pipelines—you can ensure that unprocessable messages never compromise the integrity, reliability, or scalability of your system.

In the next section, we'll look at **Event Sourcing and CQRS Patterns**, exploring how messaging and state changes can be modeled as events to unlock powerful patterns in system design, auditability, and scalability.

Event Sourcing and CQRS Patterns

Event-driven architecture is not just about decoupling services; it also enables powerful patterns for modeling state, behavior, and interactions. Among the most transformative of these are **Event Sourcing** and **CQRS (Command Query Responsibility Segregation)**. These architectural styles shift the way systems capture and persist data, emphasizing immutable events and separation of concerns between commands and queries.

This section explores the principles, benefits, and implementation strategies of Event Sourcing and CQRS in Azure-based architectures. We'll cover how they support auditability, scalability, and resiliency, along with concrete examples using Azure services like **Event Grid**, **Event Hubs**, **Cosmos DB**, and **Azure Functions**. We'll also address common pitfalls and how to overcome them.

What is Event Sourcing?

In a traditional system, data is stored in its current state—often in relational tables. Event Sourcing, by contrast, **stores all changes to application state as a sequence of immutable events**.

Example: Instead of storing a user's profile as a mutable record, Event Sourcing records events such as:

- `UserRegistered`

- `EmailUpdated`

- `ProfilePictureChanged`

The current state is derived by **replaying these events** in order.

Characteristics:

- Events are **append-only**.
- The **event log** becomes the source of truth.
- State is derived, not directly stored.

Benefits:

- Full audit trail of all changes.
- Easy to reconstruct past states.
- Natural fit for asynchronous processing.
- Enables time-travel debugging and analytics.

What is CQRS?

CQRS stands for **Command Query Responsibility Segregation**. It separates read and write operations into distinct models.

- **Commands** change state and are handled by a command model.
- **Queries** read state and are served by a read model optimized for performance.

Why CQRS?

- Optimizes for scalability by decoupling reads from writes.

- Enables independent scaling and modeling of data for reads vs. writes.

- Supports different data stores or formats for different concerns.

Event Sourcing + CQRS = Powerful Synergy

Combining Event Sourcing with CQRS allows:

- Commands to produce events.

- Events to update one or more read models.

- Queries to hit denormalized or pre-aggregated views.

Flow Example:

1. User submits `ChangeEmailCommand`.

2. Command handler emits `EmailChanged` event.

3. Event is stored in event log.

4. A projection updates the read model.

5. Queries access the read model directly.

Implementing Event Sourcing in Azure

1. Event Log Storage Options

- **Azure Cosmos DB**: Ideal for high-throughput event storage.

- **Azure Blob Storage**: Cost-effective for large, append-only event logs.

- **Azure Table Storage**: Simple schema, good for ordered events.

Each event should include:

- Event   ID

- Aggregate   ID   (e.g.,   User   ID)

- Event   Type

- Timestamp

- Payload

Event Example (Cosmos DB):

```json
{

  "id": "evt-123",

  "aggregateId": "user-789",

  "eventType": "UserRegistered",

  "timestamp": "2025-01-01T12:00:00Z",

  "data": {

    "email": "user@example.com",

    "name": "Jane Doe"

  }

}
```

2. Event Producers and Consumers

Use **Azure Functions**, **Event Grid**, or **Event Hubs** to publish and subscribe to events.

```csharp
[FunctionName("HandleUserRegistered")]

public static async Task Run(

    [EventGridTrigger] EventGridEvent eventGridEvent)

{

    var                            data                            =
eventGridEvent.Data.ToObjectFromJson<UserRegisteredData>();
```

```
await UpdateUserProjection(data);

}
```

Implementing CQRS in Azure

Command Side (Write Model)

- Azure Functions or ASP.NET APIs receive commands.

- Validate and authorize the command.

- Store events in an event store (Cosmos DB, Blob, SQL).

- Publish events via Event Grid or Service Bus.

Query Side (Read Model)

- Azure Functions or Cosmos DB change feed update projections.

- Read model stored in:

  - Cosmos DB for document views.

  - Azure SQL for reporting.

  - Redis for fast lookups.

Example: Projection Update

```
public async Task ApplyEmailChanged(string userId, string newEmail)

{

    var user = await _readRepo.GetUser(userId);

    user.Email = newEmail;

    await _readRepo.SaveUser(user);

}
```

Ensuring Consistency and Resilience

Eventual consistency is a natural aspect of Event Sourcing + CQRS.

Resilience Patterns:

- **Retry logic** in projection updaters.
- **Idempotent projections** to handle duplicate events.
- **Dead-lettering** failed events for offline processing.

Ordering Guarantees:

- Use partition keys and sequence numbers in Cosmos DB.
- Use Azure Event Hubs' partitioned consumers.

Versioning and Schema Evolution

Over time, event schemas change. Event Sourcing must support **versioned events**.

Strategies:

- Include version number in event payload.
- Use upcasters to transform old events to new format at runtime.
- Keep consumers backward-compatible.

Testing and Debugging

- Rebuild state by replaying events into an in-memory model.
- Snapshot intermediate states for performance tuning.
- Use Application Insights for tracing event flow.

Snapshot Example:

- Store a snapshot after every 100 events.
- On load, apply snapshot + subsequent events.

Real-World Use Case

Scenario: A logistics company implements a parcel tracking system.

Command Model:

- Commands: `CreateParcel`, `AssignDriver`, `MarkDelivered`
- Stored in Event Store (Cosmos DB)

Events:

- `ParcelCreated`, `DriverAssigned`, `DeliveryCompleted`

Read Models:

- Parcel Status View (Cosmos DB)
- Driver Schedule View (SQL)
- Notifications Queue (Event Grid)

Outcomes:

- Improved observability into parcel lifecycle.
- Enabled rollback of status updates.
- Reduced query latency by 70% through optimized read models.

Challenges and Considerations

- **Event ordering**: Must be preserved for correct projections.
- **Read model lag**: Design UI/UX to accommodate eventual consistency.

- **Complexity**: Event Sourcing adds cognitive load—apply only where justified.

- **Tooling**: No native Azure Event Store—build or integrate third-party tools like EventStoreDB.

Best Practices Summary

- Use **immutable, versioned events** to capture business facts.

- Persist events in scalable and reliable storage like **Cosmos DB**.

- Design **projections** to build read models tailored to query needs.

- Apply **CQRS** to separate command and query responsibilities.

- Implement **idempotent event handlers** and **retry logic**.

- Monitor event flows and failures with Azure Monitor and Application Insights.

- Introduce **snapshots** for efficient replay in high-velocity systems.

- Always consider **eventual consistency** in UI and data design.

Conclusion

Event Sourcing and CQRS are powerful patterns that change the way we think about data, behavior, and state in distributed systems. They enable high scalability, rich audit trails, and adaptability to change—qualities that are essential in resilient architectures. Azure provides all the components required to build robust implementations of these patterns, from serverless functions and messaging platforms to globally distributed storage systems.

In the next chapter, we'll move from architecture patterns to **Observability and Failure Detection**, where we'll explore how to monitor, trace, and automatically recover from faults using Azure-native tools like Application Insights, Azure Monitor, and Log Analytics.

Chapter 7: Observability and Failure Detection

Designing for Monitoring with Azure Monitor and Log Analytics

Modern cloud-native applications must be resilient by design—and observability is the lens through which resilience can be validated, measured, and improved. Without visibility into internal states, external interactions, and system performance, even the most robust architecture becomes a black box—impossible to troubleshoot and dangerous to operate at scale.

Azure offers a rich observability ecosystem led by **Azure Monitor** and **Log Analytics**, which work together to capture telemetry, generate insights, and drive automated actions. In this section, we will examine how to build a comprehensive monitoring strategy using these tools, how to instrument your application and infrastructure for maximum visibility, and how to establish meaningful, actionable observability practices aligned with business and operational objectives.

What Is Observability?

Observability is the ability to understand the internal state of a system based on the telemetry it produces. According to the **three pillars model**, observability comprises:

1. **Logs**: Structured and unstructured data about events and behavior.

2. **Metrics**: Numeric measurements over time (e.g., CPU, latency).

3. **Traces**: End-to-end paths of requests across components.

Together, these offer deep insight into:

- Performance   bottlenecks

- System   failures

- Usage   patterns

- Anomalies   and   regressions

Azure Monitor: The Central Hub

Azure Monitor is the foundational observability platform in Azure. It collects, aggregates, analyzes, and acts on telemetry data from your Azure resources and applications.

Key Capabilities:

- Data collection from VMs, containers, databases, and services.

- Alerts and dashboards for proactive monitoring.

- Querying via Kusto Query Language (KQL).

- Integration with external tools like Grafana, Power BI, and Azure Automation.

Architecture of Azure Monitoring

1. **Data Sources:**

   ○ Azure resources (e.g., App Services, SQL, AKS).

   ○ Custom applications via Application Insights SDK.

   ○ Operating systems and agents (e.g., Log Analytics agent).

   ○ Diagnostics logs from services like Azure Storage and Event Hubs.

2. **Data Platform:**

   ○ Azure Monitor ingests logs and metrics.

   ○ Data is stored in **Log Analytics Workspaces**.

3. **Insights & Actions:**

   ○ Dashboards

   ○ Alerts

   ○ Workbooks

   ○ Azure Logic Apps / Automation

Log Analytics: Query-Driven Insight

Log Analytics is the query engine and storage backend for logs in Azure Monitor. It uses **Kusto Query Language (KQL)** for querying telemetry.

Sample Query: View failed HTTP requests over the last hour

```
requests
| where success == false
| where timestamp > ago(1h)
| summarize count() by resultCode, cloud_RoleName
```

Common Tables in Log Analytics:

- `requests`: Tracks incoming HTTP requests.
- `dependencies`: Tracks outbound calls.
- `exceptions`: Captures unhandled errors.
- `traces`: Custom application logs.
- `metrics`: Standard and custom metric values.
- `heartbeat`: Agent status reports.

Instrumenting Applications with Application Insights

Application Insights is a feature of Azure Monitor designed for application-level observability. It supports:

- Automatic instrumentation for ASP.NET, Node.js, Java, and Python.
- Manual instrumentation for custom telemetry.
- Distributed tracing across services and APIs.

Enabling Application Insights in .NET Core:

```
services.AddApplicationInsightsTelemetry(configuration["APPINSIGHTS_
CONNECTIONSTRING"]);
```

Custom Event Example:

```
telemetryClient.TrackEvent("UserLoginAttempt",                      new
Dictionary<string, string>

{

    { "userId", "user123" },

    { "result", "success" }

});
```

Monitoring Infrastructure

Azure Monitor can collect metrics and logs from:

- **Azure VMs**: via Azure Monitor Agent (AMA).
- **Azure Kubernetes Service (AKS)**: via Container Insights.
- **Azure SQL, Storage, Redis, and Cosmos DB**: via Diagnostic Settings.

Enable diagnostics via CLI:

```
az monitor diagnostic-settings create \
  --resource <resource-id> \
  --name "sendToLogAnalytics" \
  --workspace <workspace-id> \
  --logs '[{"category": "AllMetrics", "enabled": true}]'
```

Building Dashboards and Workbooks

Azure Workbooks and Dashboards provide rich visualizations for real-time and historical data.

Common Monitoring Workbooks:

- App   performance   overview
- Availability   and   latency
- Failure   rate   trends
- Dependency   performance
- Infrastructure   heatmaps

Create a Workbook:

1. Go   to   Log   Analytics   Workspace   >   Workbooks.
2. Select   a   template   or   create   from   scratch.
3. Use   KQL   queries   to   drive   visualizations.

Creating Alerts

Azure Monitor supports **metric alerts**, **log-based alerts**, and **activity log alerts**.

Log Alert Example: Failed logins over 5 in 5 minutes

```
traces

| where message contains "Login failed"

| summarize count() by bin(timestamp, 5m)

| where count_ > 5
```

Create via Azure CLI:

```
az monitor scheduled-query create \

  --name "FailedLoginAlert" \
```

```
--resource-group myrg \

--workspace myworkspace \

--query "traces | where message contains 'Login failed'" \

--action
"/subscriptions/xxx/resourceGroups/myrg/providers/microsoft.insights
/actionGroups/myActionGroup"
```

Integrating with DevOps Pipelines

Embed observability into CI/CD pipelines:

- Run post-deployment health checks using KQL.
- Fail deployment if key metrics regress.
- Record deployment annotations in Application Insights.

Deployment Annotation (PowerShell):

```
Add-AzApplicationInsightsAnnotation `

  -ResourceGroupName "myrg" `

  -Name "myapp" `

  -AnnotationName "DeployV2.1" `

  -Properties @{ "status" = "Success"; "buildId" = "3015" }
```

Monitoring for Resilience

To ensure application resilience, monitor:

- **Availability**: Uptime, error rates.
- **Performance**: Response time, throughput.

- **Faults**: Exceptions, failed dependencies.
- **Saturation**: CPU, memory, IOPS.
- **Degradation**: Latency or retry increases.
- **Security**: Unauthorized access attempts, role changes.

Example Metrics:

- requests/failed
- dependencies/failed
- memory/used
- container/restart_count
- availabilityResults/availabilityPercentage

Real-World Implementation Example

Scenario: A healthcare SaaS provider uses Azure App Services, Cosmos DB, and AKS.

Monitoring Stack:

- Application Insights for App Services.
- Container Insights for AKS.
- Log Analytics for centralized querying.
- Workbooks for SLA compliance reports.
- Alerts routed to PagerDuty via Action Groups.

Results:

- 40% reduction in mean time to detection (MTTD).
- Predictive alerting based on traffic anomalies.

- Unified view of application and infrastructure health.

Best Practices Summary

- Instrument code with Application Insights for end-to-end tracing.
- Use Log Analytics and KQL to detect failure patterns.
- Enable diagnostic settings for all critical resources.
- Design dashboards tailored to ops and engineering teams.
- Create alerts on SLA thresholds and error rates.
- Regularly review observability coverage and gaps.
- Correlate telemetry using operation and trace IDs.
- Automate telemetry validation as part of CI/CD.

Conclusion

Designing for observability is not an afterthought—it's an architectural commitment. With Azure Monitor and Log Analytics, developers and operators gain the insight needed to detect, diagnose, and respond to issues proactively. By embedding observability deeply into both infrastructure and application layers, organizations can ensure continuous improvement, enhanced reliability, and faster recovery in the face of inevitable failures.

In the next section, we'll examine **Tracing with Application Insights**, focusing on distributed tracing and telemetry correlation across microservices, APIs, and user journeys.

Tracing with Application Insights

In modern distributed architectures—especially those built on microservices or serverless functions—**tracing** is essential to understanding how requests propagate through the system. It enables developers and operators to **visualize request flows**, **correlate telemetry**, and **identify performance bottlenecks** or failure points across service boundaries.

Application Insights, a core component of Azure Monitor, offers built-in support for **distributed tracing**, making it possible to track the journey of a request across APIs, queues, databases, and external services. This section explores how to use Application Insights for effective tracing, how to propagate correlation context, and how to troubleshoot complex systems using the data it provides.

What is Distributed Tracing?

Distributed tracing follows a single request across multiple systems and records the interaction at each step. Each trace typically contains:

- **Root operation** (e.g., HTTP request from a client)

- **Child operations** (e.g., downstream API calls, DB queries, queue messages)

- **Spans**: Units of work with timing and metadata

Each span is linked by a **trace ID**, allowing visualization of end-to-end workflows.

Benefits:

- Understand end-to-end request flow

- Pinpoint latency sources

- Detect broken or underperforming services

- Troubleshoot errors with context

Application Insights Telemetry Model

Application Insights automatically captures multiple telemetry types:

Telemetry Type	Description
RequestTelemetry	Incoming HTTP requests to your app
DependencyTelemetry	Outbound calls (e.g., HTTP, SQL, Cosmos)

`ExceptionTelemetry`	Unhandled exceptions
`TraceTelemetry`	Custom log messages
`EventTelemetry`	Custom business events

Each telemetry item includes:

- `operation_Id`: Correlates all telemetry for a request
- `parent_Id`: Links dependencies to their calling request
- `cloud_RoleName`: The logical service name (e.g., `auth-service`)

Enabling Tracing in .NET Applications

1. **Add Application Insights SDK**

```
dotnet add package Microsoft.ApplicationInsights.AspNetCore
```

2. **Configure in Startup.cs**

```
services.AddApplicationInsightsTelemetry();
```

3. **Propagate Correlation Headers**

When making outbound HTTP requests:

```
var client = httpClientFactory.CreateClient();
client.DefaultRequestHeaders.Add("Request-Id", Activity.Current.Id);
```

```
client.DefaultRequestHeaders.Add("Correlation-Context",
"key=value");
```

4. **Track** **Custom** **Dependencies**

```
var telemetry = new DependencyTelemetry

{

    Name = "Call Inventory API",

    Target = "inventory.api",

    Type = "HTTP",

    Data = "https://inventory/api/items/123",

    Timestamp = DateTimeOffset.UtcNow

};

telemetryClient.TrackDependency(telemetry);
```

Enabling Tracing in Azure Functions

1. **Application** **Insights** **Configuration**

Ensure `APPINSIGHTS_INSTRUMENTATIONKEY` or
`APPLICATIONINSIGHTS_CONNECTION_STRING` is set in the Function App.

2. **Function** **Binding** **Auto-Tracing**

Triggers like HTTP, Service Bus, and Cosmos DB are automatically traced.

3. **Custom** **Events** **and** **Exceptions**

```
var telemetryClient = new TelemetryClient();
```

```
telemetryClient.TrackTrace("Processing                    started",
SeverityLevel.Information);

telemetryClient.TrackException(exception);
```

Viewing Traces in Application Insights

Performance Blade

- Shows   average   response   time,   dependency   time,   and   failures.

- Breaks   down   by   operation   name,   role,   and   response   code.

End-to-End Transaction View

Visualizes request flow with nested dependencies.

- Colored   bars   show   relative   duration.

- Click   on   spans   to   view   detailed   telemetry.

Application Map

A topology graph showing dependencies between services and their health status.

- Nodes   =   services

- Edges   =   dependency   calls

- Colors   =   availability,   performance,   error   rate

Propagating Trace Context Across Services

Distributed tracing requires propagation of trace context:

- Use   **W3C**   **Trace**   **Context**   headers:

  - traceparent: Standard   format   for   trace   and   span   IDs.

o `tracestate`:   Optional   vendor-specific   context.

Example header:

```
traceparent: 00-4bf92f3577b34da6a3ce929d0e0e4736-00f067aa0ba902b7-01
```

Azure SDKs and Application Insights automatically handle this for supported platforms.

If using custom HTTP clients or messaging, propagate these headers manually.

Tracing Across Asynchronous Boundaries

Applications often use queues or event hubs, which introduce asynchronous boundaries.

To maintain traceability:

- **Embed trace context** in message metadata or payload.
- On message receipt, **resume the trace** using the original context.

Example: Azure Service Bus + Trace Context

Sender:

```
message.ApplicationProperties["traceparent"] = Activity.Current.Id;
```

Receiver:

```
ActivityContext context = ActivityContext.Parse(message.ApplicationProperties["traceparent"]);

var activity = new Activity("ProcessMessage").SetParentId(context.TraceId.ToString());

activity.Start();
```

Custom Telemetry and Enrichment

Enrich telemetry with additional properties for filtering and diagnostics.

```
var properties = new Dictionary<string, string>
{
    { "userId", "abc123" },
    { "feature", "checkout" }
};
telemetryClient.TrackEvent("CheckoutStarted", properties);
```

Telemetry Initializers automatically add custom context:

```
public class RoleNameInitializer : ITelemetryInitializer
{
    public void Initialize(ITelemetry telemetry)
    {
        telemetry.Context.Cloud.RoleName = "cart-service";
    }
}
```

Register in `Startup.cs`:

```
services.AddSingleton<ITelemetryInitializer, RoleNameInitializer>();
```

Integrating Traces with Logs and Metrics

Correlate logs and metrics using `operation_Id`:

Query: Find all telemetry related to a specific request

```
let traceId = "abc123...";
```

```
union traces, requests, dependencies, exceptions
| where operation_Id == traceId
```

You can create **workbooks** that combine logs, metrics, and traces for holistic observability.

Real-World Use Case

Scenario: A retail company deploys a microservices-based ordering system.

- Services include `frontend`, `cart`, `inventory`, `checkout`, and `notification`.
- All services emit telemetry to Application Insights.

Implementation:

- Common correlation logic using a shared tracing library.
- Azure API Management preserves trace context for downstream services.
- Service Bus messages include `traceparent`.
- Traces are visualized using Application Map and end-to-end views.

Benefits:

- Reduced MTTR from 2 hours to 15 minutes.
- Easily identified latency in checkout service due to dependency retry storm.
- Improved cross-team collaboration with shared tracing language.

Best Practices Summary

- Enable and configure Application Insights in all services.
- Use W3C trace context for consistent correlation across boundaries.
- Add trace context to messages and resume traces on consumption.

- Enrich telemetry with custom dimensions for meaningful filtering.

- Use Application Map to visualize service topology.

- Combine logs, metrics, and traces in queries and dashboards.

- Use telemetry initializers to standardize trace metadata.

- Apply alerting and SLA dashboards based on trace metrics (e.g., 95th percentile latency).

Conclusion

Tracing with Application Insights transforms how teams understand distributed applications. It provides the visibility needed to trace user journeys, diagnose failures, and optimize performance across multiple systems. By consistently applying trace correlation, instrumenting all services, and leveraging Azure's rich visual and analytical tools, you unlock the ability to build and operate truly resilient systems.

In the next section, we'll explore **Health Checks and Telemetry Pipelines**, focusing on continuous assessment of service health and building pipelines that route telemetry data for proactive and reactive remediation.

Health Checks and Telemetry Pipelines

System resilience is not just about recovering from failures—it's about **detecting them early, mitigating them swiftly**, and informing the right teams or systems before customers are affected. Health checks and telemetry pipelines are key tools in achieving this. They form the **early warning systems** and **feedback loops** that help distributed applications remain healthy and performant.

In this section, we will examine how to implement robust health checks in Azure-hosted applications, how to design telemetry pipelines that collect and route signals effectively, and how to use this data to trigger automated or manual responses. We'll cover best practices for infrastructure and application-level health checks, using tools like Azure Application Gateway, Azure Monitor, Azure Functions, and custom telemetry.

The Purpose of Health Checks

Health checks serve two core purposes:

1. **Liveness**: Is the application or service running?

2. **Readiness**: Is the application able to handle requests?

These checks can:

- Drive auto-healing logic (e.g., restart containers).
- Feed into load balancers to route traffic appropriately.
- Notify operations teams of degradation or failures.

Application-Level Health Checks

For web applications and microservices, implementing HTTP-based health checks is a common pattern. Most platforms (ASP.NET, Node.js, Java Spring) support health endpoints like:

```
GET /healthz
GET /readiness
GET /liveness
```

ASP.NET Core Example

```
public void ConfigureServices(IServiceCollection services)
{
    services.AddHealthChecks()
.AddSqlServer(Configuration["ConnectionStrings:DefaultConnection"])
.AddAzureBlobStorage(Configuration["BlobStorageConnection"]);
}
public void Configure(IApplicationBuilder app)
{
    app.UseEndpoints(endpoints =>
```

```
    {
        endpoints.MapHealthChecks("/healthz");
    });
}
```

Response Example:

```json
{
  "status": "Healthy",
  "results": {
    "sql": {
      "status": "Healthy"
    },
    "blob": {
      "status": "Healthy"
    }
  }
}
```

Azure Services and Health Probes

1. Azure Application Gateway

- Uses custom probes to check backend health.
- Supports custom paths (e.g., /healthz) and intervals.

```
az network application-gateway probe create \
```

```
--gateway-name myGateway \

--resource-group myRG \

--name myHealthProbe \

--protocol Http \

--host www.example.com \

--path /healthz \

--interval 30 \

--timeout 20 \

--unhealthy-threshold 3
```

2. Azure Kubernetes Service (AKS)

- Supports `livenessProbe` and `readinessProbe` for Pods.

```
livenessProbe:
  httpGet:
    path: /healthz
    port: 80
  initialDelaySeconds: 5
  periodSeconds: 10
```

3. Azure Front Door

- Integrates with health probes to exclude unhealthy backends.

Custom Health Checks for Dependencies

Dependencies like databases, caches, or APIs should be tested periodically.

Examples:

- Can the app connect to SQL and run a query?
- Is Redis available and responsive?
- Are storage accounts returning expected results?

Consider wrapping these checks with **timeouts** and **circuit breakers** to avoid cascading failures.

Building Telemetry Pipelines

A telemetry pipeline is the flow of metrics, logs, and traces from their source to destinations where they can be analyzed or trigger actions.

Telemetry Sources:

- Applications (via Application Insights SDK)
- Azure services (via Diagnostic Settings)
- Infrastructure (via Azure Monitor Agent)
- Custom events and logs (via REST APIs or SDKs)

Pipeline Components:

1. **Collection**: App Insights, Log Analytics agents.
2. **Processing**: Filters, aggregators, transformation layers.
3. **Routing**: Logic Apps, Event Hub, Azure Monitor Export.
4. **Storage**: Log Analytics, Azure Blob, Cosmos DB.
5. **Action**: Alerts, dashboards, automated remediation.

Sample Pipeline: Application Insights to Alerting and Dashboard

Flow:

- App emits `RequestTelemetry` and `ExceptionTelemetry`.
- Data goes to Log Analytics workspace.
- Queries detect error spikes or threshold violations.
- Alerts sent via Action Groups (email, SMS, webhook).
- Dashboard displays real-time health status.

Combining Health Checks with Telemetry

Health checks provide **point-in-time binary status**, while telemetry provides **rich continuous insight**.

Pattern:

- Run health checks periodically (e.g., every 30s).
- Emit custom telemetry based on results.

```
if (!CheckDatabaseConnection())

{

    telemetryClient.TrackTrace("DB                check              failed",
SeverityLevel.Error);

    return HealthCheckResult.Unhealthy("Cannot connect to SQL");

}
```

Aggregate with:

```
customMetrics

| where name == "health_status"

| summarize count() by value, bin(timestamp, 1m)
```

Auto-Healing and Automated Response

1. Azure Auto-Heal (App Services):

- Restart app based on memory, request count, or status code patterns.

2. Azure Functions + Alerts:

- Trigger Azure Function when alert fires (e.g., service is unhealthy).
- Function restarts a container, scales up a resource, or notifies support.

3. Logic Apps / Power Automate:

- Integrate telemetry-based alerts into business processes (e.g., ITSM ticket creation).

Real-World Use Case

Scenario: A fintech platform runs microservices in AKS and uses Azure Front Door.

Implementation:

- Each service exposes `/healthz` and `/readiness`.
- Front Door probes each region to route traffic intelligently.
- Application Insights logs health failures and HTTP 5xx.
- Azure Monitor alerts notify on three consecutive failures.
- A Logic App escalates to PagerDuty and restarts pods via Azure CLI.

Outcomes:

- Reduced false positives through readiness vs. liveness separation.
- 5x improvement in incident response time.
- Higher availability through automatic traffic failover.

Best Practices Summary

- Implement both **liveness** and **readiness** checks.
- Use **dependency-aware health checks** (e.g., SQL, Redis, queues).
- Integrate health status with **load balancers** and **orchestration platforms**.
- Design **telemetry pipelines** that route key signals to the right consumers.
- Monitor **health trends** over time for anomaly detection.
- Automate actions (restart, scale, alert) based on health degradation.
- Regularly test and simulate health check failures.

Conclusion

Health checks and telemetry pipelines form the nervous system of resilient cloud systems. While health checks enable services to declare their status to the outside world, telemetry pipelines provide the depth, nuance, and history needed to act on those signals. By designing both in tandem, teams can gain real-time situational awareness, shorten incident lifecycles, and build self-healing systems that detect and resolve issues with minimal human intervention.

In the next section, we'll explore **Automating Recovery with Azure Automation**, focusing on self-remediation strategies triggered by health failures, alerts, and predictive insights.

Automating Recovery with Azure Automation

As modern systems grow in scale and complexity, **manual recovery from incidents** becomes untenable. While monitoring and alerts are essential for detecting issues, the next evolutionary step toward resilience is **automated recovery**—systems that **identify**, **diagnose**, and **remediate** issues without human intervention.

Azure Automation is a powerful platform that enables such intelligent, hands-off remediation. It combines capabilities like **runbooks**, **update management**, **PowerShell and Python scripting**, **hybrid workers**, and **integration with Azure Monitor**, to respond to signals across your Azure and hybrid environment. This section explores how to use Azure Automation to implement automated recovery processes, integrate with monitoring signals, and build a framework for continuous, intelligent system healing.

The Case for Automated Recovery

Manual recovery challenges:

- Delayed response due to human bottlenecks.
- Increased MTTR (Mean Time To Repair).
- Inconsistent remediation actions.
- Human error under stress.

Automated recovery benefits:

- Faster response times.
- Consistency and repeatability.
- 24/7 operations without fatigue.
- Integration with monitoring for closed-loop systems.

Automated recovery is especially important for **scaling systems**, **mission-critical apps**, and **compliance-driven environments**.

What Is Azure Automation?

Azure Automation is a cloud-based platform for **process automation**, **configuration management**, **update deployment**, and **shared runbooks**.

Key components:

- **Runbooks**: Workflows written in PowerShell or Python.
- **Automation Accounts**: Containers for scripts, assets, and credentials.
- **Schedules**: Time-based triggers.
- **Webhooks**: Event-based triggers from external systems.
- **Hybrid Workers**: Agents to run scripts on-premises or in specific networks.

Types of Runbooks

1. **Graphical**   **Runbooks**
   - Built with a visual designer.
   - Good for simple workflows.

2. **PowerShell**   **Runbooks**
   - Written in PowerShell; ideal for Windows and Azure tasks.

3. **Python**   **Runbooks**
   - Useful for Linux tasks or cross-platform scripting.

4. **Webhook-Triggered**   **Runbooks**
   - Used to invoke recovery actions via alert rules or third-party systems.

Example Recovery Use Cases

1. Restart a Web App on Failure

Trigger: CPU > 90% for 5 minutes or app returns HTTP 500 repeatedly.

```
Restart-AzWebApp -ResourceGroupName "prod-rg" -Name "my-api"
```

2. Scale Out an App Service Plan

Trigger: App latency exceeds SLA for 10 minutes.

```
Set-AzAppServicePlan -Name "prod-plan" -ResourceGroupName "prod-rg" -
NumberofWorkers 5
```

3. Redeploy VM from Latest Snapshot

Trigger: VM heartbeat lost or unhealthy probe status.

```
Stop-AzVM -Name "db-vm" -ResourceGroup "prod-rg" -Force

Restore-AzSnapshot -SnapshotName "db-vm-snapshot-latest" -
ResourceGroupName "prod-rg"
```

4. Rotate Secrets or Certificates

Trigger: Secret near expiry (detected via Key Vault events or schedule).

```
Start-AzKeyVaultSecretRotation  -VaultName  "prod-kv"  -Name  "sql-
connection"
```

Integrating Azure Automation with Azure Monitor

You can link alerts from Azure Monitor to Automation runbooks to create a **self-healing loop**.

Steps:

1. Create a runbook that performs a corrective action.
2. Publish the runbook and generate a webhook.
3. Create an alert in Azure Monitor that triggers when a condition is met.
4. Set the alert action group to call the webhook.

Webhook Trigger Example:

```
param([object]$WebhookData)


$vmName = $WebhookData.RequestBody.vmName

Stop-AzVM -ResourceGroupName "rg-prod" -Name $vmName -Force

Start-AzVM -ResourceGroupName "rg-prod" -Name $vmName
```

Creating Webhook in PowerShell:

```
New-AzAutomationWebhook -Name "vm-recovery" `

  -ResourceGroupName "rg-prod" `

  -AutomationAccountName "auto-acc" `
```

```
-RunbookName "RestartVMOnFailure" `

-IsEnabled $true
```

Securing Automation Runbooks

- **Use Managed Identities** to securely authenticate to Azure resources.
- Store credentials in **Azure Key Vault**.
- Use **Azure RBAC** to scope permissions to least privilege.
- Audit runbook execution with **Activity Logs** and **Log Analytics**.

Assign Managed Identity Example:

```
az automation account identity assign \

  --name auto-acc \

  --resource-group rg-prod
```

Building a Recovery Framework

A resilient system should include:

1. **Detection Layer**: Azure Monitor, Log Analytics alerts.
2. **Routing Layer**: Action groups, Logic Apps, Event Grid.
3. **Remediation Layer**: Azure Automation runbooks or Logic Apps.
4. **Validation Layer**: Post-recovery health checks or confirmation alerts.
5. **Escalation Layer**: Notify humans if automation fails.

Advanced Patterns

1. Conditional Logic in Runbooks

```
if ($cpuUsage -gt 80) {

    Restart-AzWebApp -Name "api-service"

}

else {

    Write-Output "CPU usage normal; no action taken."

}
```

2. State Machine Recovery (multi-step)

- Use tags or metadata to store the recovery state.
- Example: `vmStatus = "NeedsRestore"` or `attemptCount = 2.`

3. Event-Driven Recovery with Event Grid

- Event Grid can route platform events (e.g., Key Vault expiration) directly to Automation or Functions.

4. GitOps for Runbooks

- Store scripts in GitHub.
- Use CI/CD (e.g., GitHub Actions) to publish to Automation Account.

Real-World Example

Scenario: A SaaS platform experiences random database connection issues under load.

Solution:

- Azure Monitor detects SQL errors > threshold.
- Action group triggers webhook to Automation.

- Runbook checks app connection pool status and restarts App Service if needed.
- Health check confirms recovery.
- Summary sent to on-call team via Microsoft Teams.

Results:

- MTTR reduced from 45 minutes to under 3 minutes.
- Fewer on-call escalations.
- Improved availability and customer trust.

Best Practices Summary

- Automate **routine recovery tasks** for known failure modes.
- Use **Azure Monitor + Automation** for end-to-end self-healing.
- **Secure** scripts with identities and RBAC.
- Always **test runbooks** with dry-run scenarios.
- Log and monitor **all automated actions**.
- Escalate when automation fails or hits retry limits.
- Version control runbooks and treat them as infrastructure-as-code.

Conclusion

Automated recovery is the bridge between observability and resilience. With Azure Automation, you can proactively respond to degradation, prevent incidents from escalating, and build confidence in your platform's reliability. By integrating telemetry, triggering logic, and secure remediation scripts, teams can scale operations without scaling burnout—achieving stability through software, not manual intervention.

In the next chapter, we shift from operational readiness to governance with **Security and Compliance in Resilient Systems**, where we explore how identity, secrets, and policy-driven controls contribute to secure, compliant resilience at scale.

Chapter 8: Security and Compliance in Resilient Systems

Designing with Zero Trust Principles

In a world where distributed systems span multiple networks, devices, identities, and geographies, traditional perimeter-based security is no longer sufficient. The increasing frequency and sophistication of cyberattacks demand a **paradigm shift** in how we approach security, especially for cloud-native and resilient architectures.

Enter **Zero Trust**—a security model that assumes **breach is inevitable** and therefore requires **continuous verification** of every access request, regardless of source or destination. Zero Trust is not a product; it is a framework built around core principles that, when applied correctly, **dramatically improve the security posture** of your applications and infrastructure while enabling flexible and scalable access models.

In this section, we explore how to design and implement Zero Trust in Azure, with a particular focus on how it intersects with the goals of resilience. We will cover principles, Azure-native implementations, identity, network controls, monitoring, and how to embed Zero Trust into every layer of your architecture.

What is Zero Trust?

Zero Trust is founded on the assumption that:

- **No user, device, or system is inherently trustworthy**.

- **Access must be explicitly granted** based on identity, location, device state, and behavior.

- **Least privilege** must be enforced for all operations.

- **Telemetry and analytics** must be used continuously to monitor, audit, and improve.

Zero Trust applies across:

- **Identities** (users, apps, services)

- **Devices** (managed, BYOD, IoT)

- **Data** (sensitive, regulated, classified)

- **Applications** (SaaS, PaaS, custom)
- **Networks** (internal, hybrid, public)

Core Principles of Zero Trust

1. **Verify** **Explicitly**
   - Authenticate and authorize every request using all available context.
2. **Use** **Least** **Privilege** **Access**
   - Limit access with Just-In-Time (JIT) and Just-Enough-Access (JEA) models.
3. **Assume** **Breach**
   - Minimize blast radius, segment access, and monitor continuously.

Applying Zero Trust on Azure

1. Secure Identities with Azure Active Directory (Azure AD)

- Use **Multi-Factor** **Authentication** **(MFA)**.
- Apply **Conditional** **Access** **Policies** based on:
  - Location
  - Device compliance
  - Risk levels

```
az ad conditional-access policy create \
  --display-name "Require MFA for Admins" \
  --conditions "{ \"users\": { \"includeRoles\":
[\"GlobalAdministrator\"] } }" \
  --grant-controls "{ \"operator\": \"OR\", \"builtInControls\":
[\"mfa\"] }"
```

- Enable **Identity Protection** for risk-based detection.

- Use **privileged identity management (PIM)** for time-bound access.

2. Secure Endpoints and Devices

- Integrate with **Microsoft Intune** for device compliance checks.

- Enforce access only from managed and compliant devices.

- Use Defender for Endpoint to detect compromised devices.

3. Protect Applications

- Use **Azure AD App Registrations** with scopes and permissions.

- Secure APIs with **OAuth2 and OpenID Connect**.

- Use **Managed Identities** to avoid hardcoded credentials in code.

```
az identity create --name "myAppIdentity" --resource-group "rg-prod"
```

- Integrate with **Azure API Management** for rate limiting, IP filtering, and JWT validation.

Network Segmentation and Micro-Perimeters

Traditional networks use flat architectures and rely on firewalls. Zero Trust emphasizes:

- **Micro-segmentation**

- **Software-defined** **perimeters**

- **Policy-based** **network** **controls**

Azure Tools:

- **Network Security Groups (NSGs)**: Control east-west and north-south traffic.

- **Application Security Groups (ASGs)**: Group workloads dynamically.

- **Azure Firewall**: Centralized, scalable network access control.

- **Private Endpoints**: Remove public exposure from PaaS services.

- **Virtual WAN and VPN Gateway**: Secure hybrid connectivity.

```
az network nsg rule create \
  --resource-group rg-prod \
  --nsg-name app-nsg \
  --name AllowWebInbound \
  --priority 100 \
  --direction Inbound \
  --access Allow \
  --protocol Tcp \
  --destination-port-ranges 443
```

Data Security and Encryption

Protecting data under Zero Trust means:

- **Encrypting at rest and in transit**
- **Classifying and labeling sensitive data**
- **Limiting access via identity and roles**

Azure Implementations:

- Use **Azure Disk Encryption**, **Storage Service Encryption**, and **TDE** for databases.

- Leverage **Azure Information Protection (AIP)** for labeling.

- Audit data access with **Microsoft Purview**.

Monitoring and Analytics

Continuous monitoring is central to Zero Trust.

Key telemetry sources:

- **Azure AD Sign-in Logs**
- **Microsoft Defender for Cloud**
- **Azure Monitor / Log Analytics**
- **Microsoft Sentinel (SIEM)**

Sample KQL Query: Failed Sign-ins by Country

```
SigninLogs
| where ResultType != 0
| summarize Count = count() by CountryOrRegion, bin(TimeGenerated, 1h)
```

Automation and Governance

Use **Azure Policy** to enforce Zero Trust principles at scale.

Example: Block creation of public IPs

```
{
  "if": {
    "field": "type",
    "equals": "Microsoft.Network/publicIPAddresses"
  },
```

```
"then": {

  "effect": "deny"

}

}
```

- Use **Azure Blueprints** to package and deploy compliance controls.
- Use **Management Groups** for organizational-level policy application.

Real-World Scenario

Scenario: A healthcare provider moving to Azure wants to implement Zero Trust to meet HIPAA compliance and protect sensitive patient data.

Approach:

- All services use managed identities.
- Access to APIs is gated by Conditional Access and Azure AD tokens.
- No services are exposed to the public internet; Private Endpoints are enforced via policy.
- Activity is monitored in Microsoft Sentinel with custom alerts on unusual sign-ins.
- RBAC and PIM ensure JIT access to critical systems.

Result:

- Passed external compliance audit.
- Prevented multiple phishing-based credential attacks with Conditional Access.
- Reduced operational risk and surface area of attack.

Best Practices Summary

- Enforce **MFA** and **Conditional Access** for all users and admins.

- Remove all hardcoded secrets—use **Key Vault** and **Managed Identities**.

- Restrict network access with **NSGs**, **ASGs**, and **Private Endpoints**.

- Monitor continuously using **Log Analytics**, **Defender for Cloud**, and **Sentinel**.

- Apply **least privilege** with **RBAC**, **PIM**, and **JIT/JEA**.

- Use **Azure Policy** to prevent configuration drift and enforce compliance.

- Treat Zero Trust as a **journey, not a destination**—review and iterate regularly.

Conclusion

Zero Trust is the new foundation of secure, resilient cloud systems. In Azure, it is not only achievable but increasingly essential for protecting identities, data, applications, and networks. By embedding these principles across all layers of your architecture, you reduce risk, limit the blast radius of attacks, and lay the groundwork for compliance, scalability, and operational maturity.

In the next section, we'll explore **Key Vault and Secrets Management**, focusing on how secure key management underpins not only Zero Trust but also the overall resilience of modern applications.

Key Vault and Secrets Management

In resilient architectures, **security and availability go hand in hand**. One of the most critical aspects of securing modern cloud applications is the **management of secrets**—API keys, connection strings, certificates, passwords, and encryption keys. Improper handling of these sensitive assets can lead to devastating breaches and downtime, undermining the very resilience you're trying to build.

Azure Key Vault is Microsoft's cloud-native solution for secure secret management. It enables centralized control, access auditing, high availability, and integration with identity-based access controls. In this section, we'll explore how to design, implement, and manage a robust secret management strategy using Azure Key Vault, while aligning with best practices for zero trust, automation, DevSecOps, and compliance.

Why Secrets Management Matters

Without proper management, secrets:

- **Leak** **in** **source** **code** or logs
- **Expire** **unexpectedly**, causing app failures
- **Get** **overprivileged**, leading to lateral movement during breaches
- **Are** **reused**, increasing blast radius

A secure secrets management system ensures:

- Centralized control and visibility
- Time-bound, least-privilege access
- Auditable access logs
- Secure storage and transmission

Azure Key Vault Overview

Azure Key Vault is a cloud-based service that safeguards cryptographic keys and secrets used by cloud applications and services. It supports:

- **Secrets**: Connection strings, passwords, API tokens
- **Keys**: RSA, EC keys for encryption/signing
- **Certificates**: SSL/TLS certs from integrated or BYO CAs
- **Managed HSM**: For FIPS 140-2 Level 3 compliance

Key Vault Design Considerations

1. Vault Per Environment

Use **separate vaults** for dev, staging, and production to ensure isolation.

```
az keyvault create --name myvault-prod --resource-group rg-prod --
location eastus
```

2. Vault Per Application or Team

Avoid overly shared vaults to reduce blast radius and simplify RBAC.

3. Naming Convention

Standardize with purpose, app name, and environment:

```
kv-appname-env-region
```

```
e.g., kv-ordering-prod-eus
```

Storing and Accessing Secrets

Storing a Secret:

```
az keyvault secret set --vault-name kv-orders-prod --name
"DbConnectionString" --value "<secret-value>"
```

Accessing a Secret Programmatically (C#):

```
var client = new SecretClient(new Uri("https://kv-orders-
prod.vault.azure.net"), new DefaultAzureCredential());

KeyVaultSecret secret = await
client.GetSecretAsync("DbConnectionString");
```

This uses **Managed Identity**, avoiding credential storage in code.

Controlling Access with Azure RBAC

Access models:

- **Vault access policy (legacy)**: Assign permissions per principal.
- **Azure RBAC (recommended)**: Use built-in roles like:
  - Key Vault Reader

- Key   Vault   Secrets   User
- Key   Vault   Administrator

Assign via CLI:

```
az role assignment create \

  --assignee <principal-id> \

  --role "Key Vault Secrets User" \

  --scope          "/subscriptions/<sub-id>/resourceGroups/rg-prod/providers/Microsoft.KeyVault/vaults/kv-orders-prod"
```

Use **Managed Identities** for apps and services to fetch secrets securely without credentials.

Secret Rotation and Expiration

Secret sprawl and static credentials are major security risks. **Automation of secret rotation is critical to maintaining security without operational disruption.**

Rotation Strategies:

1. **Manual   +   Expiry   Alerts**
   - Set   expiry   date
   - Monitor   SecretNearExpiry   events
2. **Azure   Automation**
   - Trigger a runbook to generate a new secret and update the application
3. **Azure   Key   Vault   Event   Grid**
   - Hook into secret change events to trigger CI/CD or config reload
4. **Key   Vault   Certificates   Auto-Renewal**
   - Configure Key Vault to auto-renew certificates from integrated CAs

Set Expiration Date on Secret:

```
az keyvault secret set-attributes --vault-name kv-app-prod --name
"ApiKey" --expires "2025-12-31T23:59:00Z"
```

Monitoring and Auditing

Auditing who accessed what secrets, when, and from where is essential for compliance.

Enable Diagnostic Settings:

```
az monitor diagnostic-settings create \

  --resource                /subscriptions/<sub-id>/resourceGroups/rg-
prod/providers/Microsoft.KeyVault/vaults/kv-orders-prod \

  --name "sendToLogAnalytics" \

  --workspace <workspace-id> \

  --logs '[{"category": "AuditEvent", "enabled": true}]'
```

Audit Query Example (KQL):

```
AzureDiagnostics

| where ResourceType == "VAULT"

| where OperationName == "SecretGet"

| summarize count() by Identity, TimeGenerated, ResultType
```

Export logs to **Log Analytics**, **Storage**, or **Event Hubs**.

Integrating Key Vault into CI/CD Pipelines

Use Azure DevOps or GitHub Actions to access secrets during builds/deployments.

Azure DevOps Example:

1. Add Key Vault as a linked service in the pipeline.
2. Reference secrets in pipeline variables.

```
variables:
  - group: kv-orders-prod


steps:
  - script: echo "Using connection string $(DbConnectionString)"
```

GitHub Actions Example:

Use Azure/login and Azure/keyvault actions.

```
- uses: azure/login@v1
  with:
    creds: ${{ secrets.AZURE_CREDENTIALS }}


- uses: azure/get-keyvault-secrets@v1
  with:
    keyvault: kv-orders-prod
    secrets: DbConnectionString
```

Common Anti-Patterns to Avoid

- **Embedding secrets in code or config files**
- **Granting blanket Key Vault Administrator access to all users**
- **Not enabling diagnostics or audits**

- **Using shared credentials between apps or teams**
- **Not rotating secrets regularly**
- **Using key vault without a private endpoint (for sensitive workloads)**

High Availability and Resilience

Azure Key Vault is a **globally distributed** service with high availability built-in. Still, resilience best practices include:

- Use **soft delete** and **purge protection** to prevent accidental deletion.
- **Geo-replicate secrets** if necessary (Premium tier).
- Use **regionally distributed instances** for multi-region workloads.
- **Gracefully handle throttling** (HTTP 429) in code.

Enable Soft Delete:

```
az keyvault update --name kv-orders-prod --enable-soft-delete true
```

Real-World Implementation Example

Scenario: A payment processing platform integrates multiple third-party providers and must secure tokens, certs, and API keys.

Approach:

- Each app component has its own managed identity.
- All secrets and certs are stored in Azure Key Vault Premium.
- Certificates are rotated automatically every 90 days.
- Secret access is logged and analyzed in Sentinel for anomaly detection.
- DevOps pipelines retrieve secrets via Key Vault integration, not config files.

Benefits:

- No credential leakage incidents in over 2 years.

- Instant revocation of access via identity disablement.

- Meets PCI DSS and ISO 27001 audit requirements.

Best Practices Summary

- Store all secrets in **Azure Key Vault**—never in code.

- Use **managed identities** to access secrets securely.

- Implement **expiration dates**, **rotation**, and **access control**.

- Use **Azure Policy** to enforce Key Vault usage.

- Enable **audit logging** and **alerting** on suspicious access patterns.

- Integrate Key Vault into **DevSecOps pipelines**.

- Prefer **Azure RBAC** over vault access policies.

- Use **private endpoints** for production-grade vaults.

Conclusion

Secrets management is foundational to security and resilience in the cloud. With Azure Key Vault, organizations can centralize control, reduce risk, and simplify compliance, all while enabling secure and seamless access for apps and users. When secrets are managed well, systems become safer, easier to audit, and more resilient in the face of both failure and attack.

In the next section, we'll explore **Identity and Access Resilience**, which builds on the principles of Zero Trust to ensure your identity infrastructure—often the first line of defense—remains secure and highly available under stress.

Identity and Access Resilience

Identity is the cornerstone of modern cloud security. In Azure, **Azure Active Directory (Azure AD)** is the backbone of authentication and authorization for users, services, and applications.

If your identity layer becomes unavailable, misconfigured, or compromised, the availability of your entire system—and your ability to recover from incidents—may be severely impacted.

In a Zero Trust model, **identity is the new perimeter**. But resilience requires more than strong authentication. It demands **redundancy**, **role-based segmentation**, **privileged access protections**, and **incident response playbooks** for identity outages. This section explores the principles and practices for building resilient identity and access management on Azure. We'll cover fault-tolerant identity architecture, managed identities, RBAC hardening, privileged access workflows, and best practices for ensuring access continuity during disruptions.

The Role of Identity in Resilience

Why identity failures break everything:

- Users   can't   sign   in.

- Applications   lose   access   to   APIs   and   databases.

- Automated   pipelines   fail   due   to   missing   credentials.

- Access   reviews   and   compliance   controls   become   unavailable.

Your resilience strategy must address:

- **Authentication**   resilience

- **Authorization**   consistency

- **Access   lifecycle**   and   recovery

- **Privilege   isolation**   and   break-glass   procedures

Azure Identity Fundamentals

Key Azure identity mechanisms include:

- **Azure   AD   Tenants**   –   Central   identity   provider.

- **User   identities**   –   Human   sign-ins   with   MFA,   Conditional   Access.

- **Service   principals**   –   Represent   applications   and   APIs.

- **Managed identities** – Secure app-to-Azure authentication.

- **Azure RBAC** – Grant fine-grained access at the resource level.

- **Privileged Identity Management (PIM)** – JIT access for admins.

Designing for Authentication Resilience

1. Multi-Factor Authentication (MFA)

- Enforce MFA for all users, especially admins.

- Use **multiple authentication methods** (e.g., Authenticator app, SMS, FIDO2 keys) to avoid lockouts.

```
az ad conditional-access policy create \
  --display-name "Require MFA for All Users" \
  --conditions "{ \"users\": { \"includeUsers\": [\"All\"] } }" \
  --grant-controls "{ \"builtInControls\": [\"mfa\"] }"
```

2. Conditional Access Resilience

- Avoid overly restrictive Conditional Access policies that could lock out legitimate users or services.

- Implement **named locations**, **sign-in risk thresholds**, and **emergency access exclusions**.

- Always test policies in **report-only mode** before enforcing.

3. Emergency Access Accounts (Break Glass)

Create **two or more emergency access accounts**:

- Global Administrator role
- Exempt from Conditional Access

- MFA enabled with alternative methods

Store credentials securely in a **vault** with controlled offline access.

Ensuring Authorization Resilience

1. Use Role-Based Access Control (RBAC)

- Assign **least** **privilege** **roles** to users and apps.
- Avoid using **Owner** or **Contributor** roles where unnecessary.
- Break access by **resource**, **team**, and **environment** (dev/staging/prod).

2. Use Role Assignments via ARM or Terraform

Codify access so that it can be re-applied in case of drift or accidental revocation.

```
az role assignment create \
  --assignee <principalId> \
  --role "Reader" \
  --scope "/subscriptions/<subId>/resourceGroups/<rg>"
```

3. Review and Expire Assignments

- Use **Azure** **PIM** to assign roles with an expiration time.
- Require **approval** **workflows** and **justifications**.

```
Start-AzRoleAssignment -RoleDefinitionName "Contributor" -ObjectId $userId -Scope $scope -ExpirationTime (Get-Date).AddHours(2)
```

Securing Application Access with Managed Identities

Avoid using client secrets or certificates for app authentication.

Instead:

- Use **System-Assigned Managed Identities** (one per resource).

- Or **User-Assigned Managed Identities** (reused across resources).

Assign a managed identity to a Function App:

```
az functionapp identity assign --name myfunc --resource-group rg-prod
```

Grant access to Key Vault:

```
az role assignment create \

  --assignee <identityPrincipalId> \

  --role "Key Vault Secrets User" \

  --scope
"/subscriptions/<subId>/resourceGroups/<rg>/providers/Microsoft.KeyVault/vaults/myvault"
```

This creates **resilient, credential-free** authentication.

Monitoring Identity Health

Use **Azure AD Sign-in Logs**, **Audit Logs**, and **Azure Monitor** to track:

- Failed logins

- Conditional Access failures

- Token issuance patterns

- Unusual privilege escalations

Kusto Query Example: Failed Admin Sign-ins

```
SigninLogs

| where ResultType != 0
```

```
| where UserPrincipalName endswith "@company.com"

| where Roles contains "Global Administrator"

| summarize count() by UserPrincipalName, Location, TimeGenerated
```

Identity Backup and Recovery

- Document break-glass credentials and test recovery quarterly.
- Backup role assignments and Azure RBAC state in ARM templates or Terraform.
- Automate role re-assignments after disaster recovery failovers.

Backup Role Assignments with Azure Resource Graph:

```
resourcecontainers

| where type == "microsoft.authorization/roleassignments"

| project principalName, roleDefinitionName, scope
```

Resilience for Federated Identities

If you federate sign-in (e.g., with ADFS, Okta):

- Ensure **failover** **paths** exist (cloud fallback).
- Monitor token issuance delays and outages.
- Consider **hybrid** **identity** **with** **cloud-first** **fallback**.

Azure AD now supports **seamless SSO** and **pass-through authentication**, which can reduce dependency on external IDPs.

Real-World Example

Scenario: A logistics SaaS platform relies on Azure AD for all user access and app-to-app authentication.

Challenges:

- Admins were accidentally locked out due to misconfigured Conditional Access.

- Production API apps were using expiring secrets stored in config files.

Improvements:

- Break-glass accounts created and exempt from policies.

- All service principals migrated to managed identities.

- Privileged roles moved to PIM with 4-hour expirations.

- Role assignments codified in Terraform with daily state checks.

Results:

- No lockout incidents in 12 months.

- Secrets rotation fully eliminated for internal services.

- Mean time to recover from privilege loss reduced to 2 minutes.

Best Practices Summary

- Enable **MFA** for **all** **users** **and** **admins**.
- Create and test **emergency access accounts** with vault-based credential storage.
- Use **RBAC** with least privilege and time-bound assignments.
- Implement **managed** **identities** for all Azure services.
- Monitor identity operations continuously via **Azure** **Monitor** and **KQL**.
- Backup and codify role assignments for fast redeployment.
- Use **Azure** **PIM** for secure, auditable role elevation.

- Document identity dependency chains for DR planning.

Conclusion

Identity resilience is not just a security concern—it's a core pillar of system availability. By planning for identity failures, minimizing credential sprawl, enforcing least privilege access, and integrating identity with your DevSecOps pipelines, you build a foundation that protects your systems, your data, and your users—even under attack or operational stress.

In the next section, we'll cover **Policy-Driven Governance and Compliance**, where we explore how Azure Policy, Blueprints, and governance structures enforce and scale security, compliance, and best practices across complex environments.

Policy-Driven Governance and Compliance

As cloud adoption scales across an organization, enforcing consistency, compliance, and secure configurations becomes increasingly complex. Ad hoc controls and manual reviews cannot scale effectively or ensure organizational trust, especially when systems span multiple subscriptions, regions, and teams.

Policy-driven governance provides a scalable, automated, and enforceable way to maintain security, operational excellence, and compliance. In Azure, this is achieved primarily through **Azure Policy**, **Azure Blueprints**, **Management Groups**, and **Compliance Manager**. These tools empower organizations to define and enforce rules across their cloud estate—ensuring that workloads are configured correctly, meet regulatory standards, and operate within defined guardrails.

In this section, we'll explore how to design, implement, and maintain policy-driven governance in Azure. We'll focus on building resilient systems that remain compliant, secure, and operationally sound—even as they evolve.

Why Policy-Driven Governance?

Cloud environments are dynamic by nature. Developers deploy frequently, infrastructure scales elastically, and changes occur continuously. This agility can easily lead to:

- Drift from best practices.

- Accidental security exposures.

- Non-compliance with standards.

- Operational misconfigurations.

Policy-driven governance addresses these issues by:

- Enforcing **configuration standards**.
- Preventing **unsafe deployments**.
- Monitoring for **non-compliant resources**.
- Automatically **remediating drift**.
- Supporting **auditing** **and** **reporting** for regulatory compliance.

Governance Architecture in Azure

1. Management Groups

- Allow policy inheritance across subscriptions.
- Typically aligned with organizational structure:
  - Root Management Group
    - Corp
      - Production
      - Staging
    - Dev
      - Sandbox

Assign policies at the **management group** level for consistency across environments.

2. Azure Policy

- Enforce rules at the **resource**, **resource group**, **subscription**, or **management group** level.
- Supports:

- **Deny**: Block deployments that violate rules.
- **Audit**: Log non-compliance.
- **Append**: Add properties during deployment.
- **DeployIfNotExists**: Enforce configuration via automation.

3. Azure Blueprints

- Package policies, role assignments, ARM templates, and resource groups into **repeatable, versioned definitions**.

- Ideal for landing zones, compliance frameworks, and organizational onboarding.

Common Policy Examples

Block Public IPs on Virtual Machines

```
{

  "if": {

    "field":
"Microsoft.Network/networkInterfaces/ipConfigurations.publicIpAddres
s.id",

    "notEquals": null

  },

  "then": {

    "effect": "deny"

  }

}
```

Enforce Resource Tags

```
{
```

```
"if": {

  "not": {

    "field": "tags['costCenter']",

    "exists": "true"

  }

},

"then": {

  "effect": "deny"

}

}
```

Require Encryption for Storage Accounts

```
{

  "if": {

    "allOf": [

      {

        "field": "type",

        "equals": "Microsoft.Storage/storageAccounts"

      },

      {

        "field":
"Microsoft.Storage/storageAccounts/encryption.services.blob.enabled"
,

        "equals": false

      }
```

```
    ]

  },

  "then": {

    "effect": "deny"

  }

}
```

Assign a policy using CLI:

```
az policy assignment create \

  --name "enforce-tagging" \

  --scope "/subscriptions/<sub-id>" \

  --policy <policy-definition-id> \

  --params '{

    "tagName": {

      "value": "costCenter"

    }

  }'
```

Azure Policy Initiatives

Policies can be grouped into **initiatives** for collective application.

Example: Azure Security Benchmark v3 Initiative

- Combines   dozens   of   policies   addressing:

  - Network   security

- Data   protection
- Identity   management
- Logging   and   monitoring

Apply a policy initiative:

```
az policy set-definition create \

  --name "SecurityBenchmark" \

  --definitions                        '[{"policyDefinitionId":
"/providers/Microsoft.Authorization/policyDefinitions/enforce-
https"}]' \

  --description "Org-wide security baseline"
```

Auto-Remediation with DeployIfNotExists

Policies don't just audit—they can **remediate drift**.

Example: Ensure Diagnostic Settings are enabled

- If a resource lacks diagnostics, Azure Policy can:
  - Trigger a deployment to enable it.
  - Route logs to a central workspace.

Remediation can be applied via:

```
az policy remediation create \

  --name "remediate-missing-diagnostics" \

  --policy-assignment "assign-diagnostics" \

  --scope "/subscriptions/<sub-id>/resourceGroups/<rg>"
```

Auditing Compliance

Azure Policy provides compliance reports at the:

- Management   group
- Subscription
- Resource   group
- Resource

Use **Azure Monitor Logs** and **Azure Resource Graph** to build dashboards and alerts.

KQL Query: Non-Compliant Resources by Policy

```
PolicyResources
| where ComplianceState == "NonCompliant"
| summarize count() by PolicyAssignmentName, ResourceGroup
```

Export compliance data to:

- Power   BI
- Sentinel   (for   SecOps   correlation)
- Logic   Apps   (to   notify   owners)

Blueprint-Based Governance

Blueprints are ideal for **governance at scale,** such as:

- Building   secure   **landing**   **zones.**
- Enforcing   **CIS,**   **NIST,**   **or**   **ISO**   compliance   from   day   one.
- Onboarding   new   projects   with   pre-approved   templates.

Blueprints include:

- **Artifacts**: Policy assignments, ARM templates, role assignments.
- **Parameters**: To customize deployments across environments.
- **Versions**: For controlled updates and rollbacks.

Assign a blueprint:

```
az blueprint assignment create \
  --name "corp-compliance" \
  --location eastus \
  --blueprint-name "corp-standards" \
  --parameters "@params.json"
```

Real-World Governance Implementation

Scenario: A global enterprise with 150 subscriptions needed to ensure PCI compliance across all environments.

Actions Taken:

- Structured management groups by geography and business unit.
- Applied baseline policies (deny public IPs, enforce encryption).
- Used blueprints to deploy shared services (Log Analytics, Key Vault).
- Centralized diagnostics and role assignments.
- Integrated policy compliance with Sentinel for real-time alerts.

Outcomes:

- Passed annual PCI audit with reduced effort.
- Stopped 100% of policy violations before deployment.
- Decreased misconfigured deployments by 90%.

Best Practices Summary

- Define a **management group hierarchy** and apply policies at the top.

- Use **initiatives** to group related policies by goal or compliance framework.

- Enforce **tagging standards** for chargeback and accountability.

- Implement **DeployIfNotExists** for proactive configuration enforcement.

- Monitor compliance with **Azure Monitor**, **Log Analytics**, and **dashboards**.

- Use **Blueprints** to automate secure landing zone deployments.

- Treat governance as **code** and version control your policies.

- Schedule regular **compliance reviews** and adjust policies as needed.

Conclusion

Policy-driven governance is not a restriction—it's a **foundation for resilience, scalability, and trust**. By leveraging Azure Policy, Blueprints, and Management Groups, you empower your teams to move fast while staying within safe, auditable boundaries. Resilient systems are not just ones that survive failure—they are ones that prevent misconfigurations, enforce best practices, and continuously evolve with your compliance and security needs.

In the next chapter, we'll shift our focus to **DevOps for Resilient Deployments**, where we'll explore infrastructure as code, safe release strategies, and CI/CD pipelines built for operational integrity and fast recovery.

Chapter 9: DevOps for Resilient Deployments

Infrastructure as Code with Bicep and ARM Templates

Resilience in the cloud is not just about runtime stability—it begins with **how infrastructure is deployed and managed**. Inconsistent manual provisioning, undocumented configurations, and environment drift are major contributors to outages and unpredictable behavior. To build truly resilient systems, infrastructure must be **automated, version-controlled, and repeatable**.

This is where **Infrastructure as Code (IaC)** comes in. Azure supports two robust IaC solutions: **ARM (Azure Resource Manager) templates** and **Bicep**, a newer, more readable domain-specific language that compiles down to ARM. Together, they empower teams to deploy Azure resources reliably, consistently, and idempotently across environments.

In this section, we'll explore how to use Bicep and ARM to define resilient infrastructure, enforce standards, reduce misconfigurations, and integrate deployments into DevOps workflows that support observability, security, and high availability.

Why Infrastructure as Code?

Benefits of IaC in Resilient Systems:

- **Repeatability**: Deploy the same configuration across dev, staging, and prod without drift.

- **Versioning**: Track infrastructure changes with source control.

- **Auditability**: Know who changed what and when.

- **Recoverability**: Re-deploy infrastructure after failure with confidence.

- **Consistency**: Enforce naming, tagging, and security rules at scale.

Manual configurations introduce **variability**. IaC removes that variability.

Bicep vs. ARM Templates

Feature	ARM Templates	Bicep
Syntax	JSON (verbose, rigid)	Declarative, simplified DSL
Readability	Low	High
Tooling	Visual Studio Code, CLI	VS Code extension, CLI
Reusability	Limited	Modules and parameters supported
Compilation	Native JSON	Compiles to ARM JSON
Learning Curve	Steep	Moderate

Recommendation: Use **Bicep** for authoring, compile to ARM for deployment.

Basic Bicep Example

```
resource storage 'Microsoft.Storage/storageAccounts@2022-09-01' = {
  name: 'resilientstorage'
  location: resourceGroup().location
  sku: {
    name: 'Standard_LRS'
  }
  kind: 'StorageV2'
  properties: {
    accessTier: 'Hot'
```

```
      supportsHttpsTrafficOnly: true

  }

}
```

Deploy via CLI:

```
az deployment group create \

  --resource-group rg-resilient \

  --template-file main.bicep
```

Designing Resilient Infrastructure with IaC

1. Use Resource Modules

Break down large templates into **modules** to promote reuse and isolation.

```
module appService './modules/appService.bicep' = {

  name: 'appServiceDeployment'

  params: {

    appName: 'resilient-api'

    location: 'eastus'

  }

}
```

2. Enforce Tags and Naming Conventions

Centralize organizational metadata in parameters or variables.

```
tags: {

  environment: 'production'
```

```
owner: 'devops@company.com'

costCenter: 'IT'

}
```

3. Integrate with Azure Policy

Ensure compliance and resilience requirements are met automatically.

Examples:

- Force   geo-redundant   storage

- Require   diagnostic   settings

- Deny   insecure   SKUs   or   regions

4. Design for Idempotency

IaC deployments should be **repeatable** without causing errors or duplicate resources.

Automating Resilient Deployments

Integrate Bicep or ARM templates into **CI/CD pipelines** to enable continuous, safe infrastructure changes.

Azure DevOps Example

```
trigger:

  branches:

    include:

      - main


stages:

- stage: Deploy

  jobs:
```

```
- job: DeployInfra

  pool:

    vmImage: ubuntu-latest

  steps:

  - task: AzureCLI@2

    inputs:

      azureSubscription: 'my-azure-conn'

      scriptType: 'bash'

      scriptLocation: 'inlineScript'

      inlineScript: |

        az deployment group create \

          --resource-group rg-resilient \

          --template-file main.bicep
```

GitHub Actions Example

```
name: Deploy Bicep to Azure


on:

  push:

    branches:

      - main


jobs:

  deploy:
```

```
runs-on: ubuntu-latest

steps:

  - uses: azure/login@v1

    with:

      creds: ${{ secrets.AZURE_CREDENTIALS }}

  - name: Deploy Bicep

    run: |

      az deployment group create \

        --resource-group rg-resilient \

        --template-file main.bicep
```

Idempotency and Drift Detection

IaC enables detection and resolution of configuration drift. For example:

- If a user modifies a resource outside the pipeline, re-running the Bicep deployment **reverts** **it** **to** **the** **desired** **state**.

- Azure DevOps and Terraform provide **drift reports** as part of pre-deployment steps.

Managing Secrets Securely

Use **parameter files**, **Key Vault integration**, or **secure pipeline secrets** to avoid leaking sensitive values.

Secure Parameter Reference in Bicep:

```
@secure()

param dbPassword string
```

In pipeline:

```
parameters:

  - name: dbPassword

    value: ${{ secrets.DB_PASSWORD }}
```

Resilient Design Patterns in Bicep

Deploy High-Availability App Service

```
resource plan 'Microsoft.Web/serverfarms@2022-03-01' = {

  name: 'resilient-app-plan'

  location: 'eastus'

  sku: {

    name: 'P1v2'

    tier: 'PremiumV2'

  }

  properties: {

    maximumElasticWorkerCount: 20

  }
}
```

Enable Geo-Replication for Storage

```
sku: {

  name: 'Standard_GRS'

}
```

Log Analytics Workspace + Diagnostic Settings

```
resource workspace 'Microsoft.OperationalInsights/workspaces@2021-
06-01' = {

  name: 'resilient-logs'

  location: 'eastus'

}



resource diagSettings 'Microsoft.Insights/diagnosticSettings@2021-
05-01-preview' = {

  name: 'sendToLogAnalytics'

  scope: storage

  properties: {

    workspaceId: workspace.id

    logs: [

      {

        category: 'StorageRead'

        enabled: true

      }

    ]

  }

}
```

Real-World Use Case

Scenario: A financial services platform needs to deploy PCI-compliant infrastructure across 6 environments.

Solution:

- Created Bicep modules for network, compute, databases, and security policies.
- Integrated IaC into Azure DevOps for gated deployments.
- Used RBAC and management groups to scope permissions.
- Applied Azure Policy to deny unencrypted storage or public IPs.
- Parameterized all regional values to support multi-region failover.

Results:

- Reduced infrastructure deployment time from days to 15 minutes.
- Detected and corrected drift in pre-production before go-live.
- Achieved consistent, compliant infrastructure with full auditability.

Best Practices Summary

- Use **Bicep** for cleaner, more manageable templates.
- Structure IaC into **modules** and **parameter** **files**.
- Automate deployments via **DevOps** **pipelines**.
- Enforce **security** **and** **compliance** with Azure Policy.
- Avoid hardcoded values—parameterize and secure secrets.
- Design IaC to be **idempotent** **and** **repeatable**.
- Test infrastructure changes in **sandbox** **environments** before promotion.
- Maintain all templates in **source** **control** with PR reviews and versioning.

Conclusion

Infrastructure as Code is the foundation of resilient deployments. By using Bicep and ARM templates, you gain the ability to declare, automate, and enforce the configuration of every

Azure resource your applications depend on. When integrated into your DevOps pipelines, IaC becomes a force multiplier—enhancing stability, security, and scalability, while reducing risk and manual toil.

In the next section, we'll explore **Safe Deployment Strategies**, including canary releases, blue/green deployments, and other methods to reduce deployment risk and accelerate recovery when things go wrong.

Safe Deployment Strategies (Canary, Blue/Green)

Deploying code into production is one of the highest-risk activities in any software lifecycle. Despite extensive testing, configuration mismatches, unforeseen edge cases, and infrastructure-specific behaviors can cause new deployments to fail—sometimes catastrophically. Safe deployment strategies mitigate this risk by **gradually introducing changes**, **isolating impact**, and **enabling quick rollback** when necessary.

In Azure, you have access to multiple tools and patterns that enable **resilient, low-risk releases**, including **canary deployments**, **blue/green deployments**, **feature flags**, and **traffic routing via Application Gateway, Front Door, and Azure DevOps**. This section explores how to implement these strategies, how they support system resilience, and how to design processes and infrastructure that embrace failure as a learning opportunity—not a disaster.

Why Safe Deployment Strategies Matter

Software changes are a leading cause of downtime. Even highly available and fault-tolerant systems can be taken down by:

- Unhandled   code   errors

- Resource   misconfiguration

- Dependency   incompatibility

- Inefficient   queries   or   memory   leaks

Safe deployments:

- Minimize   **blast**   **radius**   of   bad   **deployments**

- Provide   **real-world**   **feedback**   before   full   release

- Enable   **instant**   **rollback**

- Support **experimentation** in production

Deployment Strategy Comparison

Strategy	Risk Level	Rollback Time	User Impact	Use Case
All-at-once	High	Medium	High	Simple systems, MVPs
Blue/Green	Low	Fast	Minimal	Web apps, microservices
Canary	Low	Fast	Minimal	Gradual rollouts, A/B testing
Feature Flags	Very Low	Instant	None	User-targeted features
Ring Deployment	Low	Moderate	Medium	Internal tools, multi-region apps

---

Blue/Green Deployment on Azure

In a **blue/green deployment**, you maintain two identical environments:

- **Blue**: Current production
- **Green**: New version

After validation, you switch traffic from blue to green instantly.

Example: Azure App Service with Deployment Slots

1. Create a staging slot:

```
az webapp deployment slot create \
```

```
--name resilient-api \

--resource-group rg-prod \

--slot staging
```

2. Deploy your new version to the staging slot.

3. Validate the deployment via staging URL.

4. Swap the slots:

```
az webapp deployment slot swap \

--name resilient-api \

--resource-group rg-prod \

--slot staging \

--target-slot production
```

Advantages:

- Fast rollback via slot swap
- Same configuration (network, identity, settings)
- Isolated environment for real testing

Canary Deployments on Azure

Canary deployments involve releasing a new version to a **small subset of users** or traffic, gradually increasing exposure as confidence grows.

Approaches in Azure:

1. Azure Front Door Split Traffic

Use Front Door's **routing rules** to direct a percentage of traffic to different backends.

```
az network front-door routing-rule update \

  --front-door-name resilient-frontend \

  --resource-group rg-prod \

  --name canaryRule \

  --accepted-protocols Http Https \

  --patterns-to-match "/*" \

  --frontend-endpoints prod-endpoint \

  --route-configuration \

    '{"backendPool": "canary-backend", "weight": 10}'
```

2. Azure Traffic Manager

Route traffic based on weighted endpoints:

- `production:`   90%

- `canary:`   10%

You can adjust weights incrementally until 100% is routed to the canary.

```
az network traffic-manager endpoint update \

  --name canary-api \

  --profile-name resilient-profile \

  --resource-group rg-prod \

  --type externalEndpoints \

  --weight 10
```

3. Azure Application Gateway URL-based Routing

Canary based on headers, cookies, or URLs (e.g., `canary.example.com`).

Feature Flags and Targeted Rollouts

Feature flags let you ship code to production **with features turned off**. You can enable features for:

- Internal   users

- Specific   customers

- A/B   test   groups

- Random   sampling

Azure App Configuration with Feature Management SDK supports .NET, Java, Python, and JavaScript.

```
services.AddFeatureManagement()

    .UseDisabledFeaturesHandler<CustomFeatureHandler>();
```

Config in Azure App Configuration:

```
FeatureManagement:NewCheckoutExperience = true
```

Rollout Strategy:

- Set   initial   state: off

- Turn   on   for   test   users

- Gradually   expand   to   all   users

- Rollback   by   setting   value   to   false

Advantages:

- Zero   downtime

- Instant   rollback

- Safe   experimentation

Safe Rollback Patterns

Resilience includes **not just deployment success**, but **quick recovery from failure**.

Strategies:

- **Slot   swap   back**   (for   App   Services)
- **Revert   traffic   routing**   (Traffic   Manager   or   Front   Door)
- **Rollback   pipeline   steps**   (e.g.,   previous   container   version)
- **Disable   features   via   flags**
- **Database   versioning   and   rollback   scripts**

Container rollback example (Azure Kubernetes Service):

```
kubectl rollout undo deployment resilient-api
```

Terraform rollback:

```
git checkout previous-tag
terraform apply
```

Monitoring During Deployment

Safe deployments are only possible with **observability**:

- Track   error   rates,   latency,   throughput
- Use   Application   Insights   or   Log   Analytics
- Alert   on   abnormal   behavior   immediately

Example KQL for spike detection:

```
requests
| where timestamp > ago(10m)
| summarize count(), avg(duration) by cloud_RoleName, success
| order by count_ desc
```

Monitor:

- CPU/memory   usage
- Dependency   failures
- User   error   feedback
- Rollout   success   metrics

Automation and Pipelines

Use Azure DevOps, GitHub Actions, or any CI/CD system to script deployment and rollback.

Safe Deployment Workflow:

1. Deploy   to   canary/staging
2. Run   smoke   tests
3. Deploy   to   wider   audience
4. Validate   metrics
5. Promote   or   rollback

Azure DevOps Example with Slots:

```
- task: AzureAppServiceManage@0
  inputs:
    action: 'Swap Slots'
```

```
appName: 'resilient-api'

resourceGroupName: 'rg-prod'

sourceSlot: 'staging'

targetSlot: 'production'
```

Real-World Use Case

Scenario: A consumer banking app rolls out a new loan calculator feature.

Strategy:

- Feature is behind a flag.
- Enabled for 1% of users on Day 1.
- Errors monitored via App Insights.
- Rolled back instantly for all users when a regression caused incorrect APR calculations.
- Root cause fixed and tested in staging.
- Feature re-enabled incrementally.

Outcome:

- No customer impact.
- No incident escalation.
- Business team confident in delivery approach.

Best Practices Summary

- Use **deployment slots** or traffic managers for blue/green and canary strategies.
- Always **validate in staging** before exposing to users.

- **Automate monitoring and alerting** during rollout.

- Prefer **feature flags** for user-facing changes.

- Design pipelines to **support instant rollback.**

- **Log all deployment actions** for traceability.

- Collaborate with product teams on **rollout criteria** and rollback thresholds.

- Document **failure playbooks** and rehearse them regularly.

Conclusion

Safe deployment strategies transform the way teams ship software. They empower developers to innovate quickly while shielding users from failure. In Azure, powerful tools like Front Door, Traffic Manager, App Configuration, and deployment slots provide the building blocks for rolling out changes with confidence and recovering from incidents gracefully.

In the next section, we'll explore how to design resilient **CI/CD pipelines** using Azure DevOps and GitHub Actions, ensuring that every step from code to production is fast, secure, and failure-aware.

CI/CD Resilience with Azure DevOps and GitHub Actions

Continuous Integration and Continuous Deployment (CI/CD) pipelines are the arteries of modern software delivery. They automate the journey from code to production, enabling fast, reliable, and repeatable releases. However, without resilience baked into the pipeline itself, even the most carefully crafted infrastructure and application code can fail to reach production—or worse, deploy in a corrupted state.

CI/CD resilience is about making the **delivery process fault-tolerant, observable, recoverable, and secure**. This includes handling failed builds gracefully, rolling back broken deployments, validating infrastructure before changes go live, securing secrets, and ensuring your pipeline is not a single point of failure.

In this section, we'll explore how to architect resilient CI/CD pipelines using **Azure DevOps** and **GitHub Actions**, including best practices for recovery, security, redundancy, and maintainability.

Why CI/CD Resilience Matters

While resilient architecture ensures uptime in production, resilient pipelines ensure that:

- Your system can **safely** **evolve**.
- **Breakages** **are** **caught** **early**, not in production.
- Deployment issues don't become outages.
- Teams can trust automation and **move** **fast** **without** **fear**.

Failures can occur in:

- Build servers (e.g., network timeout, storage full)
- Dependency downloads (e.g., NPM registry outage)
- Misconfigured secrets or environments
- Broken tests, infrastructure drift, or version mismatches

A resilient pipeline identifies, isolates, and recovers from these issues predictably.

Azure DevOps and GitHub Actions Overview

Azure DevOps:

- Mature enterprise-grade pipeline tool.
- Deep Azure integration (RBAC, Key Vault, ARM/Bicep).
- Supports YAML pipelines and classic UI pipelines.
- Built-in support for test reporting, artifact management, and environments.

GitHub Actions:

- Natively integrated with GitHub repositories.
- Lightweight, developer-friendly YAML workflows.
- Built-in secrets store, environments, and protection rules.
- Supports reusable workflows and matrix builds.

Both tools can build resilient delivery systems with the right patterns.

Core CI/CD Resilience Patterns

1. Fail Fast, Fail Safe

- Use `continue-on-error: false` by default.
- Break builds immediately on critical failure.
- Separate destructive operations into approval gates.

2. Pipeline as Code

Define your pipeline using YAML and store it in your repository.

Example (GitHub Actions):

```
on:
  push:
    branches: [ main ]


jobs:
  build:
    runs-on: ubuntu-latest
    steps:
      - uses: actions/checkout@v2
      - name: Install Dependencies
        run: npm install
      - name: Run Tests
        run: npm test
```

Changes to the pipeline are **version-controlled**, **auditable**, and **revertible**.

3. Use Environments with Approvals

Introduce environments like `dev`, `qa`, `prod`, and use gated approvals.

Azure DevOps:

- Assign manual or automated checks before promoting to the next stage.

GitHub Actions:

```
environment:
  name: production
  url: https://example.com
```

You can require approval via branch protection rules and environment secrets.

Secrets Management and Resilience

Secrets are often the **Achilles' heel** of CI/CD systems.

Avoid:

- Storing secrets in plain YAML
- Printing secrets in logs
- Long-lived secrets

Use:

- **Azure Key Vault** in Azure DevOps
- **GitHub Encrypted Secrets** for GitHub Actions
- **Managed identities** and service connections for Azure resources

GitHub Secrets Example:

```
- name: Deploy
```

```
run: az deployment group create --resource-group rg-prod --template-
file main.bicep

env:

  AZURE_CLIENT_SECRET: ${{ secrets.AZURE_CLIENT_SECRET }}
```

Test Resilience in the Pipeline

1. Run Unit, Integration, and Smoke Tests

Resilient pipelines validate all layers before promotion.

- **Unit tests**: Validate logic

- **Integration tests**: Validate systems

- **Smoke tests**: Validate deployments

2. Test Failure Recovery

Simulate failure scenarios in staging:

- Service unavailable

- Secret expired

- Container crashes

Ensure failures are **detected and don't propagate**.

Artifact Handling and Versioning

Store build outputs in centralized, redundant storage:

- Azure Artifacts

- GitHub Packages

- Azure Blob Storage

Version all artifacts using commit SHA or semantic versioning.

GitHub Example:

```
- name: Upload Artifact

  uses: actions/upload-artifact@v2

  with:

    name: build-${{ github.sha }}

    path: ./dist
```

Deployment Validation Steps

Deployments must be **validated automatically** to confirm success.

Add post-deploy health checks:

- Call `/healthz` endpoint
- Check logs for startup errors
- Validate infra (e.g., DNS, TLS certs, port binding)

```
- name: Verify Health

  run: curl -f https://resilient-app.azurewebsites.net/healthz
```

Fail the pipeline if health checks do not pass.

Rollback and Re-deploy Safety Nets

Design pipelines to support:

- **Re-deploying previous version**
- **Rolling back infrastructure**

- **Cancelling** **in-flight** **deployments**

Azure DevOps Example:

```
- task: AzureAppServiceManage@0

  inputs:

    action: 'Swap Slots'

    sourceSlot: 'staging'

    targetSlot: 'production'
```

GitHub Actions: Use prior artifacts or image tags to re-deploy.

Resilience for Long-Running Pipelines

Break large deployments into:

- Independent pipeline stages
- Parallel jobs
- Retryable steps

Use **timeouts** and **retries** to handle transient failures.

Example: Retry Azure CLI Step

```
- name: Retry Deployment

  run: |

    for i in {1..5}; do

      az deployment group create --resource-group rg-prod --template-
file main.bicep && break

      sleep 10

    done
```

Monitoring CI/CD Pipelines

Track:

- Build success/failure rates
- Deployment duration
- Approval delays
- Test coverage trends
- Environment drift

Tools:

- Azure DevOps Analytics
- GitHub Insights
- Custom dashboards with Azure Monitor or Power BI

Real-World Case Study

Scenario: A fintech company needs zero-downtime updates with rollback for regulatory reasons.

Solution:

- CI/CD defined via Azure DevOps YAML pipelines
- Bicep used to deploy infrastructure consistently
- Canary slots used for all production apps
- All secrets pulled from Key Vault
- Smoke tests run before and after deployment
- Slack and PagerDuty integrated for alerts

Outcomes:

- 90% reduction in production failures
- CI/CD adoption across all teams
- Weekly deploys to prod without fear

Best Practices Summary

- Use **pipeline-as-code** in source control
- Create **distinct** **environments** with approvals
- Run **automated** **tests** at every stage
- Secure secrets with **vaults** **and** **identities**
- Break up pipelines into **retryable** **steps**
- Validate deployments with **health** **checks**
- Maintain **versioned** **artifacts** for rollback
- Monitor pipeline metrics and failures continuously

Conclusion

CI/CD pipelines are not just automation—they are **critical infrastructure**. Resilient pipelines ensure that code reaches production safely, that breakages are caught early, and that teams can move fast with confidence. Whether using Azure DevOps or GitHub Actions, the key to resilience is **defensive design, observability, and trust in automation**.

In the next section, we'll explore **Rollbacks and Rollforwards Best Practices**, detailing how to respond when deployments go wrong and how to restore service swiftly, cleanly, and safely.

Rollbacks and Rollforwards Best Practices

In complex systems, deployments occasionally go wrong despite robust testing and automation. Whether it's due to a code bug, infrastructure misconfiguration, dependency mismatch, or external failure, the ability to recover quickly is critical to system resilience. This is where **rollback** and **rollforward** strategies come into play.

Rollbacks restore a previous known-good version of the system, while rollforwards apply a fix that supersedes the failed deployment. Both approaches require careful planning, automation, and observability. In this section, we'll explore best practices, patterns, tooling, and real-world techniques for handling deployment failures using Azure-native and platform-agnostic strategies.

Rollback vs. Rollforward

Strategy	Description	When to Use
Rollback	Revert to a previous version or state	When the last known good state is safe, tested, and restorable
Rollforward	Deploy a fix that supersedes the faulty deployment	When rollback is impractical or system state has changed irreversibly

Key insight: Rollback is ideal for **stateless and versioned systems**, whereas rollforward is often necessary for **stateful or data-modifying systems**.

Preparing for Rollbacks

Rollback should never be an afterthought—it must be designed into your pipeline and deployment process.

1. Immutable Deployments

Treat builds and artifacts as **immutable units** that can be re-deployed at any time.

Best practice:

- Use versioned container tags (e.g., `api:v1.2.3`)

- Never overwrite images with `latest` in production

- Store artifacts in Azure Artifacts, GitHub Packages, or blob storage

2. Maintain Deployment History

Always retain:

- Last   N   versions

- Deployment   metadata   (who,   when,   what)

- Hash   or   commit   SHAs

Use **tags**, **branches**, and **pipelines logs** to support this.

3. Validate Post-Deployment State

Ensure deployments run **smoke tests and health checks**. If these fail, trigger an automatic rollback.

```
- name: Run Smoke Test

  run: curl -f https://resilient-api.azurewebsites.net/health
```

If this step fails, initiate rollback:

```
- name: Rollback Deployment

  run: kubectl rollout undo deployment resilient-api
```

Rollback Techniques by Platform

Azure App Service (Deployment Slots)

Use **staging slots** for blue/green or canary deployment. If issues arise post-swap, simply swap back.

```
az webapp deployment slot swap \

  --name resilient-api \

  --resource-group rg-prod \

  --slot production \

  --target-slot staging
```

This approach enables **instant rollback** with no redeployment.

Azure Kubernetes Service (AKS)

Leverage native rollback capabilities:

```
kubectl rollout undo deployment resilient-api
```

Ensure that:

- Deployment history is retained (default is 10)
- Rollbacks are automated on failure detection

Azure DevOps / GitHub Actions

Use pipeline artifacts and deployment environments to promote/demote builds.

```
- task: DownloadBuildArtifacts@0

  inputs:

    buildType: 'specific'

    project: 'resilient'

    buildVersionToDownload: 'latestFromBranch'

    branchName: 'refs/heads/main'
```

Then redeploy previous version to production.

Rollforward Strategy

Rollforward is required when:

- The faulty deployment changed data or schema
- Rolling back would cause inconsistencies
- A fix is known and testable faster than a rollback

Example: Rollforward a Hotfix

1. Detect deployment failure

2. Triage issue and apply fix

3. Patch code (hotfix branch)

4. Test in staging

5. Promote patch build to production

Rollforward **requires excellent test coverage** and **fast build pipelines**.

Database and Schema Changes

Rollbacks involving databases are inherently risky.

Best Practices:

- Use **backward-compatible schema migrations**
- Avoid destructive changes (e.g., dropping columns) in the same release
- Use **feature toggles** to gate access to new schema
- Apply **data migrations in phases**

Example using Flyway or Liquibase:

- Migration script v1: Adds nullable column
- v2: Application starts writing to column
- v3: Remove old column after stable usage

This pattern enables **safe schema evolution with rollback points**.

Monitoring and Alerting

Detect bad deployments early with metrics like:

- Spike in HTTP 500s

- Drop   in   successful   requests
- User   behavior   changes   (logins,   transactions)
- Failed   health   checks

Use **Application Insights**, **Azure Monitor**, **Prometheus**, or **Datadog**.

KQL Query: Failed Requests Post-Deployment

```
requests
| where timestamp > ago(30m)
| where resultCode startswith "5"
| summarize count() by name
```

Tie alerts to deployment timestamps and correlate with release metadata.

Automating Rollbacks

Create pipelines that **automatically trigger rollback** upon failure signals.

Example: Azure DevOps with Environment Checks

- Deploy   to   production
- Run   health   tests
- If   health   fails,   trigger   rollback   job

```
- job: rollback
  condition: failed()
  steps:
    - script: kubectl rollout undo deployment resilient-api
```

For GitHub Actions, use `if: failure()` and environment protection rules.

Real-World Example

Scenario: A retail e-commerce site deployed a new checkout flow which caused increased cart abandonment.

Issue: The UI interacted incorrectly with the payment API due to a logic bug.

Response:

- Deployment triggered alerts based on App Insights spike in `Http 400` errors.

- CI/CD pipeline automatically swapped back to staging slot.

- Incident was logged, and fix was issued within 2 hours via rollforward.

Result:

- No customer complaints

- Revenue protected

- Root cause addressed and regression tests added

Best Practices Summary

- **Design for rollback** from the start.

- Use **immutable deployments** and retain previous versions.

- **Test deployments post-release** to trigger early alerts.

- Avoid one-way schema changes; prefer **backward compatibility**.

- Automate rollback on **failed health checks** or alerts.

- Keep deployment metadata tied to build artifacts.

- Monitor user behavior and system metrics during and after rollout.

- Treat rollbacks and rollforwards as **routine, not exceptional**.

Conclusion

Failure is inevitable in modern software delivery—but **prolonged failure is not**. With rollbacks and rollforwards designed into your CI/CD and deployment processes, you gain confidence, agility, and resilience. When the unexpected happens, your systems don't crash—they recover.

In the next chapter, we'll shift our focus from patterns and practices to practical examples with **Real-World Case Studies and Architectural Reviews**, analyzing how leading organizations have applied these resilient principles at scale.

Chapter 10: Real-World Case Studies and Architectural Reviews

E-Commerce Platform at Scale

Resilience in e-commerce is not optional—it is existential. Outages during flash sales, Black Friday, or seasonal promotions can result in lost revenue, damaged reputation, and customer churn. In this section, we dive into a real-world case study of a global e-commerce platform built on Microsoft Azure, analyzing the architectural decisions, resilience strategies, failures encountered, and lessons learned.

The platform processes millions of transactions daily, supports high-volume flash sales, integrates with payment providers, logistics, inventory systems, and content delivery networks—all while maintaining stringent performance and availability SLAs.

Business Requirements and Constraints

Key Requirements:

- Global   availability   (multi-region)

- 99.99%   uptime   SLA

- Elastic   scalability   to   handle   50x   traffic   surges

- Secure   customer   and   payment   data   (PCI-DSS   compliance)

- Fast   checkout   (<2s   P95   latency)

- Integration   with   3PL   and   ERP   systems

- Real-time   order   tracking   and   alerts

Constraints:

- No   downtime   during   deployments

- Multi-team   development   across   microservices

- Legacy   systems   must   co-exist   and   evolve   gradually

---

High-Level Architecture Overview

The e-commerce platform was divided into logical domains:

- **Web Front-End**: React SPA hosted on Azure Static Web Apps
- **API Gateway**: Azure API Management with custom policies
- **Microservices**: Azure Kubernetes Service (AKS), with each domain (orders, cart, inventory, etc.) deployed independently
- **Database Tier**:
  - Azure Cosmos DB for product catalog and session data
  - Azure SQL Database for transactional data (orders, payments)
  - Redis Cache for session state and inventory hot-path
- **Asynchronous Messaging**: Azure Service Bus and Event Grid
- **Observability**: Azure Monitor, Application Insights, Log Analytics
- **CI/CD**: Azure DevOps with gated, canary releases and feature flags

---

Resilience Strategy by Layer

1. Front-End Resilience

- Deployed to Azure Front Door for global edge caching and routing
- Configured static SPA fallbacks for 503s
- Client-side retries and exponential backoff for API calls
- Lazy loading and CDN for images and bundles

2. API Gateway

- Circuit breakers on back-end APIs
- Caching policies for catalog and shipping APIs

- Rate limiting and throttling to prevent abusive behavior
- Custom error handling for graceful fallback

3. Microservices Layer

- Isolated by bounded context and deployed in AKS with independent CI/CD
- Used **Kubernetes PodDisruptionBudgets**, **liveness/readiness probes**, and **Horizontal Pod Autoscaler (HPA)**
- Resilient service-to-service communication with retries and timeouts using Dapr sidecars

```
livenessProbe:
  httpGet:
    path: /healthz
    port: 8080
  initialDelaySeconds: 10
  periodSeconds: 5
  failureThreshold: 3
```

4. Database and Data Tier

- Cosmos DB with multi-region writes and partitioned containers
- SQL Database with geo-replication and failover groups
- Redis cache with active-active clustering (Premium tier)
- Write operations designed to be idempotent and retry-safe

```
-- Sample idempotent SQL insert
MERGE INTO Orders AS target
USING (SELECT @OrderId AS OrderId) AS source
```

```
ON target.OrderId = source.OrderId

WHEN NOT MATCHED THEN

INSERT   (OrderId,   CustomerId,   TotalAmount)   VALUES   (@OrderId,
@CustomerId, @TotalAmount);
```

5. Messaging and Async Processing

- All non-critical operations (e.g., email notifications, loyalty points) processed asynchronously

- Dead-letter queues monitored via Azure Monitor alerts

- Poison message handling with retry + parking strategies

Deployment and Operations

- Canary deployments using Azure DevOps release gates and deployment slots

- Feature flags (via Azure App Configuration) controlled rollout of new features

- Chaos testing in staging environment using Gremlin and Azure Chaos Studio

- Automated smoke tests post-deployment

- Daily backups and restore drills conducted quarterly

Deployment workflow (simplified):

1. PR merged into main triggers CI build

2. Bicep templates deploy infra updates to staging

3. App deployed to staging slot, smoke tests run

4. Approval gates verify metrics and logs

5. Slot swap to production

6. Post-deployment validation via synthetic transactions

Failure Scenarios and Recovery

Scenario 1: Cosmos DB Region Outage

- East US region became partially unavailable
- Automatic failover triggered to West US
- Application leveraged SDK's preferred region config
- Observed slight latency spike, but no downtime

```
CosmosClientOptions options = new CosmosClientOptions
{
    ApplicationPreferredRegions = new List<string> { "West US", "East US" }
};
```

Scenario 2: Payment Provider Timeout

- Third-party payment API degraded during a flash sale
- Circuit breaker tripped after 5s timeout threshold
- Platform queued payments in Azure Service Bus for retry
- Users received "Payment Pending" and were notified via email

Scenario 3: Overloaded Inventory Service

- Load testing missed a spike during Black Friday
- Redis was saturated; API calls began to timeout
- HPA scaled service pods, cache tier scaled manually
- Feature flag disabled dynamic inventory check for 10 minutes
- Recovery completed with no cart loss or order failures

Observability and Alerting

- Every service exported logs to Azure Monitor via fluent-bit and App Insights SDK

- Alerts defined for:

  - 5xx error rate > 2% (per-service)

  - P95 latency over 2s

  - Service Bus dead-letter queue > 100 messages

  - Database failover events

Kusto Query Example: Error Spike

```
requests
| where resultCode startswith "5"
| where timestamp > ago(15m)
| summarize count() by name, cloud_RoleName
```

Key Lessons Learned

1. **Design for Isolation**: Microservices were isolated by both functionality and infrastructure, preventing cascading failures.

2. **Gradual Rollouts Are Crucial**: Canary deployments and feature flags saved the platform from releasing unstable features to all users.

3. **Resilience Is End-to-End**: From front-end retries to database failovers, every component contributed to platform resilience.

4. **Observability Drives Action**: Real-time telemetry enabled fast detection, triage, and recovery.

5. **Automate Recovery**: Manual processes were replaced with Azure Automation and Functions for healing and remediation.

Summary

Building a resilient e-commerce platform at scale requires more than just uptime SLAs. It involves carefully architecting systems with fail-safes, automating recovery, observing deeply, and embracing continuous delivery with confidence. This case study demonstrates how layered resilience across compute, storage, networking, and operations can enable a platform to grow and evolve—without compromising on user trust or business continuity.

In the next section, we'll explore the unique resilience challenges of multi-tenant SaaS platforms, including tenant isolation, data security, and tenant-specific scaling strategies.

Global SaaS Provider with Multi-Tenant Resilience

Designing for resilience in a multi-tenant Software-as-a-Service (SaaS) platform is inherently more complex than in a single-tenant or monolithic application. A failure in one component can impact hundreds—or even thousands—of tenants simultaneously. To mitigate this, the architecture must account for tenant isolation, dynamic scaling, operational safety, and consistent performance across varying tenant loads and geographies.

This section examines the architectural and operational resilience strategy of a global SaaS provider offering business intelligence and reporting tools to thousands of enterprises. The platform ingests data from customer systems, transforms and stores it, and provides web-based dashboards, reports, and APIs.

Platform Overview

The SaaS provider needed to support:

- **10,000+ enterprise tenants** across 4 continents

- **Uptime SLA** of **99.95%**

- **Data segregation for regulatory compliance** (e.g., GDPR, HIPAA)

- **Tenant-level isolation** to prevent noisy-neighbor issues

- **Self-service provisioning,** metering, and billing

- Integration with Azure AD for single sign-on (SSO)

Core Services:

- **Data** **ingestion** from cloud/on-prem systems
- **ETL** **pipeline** with event-driven processing
- **Visualization** **and** **dashboard** **rendering**
- **RESTful** **API** **access** for custom reporting

Multi-Tenant Resilience Strategy

1. Tenant Isolation

To prevent a failure in one tenant's workload from impacting others, the architecture enforced multiple layers of logical and physical isolation:

- **Per-tenant** **resource** **groups** for high-value tenants
- **Tenant-aware** **sharding** in data stores
- **Rate-limiting** **and** **quotas** at the API gateway
- **Dedicated queues and event topics** per tenant (for top-tier customers)

Tenant metadata was stored centrally in Cosmos DB, driving dynamic routing and resource allocation.

```
{

  "tenantId": "contoso",

  "region": "West Europe",

  "tier": "Premium",

  "storageContainer": "contoso-prod",

  "featureFlags": ["advanced_reporting", "custom_themes"]

}
```

---

2. Regional Redundancy and Failover

To support global customers, each tenant was pinned to a **primary region**, with optional failover to a secondary region.

- Cosmos DB used **multi-region writes** for metadata and tenant preferences.

- Azure Front Door distributed traffic to the **nearest healthy region**.

- Data lakes were replicated across regions using **Azure Data Factory** and **geo-redundant storage**.

During a region-wide incident (e.g., DNS resolution issue in Southeast Asia), tenants failed over to backup services with minimal latency increase.

```
failoverPriority:

  - West Europe

  - North Europe
```

---

3. Multi-Tiered Tenancy Model

The platform offered three tiers:

- **Basic** **(shared** **infrastructure)**

- **Pro** **(logical** **isolation)**

- **Enterprise** **(dedicated** **workloads)**

Basic tenants shared AKS node pools and database containers with strict quotas.

Enterprise tenants received:

- Separate resource groups

- Dedicated databases and event hubs

- SLA-backed custom domain support

This allowed targeted recovery strategies during partial outages.

---

4. Service Partitioning and Horizontal Scaling

Services were designed to be **stateless** and horizontally scalable.

- Kubernetes Deployments used **pod affinity/anti-affinity** rules to distribute tenant load.

- Azure Kubernetes Service (AKS) backed compute with **virtual node pools** using Azure Container Instances (ACI) for burst workloads.

- Azure Event Hubs with **partition keys** ensured event processing consistency per tenant.

```
eventHubClient.SendAsync(new     EventData(payload),     partitionKey:
tenantId);
```

5. Asynchronous Resilience Patterns

Synchronous workflows were minimized. Wherever possible:

- Work was decoupled via **Azure Service Bus**
- Long-running jobs used **Durable Functions**
- Processing pipelines included **dead-letter queues** and **retry logic**

Failures triggered alerts and fallback workflows, such as cached reports or degraded API responses.

CI/CD and Tenant-Aware Rollouts

Each tenant environment was tagged and version-controlled, enabling:

- Safe deployments with tenant-specific canary releases
- Per-tenant feature flag rollout using Azure App Configuration
- Automated rollback using deployment slots and versioned container images

Deployment Strategy:

1. Deploy to internal test tenants
2. Expand to canary group (e.g., 5% of Pro tier)
3. Monitor metrics (latency, errors)
4. Expand to full population

```
variables:

  tenantGroup: 'pro-canary'

  featureFlag: 'newDataExplorer'
```

Feature flags allowed fast rollbacks without redeploying:

```
"FeatureManagement": {

  "newDataExplorer": {

    "EnabledFor": [

      { "Name": "TenantFilter", "Parameters": { "TenantId": "contoso"
} }

    ]

  }

}
```

Observability at Scale

Each tenant's telemetry was segmented using **custom dimensions**:

- Logs enriched with tenant ID
- Separate Application Insights instances per tier

- Custom metrics: `request_count_by_tenant`, `report_latency`, `api_error_rate`

Azure Monitor dashboards showed:

- Hot tenants (highest traffic)
- Latency and error trends per region
- SLA compliance across the fleet

Example KQL Query:

```
requests
| extend tenantId = tostring(customDimensions["tenantId"])
| where timestamp > ago(30m)
| summarize errorRate = countif(success == false) / count() by tenantId
| order by errorRate desc
```

Failure Scenarios and Response

Scenario 1: Message Processing Backlog

- Root Cause: Misconfigured partition scaling
- Impact: 25 tenants experienced delayed ingestion
- Mitigation: Auto-scale logic revised; Dedicated Event Hub for noisy tenants

Scenario 2: AKS Node Pool Depletion

- Root Cause: Large tenant spike during reporting hours
- Resolution: ACI-backed virtual nodes provided burst capacity
- Long-Term Fix: Tiered HPA settings for critical workloads

Scenario 3: Configuration Drift in Dev Tenants

- Several dev/test tenants had unpatched versions of reporting engine
- Introduced pipeline stage to validate config drift and enforce template consistency

---

Business Impact

The platform achieved:

- 99.982% uptime over 12 months
- Zero data loss events
- SLA violations reduced by 87% year-over-year
- 3x faster incident recovery using automation and metrics

Multi-tenant resilience allowed the team to:

- Isolate and contain tenant-specific issues
- Roll out new features gradually and safely
- Handle unpredictable load surges with confidence

Key Lessons Learned

1. **Not all tenants are equal**: Tiering allowed tailored SLAs and risk profiles.
2. **Tenant metadata is foundational**: Everything from routing to features relied on metadata.
3. **Resilience is iterative**: Initial architecture didn't scale—evolved through experience.
4. **Observability must be multi-dimensional**: Visibility per tenant, per tier, per region was essential.
5. **Failovers must be tested, not assumed**: Regular regional failover drills surfaced unknowns.

Summary

Multi-tenant SaaS resilience isn't a feature—it's an architectural commitment. The ability to provide consistent, secure, and highly available services to thousands of customers, each with unique demands and sensitivities, is a hallmark of mature cloud platforms. By isolating failure domains, adopting robust messaging and scaling patterns, and automating observability, this platform achieved a level of resilience that enabled rapid innovation without sacrificing reliability.

Next, we'll analyze a real-time analytics platform, where ultra-low latency and stream processing resilience are paramount.

Real-Time Analytics Platform

Real-time analytics platforms serve as the nervous system of modern organizations, delivering insights from streaming data with minimal latency. These platforms power use cases such as fraud detection, operational monitoring, personalized recommendations, and IoT telemetry. However, building and maintaining a resilient real-time analytics system presents unique challenges: unbounded data streams, late-arriving data, processing spikes, external service dependencies, and high expectations for availability and freshness.

In this section, we examine the architecture and resilience strategy of a real-world Azure-based real-time analytics platform built to process billions of events per day, with SLAs on both latency and data accuracy. We explore its compute pipeline, storage architecture, failure modes, scaling strategies, and the role of observability in sustaining performance and reliability at scale.

Business Requirements

The platform was developed for a logistics technology provider offering live tracking and analytics for thousands of delivery fleets across North America and Europe.

Requirements:

- Ingest and process >5 billion events/day with <5s latency

- Maintain 99.99% availability for ingestion APIs and dashboards

- Detect anomalies in event patterns within 10 seconds of occurrence

- Support real-time alerting for downstream systems

- Ensure exactly-once processing for critical pipelines (e.g., shipment status)

Data Sources:

- IoT devices (vehicle sensors, GPS trackers)

- Mobile apps (driver input, photos, comments)

- ERP integrations (delivery scheduling, updates)

High-Level Architecture

The system was composed of the following layers:

1. **Ingestion**:

   o Azure Event Hubs (partitioned) for stream ingestion

   o Azure IoT Hub for device telemetry

   o API Gateway (Azure API Management) for mobile and partner apps

2. **Stream Processing**:

   o Azure Stream Analytics for simple routing

   o Azure Functions for lightweight ETL tasks

   o Azure Databricks Structured Streaming for heavy transformations, joins, windowing, and ML inferencing

3. **Persistent Storage**:

   o Azure Data Lake Gen2 (raw and processed layers)

   o Azure Cosmos DB for real-time state lookup (e.g., active shipment status)

   o Azure Synapse Analytics for batch enrichment and historical analysis

4. **Visualization & Alerting**:

   o Power BI with DirectQuery to Synapse and Cosmos DB

   o Azure Monitor + Log Analytics + Azure Alerts

   o Custom dashboards for dispatchers and operations managers

Resilience Techniques by Layer

Ingestion Resilience

- Event Hubs used **dedicated throughput units** and **capture to blob** enabled for replay

- Partitions mapped by `deviceId` to ensure ordering guarantees

- Geo-disaster recovery enabled on Event Hubs namespaces

```
{
  "properties": {
    "partitionKey": "deviceId",
    "eventTime": "2023-08-11T12:34:56Z"
  }
}
```

- IoT Hub used **device twin sync** and **message routing** with fallback queues

- API layer integrated **rate-limiting**, **throttling**, and **custom retry headers**

Processing Resilience

- Stream Analytics jobs deployed in pairs with hot standby regions

- Functions used **Durable Functions** to handle retries and compensation

- Databricks clusters autoscaled with custom thresholds on queue depth

- Output operations included retry/backoff and dead-letter policies

```
query = (
  spark.readStream
    .format("eventhubs")
```

```
.options(**event_hub_config)

.load()

.withColumn("parsed",        from_json(col("body").cast("string"),
schema))

.withWatermark("timestamp", "2 minutes")

.groupBy(window("timestamp", "1 minute"), "deviceId")

.agg(...)

)
```

- Streaming jobs wrote to **delta lake tables** with schema evolution support
- Jobs had **graceful shutdown logic** and checkpointing to Azure Blob

---

Handling Late or Out-of-Order Data

Late-arriving data was a critical challenge due to:

- Intermittent mobile connectivity
- Delays in syncing from edge devices

Mitigations:

- Watermarking strategies in Databricks and ASA
- Buffering + backfill pipelines triggered hourly
- Event payloads included logical event time (used for downstream ordering)
- Data written with partition keys that aligned to event time

```
.withWatermark("eventTime", "5 minutes")

.groupBy(window("eventTime", "1 minute"))
```

Scaling for Load Spikes

The system regularly encountered spikes due to:

- Daily logistics batch updates
- Weather-related delivery rerouting
- Flash deployment of mobile app versions

Scaling Strategies:

- Event Hub auto-inflate enabled (up to 20 TU)
- Databricks used **Autoscaling Clusters** with pre-warmed pools
- Azure Functions scaled based on Service Bus depth
- Stream Analytics queried queue length via Diagnostic Settings
- Alerts triggered when job latency > threshold, triggering Azure Automation scale scripts

```
az eventhubs eventhub update \
  --name ingestion-hub \
  --resource-group analytics-rg \
  --namespace-name logistics-ehns \
  --message-retention 72 \
  --partition-count 32
```

Observability and Failure Detection

The platform collected metrics from:

- Event Hubs (incoming message rate, throttling)

- Function App (failures, retries, durations)
- Databricks jobs (throughput, SLA miss rate)
- Cosmos DB (RU consumption, latency)
- Custom metrics via Azure Monitor SDK (e.g., "events per tenant")

Dashboards included:

- Live ingestion rates per region
- Job checkpoint lag
- Alert frequency and acknowledgment times

Sample KQL Query – Stream Failure Rates:

```
AzureDiagnostics
| where ResourceType == "STREAMINGJOBS"
| where ResultType != "Success"
| summarize count() by bin(TimeGenerated, 5m), JobName
```

Recovery Automation:

- Functions retried using exponential backoff
- If retries exceeded threshold, messages were moved to DLQ
- DLQs were monitored via Azure Logic Apps to trigger alerts and initiate reprocessing workflows

---

Incident Response and Real-World Failures

Failure Case 1: Region-wide Cosmos DB Latency

- Impact: Dashboards showed outdated data for 18 minutes

- Root Cause: Regional write latency spike due to planned maintenance

- Resolution: Switched read region to fallback, replicated stream state to Redis temporarily

- Long-Term Fix: Use Redis as hot cache for real-time reads; Cosmos for durability

Failure Case 2: Function Timeout on Peak Ingestion

- Impact: ETL bottleneck caused backlog in Event Hub

- Fix: Moved function to Premium Plan with VNET integration and increased CPU

- Added custom telemetry for queue length and processing time per message

Failure Case 3: Partition Skew

- Impact: One partition overloaded due to fleet assignment anomaly

- Resolution: Re-sharded Event Hub and updated routing logic

- Monitoring adjusted to alert on per-partition variance

Design Learnings

1. **Partitioning is strategic** – Consistent hashing and uniform load distribution avoided bottlenecks.

2. **Backpressure control is essential** – Without buffering and smart retries, downstream pressure cascaded quickly.

3. **Event time vs. ingestion time** – Watermarks and ordering logic prevented timestamp chaos.

4. **Multi-format data validation** – Schematized events with AVRO/JSON saved massive operational effort.

5. **Observability enabled automation** – Without metric-driven remediation, the system would have degraded silently.

Summary

Resilience in a real-time analytics platform is not just about uptime—it's about **continuous correctness**, **adaptive scaling**, and **systemic responsiveness**. This architecture balanced ingestion velocity, event fidelity, and operational transparency to deliver actionable intelligence in near real time. By embracing stream-first design, modular processing, and proactive observability, the platform evolved into a mission-critical part of the customer's logistics engine.

Next, we'll explore the final case study: post-mortem lessons from real-world system failures and the cultural and architectural responses that enabled teams to emerge stronger and better prepared.

Lessons Learned from Post-Mortems

Failures are inevitable in complex systems. What separates resilient organizations from the rest is not their ability to prevent every failure, but their capability to **respond, recover, and learn** from those failures. Post-mortems are the formal mechanism through which teams analyze incidents, extract insights, and improve their architecture, processes, and culture.

This section presents post-mortem examples and the resilience lessons they revealed. Drawing from real-world cloud incidents—some customer-facing, others internal—we explore how transparency, tooling, process maturity, and engineering culture contribute to a robust system over time. By institutionalizing learning, these teams turned setbacks into durable improvements.

Purpose and Anatomy of a Post-Mortem

A post-mortem (or incident retrospective) is a structured analysis conducted after a significant incident. Its goal is not to assign blame, but to:

- Understand **what** **happened**
- Identify **why** it happened
- Document **how** it was detected and resolved
- Uncover **gaps** in systems, tooling, or process
- Create **action** **items** to prevent recurrence

Key Components:

- Timeline of events
- Impact analysis (technical + business)

- Root   cause(s)

- Detection   and   diagnosis   timeline

- Recovery   steps

- Lessons   learned

- Follow-up   actions   and   owners

Incident #1: Azure Storage Key Rotation Breaks Downstream Access

Context:
A team rotated their Azure Storage access keys as part of a quarterly security review.

Symptoms:

- Event ingestion pipeline (Azure Functions) began failing intermittently

- Error logs showed `403 - AuthenticationFailed` for blob writes

Root Cause:

- Storage key was updated in Azure Key Vault

- Function App's managed identity was not used; instead, the key was hardcoded in App Settings

- KeyVault reference syntax was invalid, and error wasn't caught during deployment

Detection:

- Alert triggered on spike in ingestion failures

- Took 45 minutes to identify misconfiguration

Impact:

- Data loss for 3 low-volume tenants over 1 hour

- Retry queue overflowed in Event Hub, adding delay to all processing

Lessons:

- Hardcoding secrets violates least privilege and rotation resilience

- Secrets should always be fetched via managed identities and Key Vault

- Deployment validations must include test for environment variable resolution

Action Items:

- Migrate to managed identities for all Azure resources

- Add smoke tests to verify App Settings after each deployment

- Add alert for Event Hub retry queue depth

Incident #2: Feature Flag Misfire Causes Partial Outage

Context:

- A new checkout feature was deployed behind a feature flag using Azure App Configuration

Symptoms:

- 10% of users began seeing blank cart pages

- Mobile error rate increased by 30%

- SREs noticed spike in HTTP 500s

Root Cause:

- Feature flag evaluated to true for a segment missing required configuration

- Backend API deployed with partial support for the new logic

- Flag rollout exceeded safe segment before validation completed

Detection:

- Alert from Application Insights on response time spike

- Rollback took 15 minutes due to lack of automation

Impact:

- 7,000 checkout failures over 40 minutes
- $82K revenue impact in lost orders

Lessons:

- Rollout process must include automated validation of flag coverage
- Feature flag dependency checks should be part of pre-deployment pipeline
- Rollback of feature flags should be fully automated and decoupled from app redeploy

Action Items:

- Implement canary segment validation before global rollout
- Define feature flag schemas and validation tests
- Add toggle rollback workflow to GitHub Actions

Incident #3: Intermittent DNS Resolution Failures in AKS

Context:

- AKS cluster running microservices experienced random service resolution issues

Symptoms:

- Periodic 502/504 errors between services
- Retry logic hid the failures for several minutes
- Kube-DNS logs showed spike in unresolved names

Root Cause:

- Node-level DNS caching exhausted open file handles

- DNS daemonset was pinned to older image with bug
- Autoscaler added new nodes but they failed to join DNS mesh due to misconfigured RBAC

Detection:

- Application Insights latency metrics showed spike
- Internal dashboard flagged 10% drop in successful orders

Impact:

- 18 minutes of intermittent service degradation
- 2,000 impacted user sessions, ~250 failed transactions

Lessons:

- Platform dependencies like DNS must be observable and version-controlled
- RBAC misconfigurations are silent killers in resilience
- Circuit breakers masked the issue but delayed root cause detection

Action Items:

- Upgrade DNS daemonset and pin image versions
- Add Prometheus alert on DNS request queue depth
- Enforce RBAC validation as part of AKS node pool scale events

---

Cultural Learnings

Resilient systems are built by **resilient teams**. The most mature teams treated post-mortems as opportunities, not burdens.

Cultural patterns observed:

- **Blamelessness**: Focus was on systems, not individuals

- **Fast feedback loops**: Incidents logged and reviewed within 24–48 hours

- **Learning amplification**: Lessons shared across teams, not siloed

- **Documentation hygiene**: Knowledge base updated with playbooks and recovery guides

- **Simulation mindset**: Chaos drills used to validate assumptions and readiness

Technical Meta-Lessons

1. **Everything should be testable and observable**
   If a failure is silent, it will repeat.

2. **Feature flags are only safe when validated**
   The code path behind a flag still runs in production context.

3. **Automate all critical recovery paths**
   If rollback is manual, it's already too slow.

4. **Dependencies deserve SLAs and chaos testing**
   Storage, DNS, identity—all need SLOs, dashboards, and game days.

5. **Resilience = Architecture + Process + Culture**
   Resilience isn't only code—it's the ecosystem in which that code lives.

Implementing a Post-Mortem Practice

To operationalize learning from failure:

- Create an **incident template** with mandatory fields

- Assign **incident commander** roles with clear escalation paths

- Establish a **central incident registry**

- Link actions to OKRs, sprints, and retrospectives

- Host quarterly **incident reviews** across orgs

Recommended Tools:

- Azure DevOps Work Items
- Notion / Confluence for knowledge base
- GitHub Projects for action item tracking
- Azure Monitor Workbooks for timeline correlation

Summary

Post-mortems are not just reports—they're catalysts for change. They give teams a language for failure, a structure for accountability, and a roadmap for improvement. The most resilient platforms in the world are not the ones that never fail—but the ones where failure leads to lasting, institutional knowledge.

The next chapter explores **how to future-proof resilient systems**, by adopting proactive strategies like AI-driven anomaly detection, chaos engineering, and continuous optimization against evolving cloud platforms and business demands.

Chapter 11: Future-Proofing Resilient Systems

Leveraging AI and ML for Predictive Resilience

Modern cloud systems must do more than recover from failure—they must **anticipate it**. With the volume, velocity, and variety of telemetry data generated across distributed applications, infrastructure, and networks, traditional monitoring techniques are no longer sufficient. Enter **predictive resilience**: the use of Artificial Intelligence (AI) and Machine Learning (ML) to foresee incidents before they occur, enabling preemptive actions and intelligent automation.

In this section, we explore how Azure's AI/ML ecosystem can be integrated into your architecture to create proactive, self-healing systems. We examine common patterns, real-world use cases, reference architectures, and tooling for implementing predictive resilience using Azure-native and open-source technologies.

The Shift from Reactive to Predictive

Historically, system resilience was reactive:

- An   error   occurs
- Monitoring   detects   the   anomaly
- An   alert   is   sent
- Engineers   respond

Predictive resilience flips this model:

- **Patterns   in   data**   are   continuously   analyzed
- **Models   learn   from   past   incidents**
- **Anomalies   are   flagged**   before   SLAs   are   breached
- **Automated   responses**   prevent   degradation

This approach requires a data-centric foundation and careful integration of AI capabilities across observability and operational tooling.

Key Capabilities of Predictive Resilience

1. **Anomaly   Detection**

   o   Identify   patterns   that   deviate   from   historical   baselines

   o   Useful for detecting early signs of memory leaks, performance degradation, or
       usage   spikes

2. **Root   Cause   Analysis   (RCA)   Automation**

   o   Use   ML   to   correlate   incidents   across   logs,   metrics,   and   traces

   o   Reduce   Mean   Time   to   Identify   (MTTI)

3. **Predictive   Maintenance**

   o   Anticipate   hardware   or   VM   failures   based   on   trends

   o   Common   in   IoT,   manufacturing,   and   edge   environments

4. **Auto-remediation   and   Smart   Scaling**

   o   Trigger   scaling   actions   or   healing   scripts   based   on   forecasts

   o   Adapt   capacity   ahead   of   load   surges

Azure Services for Predictive Resilience

Azure Monitor and Application Insights (Smart Detection)

- Built-in   ML-based   anomaly   detection   on:

  o   Server   response   time

  o   Dependency   failures

  o   Exception   rates

Example alert configuration:

```
{
  "criteria": {
```

```
   "type": "DynamicThresholdCriterion",

   "metricName": "requests/duration",

   "operator": "GreaterThan",

   "alertSensitivity": "High"

  }

}
```

Use **Azure Monitor Workbooks** to visualize and contextualize anomalies over time.

Azure Metrics Advisor

- Fully managed service for real-time anomaly detection at scale
- Learns from seasonality, trends, holidays
- Integrates with Event Hubs, Azure Data Explorer, Application Insights

Key features:

- Multi-dimensional anomaly analysis
- Alerts based on correlation
- Feedback loop for improving model accuracy

Example Use Case:

```
Data Source: Application Insights

Metric: Response Time by Region

Trigger: Anomaly detected in "West Europe"

Action: Scale-out App Service + notify engineer
```

Azure Machine Learning

Use when custom models are required:

- Build time-series forecasting models (ARIMA, Prophet, LSTM)

- Use historical incidents to train classifiers for root causes

- Deploy models as REST endpoints for scoring live data

Key tools:

- Azure ML Pipelines

- AutoML (for low-code ML)

- MLflow integration for model lifecycle management

Building a Predictive Resilience Pipeline

Architecture Components:

1. **Data Collection**

   - Azure Monitor Logs

   - Log Analytics

   - Custom metrics (via SDK or Prometheus)

2. **Data Transformation**

   - Azure Data Factory

   - Azure Stream Analytics

   - Azure Synapse Pipelines

3. **Model Training and Scoring**

   - Azure ML or Databricks

   - Scheduled retraining (weekly/monthly)

4. **Operational Integration**

   - Azure Logic Apps or Functions for response automation

- Integration with Azure Alerts, Sentinel, DevOps pipelines

Example: Predicting Web API SLA Breaches

- Data: Request duration from App Insights
- Model: Forecast API response time using Prophet
- Trigger: If forecasted latency exceeds threshold in next 10 minutes
- Action: Warm up additional App Service instances

Practical Example

Scenario: A global e-commerce platform wants to detect checkout latency issues **before** they impact conversion rates.

Solution:

- Collect real-time latency metrics from App Insights
- Feed data into Azure Metrics Advisor
- Use custom model in Azure ML to predict peak loads
- Automate scale-out when thresholds are exceeded

Response Workflow:

1. Anomaly detected in `CheckoutLatency` (Metrics Advisor)
2. Model forecasts sustained latency > 2s over next 15 minutes
3. Azure Function triggers scale-out policy in App Service Plan
4. Log custom event in Application Insights
5. Notify SRE via Teams integration

Challenges and Considerations

1. **Data Volume and Quality**
   - Garbage in, garbage out: noisy or missing data degrades model accuracy
   - Pre-processing and normalization are essential

2. **False Positives**
   - High sensitivity models may generate alert fatigue
   - Include domain-specific thresholds and rules

3. **Model Drift**
   - Retrain models periodically
   - Monitor model confidence and performance

4. **Security and Privacy**
   - Ensure PII is not used in training data
   - Comply with regional data residency regulations

5. **Team Readiness**
   - Require collaboration between SRE, data science, and engineering
   - Documentation and observability must be in place before predictive tools can be effective

---

Best Practices

- Start with out-of-the-box tools like **Smart Detection** and **Metrics Advisor**
- Instrument applications with **custom dimensions** for more targeted models
- Use **historical incidents** to guide model development
- Integrate predictions into **existing alerting and incident workflows**
- Build **feedback loops** from SREs to continuously improve model relevance
- Visualize predictions with **Workbooks** for stakeholder alignment

Summary

AI and ML are no longer futuristic novelties in operations—they're becoming essential for delivering highly resilient systems at scale. Predictive resilience transforms the way teams anticipate and mitigate failure, reducing downtime and elevating user experience. By embedding intelligent forecasting, anomaly detection, and automation into your cloud architecture, you can shift from reactive firefighting to proactive excellence.

In the next section, we explore how **Chaos Engineering on Azure** complements predictive strategies by systematically validating your systems' ability to withstand failures.

Chaos Engineering on Azure

Chaos engineering is the practice of intentionally introducing faults into a system to validate its ability to withstand and recover from unexpected conditions. Originally pioneered by Netflix with their Chaos Monkey tool, chaos engineering has evolved into a discipline that plays a vital role in building resilient systems—especially in the cloud.

On Azure, chaos engineering is gaining traction as organizations seek to validate high-availability, disaster recovery, and failure-handling mechanisms proactively rather than reactively. This section dives into practical strategies, tooling, processes, and case studies to help you implement chaos engineering on Azure safely and effectively.

Why Chaos Engineering?

No amount of static code analysis, load testing, or unit testing can reveal all the potential weak points in a distributed system. Chaos engineering enables you to:

- Test your system's behavior under real-world failure conditions

- Validate monitoring and alerting accuracy

- Ensure that fallback, retry, and circuit breaker mechanisms work as intended

- Improve incident response readiness

- Build confidence across engineering, SRE, and product teams

Principles of Chaos Engineering

1. **Define a steady state**
   Identify baseline metrics that define normal behavior (e.g., average response time, error rate, throughput).

2. **Formulate a hypothesis**
   Predict how the system should behave under failure (e.g., circuit breaker should activate, traffic should reroute).

3. **Introduce controlled chaos**
   Inject a specific fault or simulate a degradation.

4. **Observe and measure**
   Monitor system behavior during and after the injection. Was the steady state preserved?

5. **Learn and improve**
   Update your architecture, configuration, or playbooks based on the outcome.

Chaos Engineering Scenarios on Azure

1. VM or Node Failures

- Terminate a virtual machine or AKS node and verify system resilience

- Validate load balancer rerouting and service autoscaling

2. Network Latency or Packet Loss

- Introduce latency or packet drops between services

- Validate retry and timeout mechanisms

3. Dependency Failures

- Simulate database outages or unavailability of third-party APIs

- Test how the application responds: degrade gracefully or fail catastrophically?

4. Region Outage Simulation

- Redirect traffic between Azure regions

322 |

- Validate geo-redundancy and DNS failover

5. Secrets and Identity Failures

- Expire a secret or rotate a key unexpectedly
- Validate detection, alerting, and auto-remediation

Tooling for Chaos Engineering on Azure

Azure Chaos Studio (Preview)

Azure Chaos Studio is Microsoft's managed chaos engineering platform. It integrates directly with Azure resources and offers agent-based and service-direct fault injections.

Capabilities:

- Resource-level chaos targeting (VMs, AKS, App Services)
- Predefined fault types (e.g., CPU pressure, network latency, disk IO)
- Safe blast radius controls
- Experiment workflows
- Integration with Azure Monitor and Log Analytics

Sample Chaos Experiment (ARM template snippet):

```
{
  "type": "Microsoft.Chaos/experiments",
  "properties": {
    "selectors": [
      {
        "type": "List",
        "id": "selector1",
        "targets": [
```

```
          {

             "type": "ChaosTarget",

             "id":
"/subscriptions/{subId}/resourceGroups/{rg}/providers/Microsoft.Comp
ute/virtualMachines/myVM"

          }

       ]

     }

  ],

  "steps": [

    {

      "name": "step1",

      "actions": [

        {

          "type": "continuous-cpu-pressure",

          "parameters": {

            "duration": "PT5M",

            "coresAffected": "50"

          },

          "selectorId": "selector1"

        }

      ]

    }

  ]

}
```

}

Other Tools

- **Gremlin**: Commercial SaaS platform with UI-driven chaos experimentation, Azure integration, and SLO validation.

- **Chaos Mesh**: Kubernetes-native chaos tool, usable with AKS for injecting latency, faults, and node disruptions.

- **LitmusChaos**: Another CNCF project focused on Kubernetes resilience testing.

- **Custom Scripts**: Use Azure CLI or PowerShell to simulate resource disruptions, restart services, or revoke permissions.

Building a Chaos Engineering Practice

1. Start Small and Safe

- Begin with non-production environments

- Use read-only workloads

- Choose low-blast-radius components

2. Automate and Schedule

- Integrate chaos tests into CI/CD pipelines or nightly jobs

- Example: Run chaos experiments after staging deployment, pre-prod promotion

3. Combine with Observability

- Pair chaos experiments with dashboards, alerts, and logs

- Use Azure Monitor Workbooks to visualize impact in real time

4. Define Escape Hatches

- Always ensure you can stop an experiment instantly

- Monitor for unintended system degradation
- Include approval workflows for live experiments

5. Build Organizational Buy-in

- Share early wins and learnings
- Collaborate with incident response and reliability teams
- Include chaos drills in SRE training and runbooks

Example Use Case: API Dependency Outage

Scenario:

- API depends on a third-party payment processor
- Business goal: Ensure the application degrades gracefully if the processor is slow or offline

Experiment:

- Inject latency (500ms–1s) into outbound HTTP calls to the payment processor
- Observe:
  - Retry logic activation
  - Circuit breaker trip
  - Fallback UI for user
  - Alert generation

Outcome:

- First run caused application-wide timeouts due to no circuit breaker
- After fix: fallback logic served cached payment options, circuit breaker tripped correctly

Learnings:

- Validate resilience patterns with live chaos, not just code review
- Real-world latency differs from synthetic tests

Measuring the Impact of Chaos Engineering

Establish KPIs to track before and after:

- MTTD (Mean Time to Detect)
- MTTR (Mean Time to Resolve)
- SLA/SLO breach rate
- Alert response time
- Coverage of chaos-tested services
- Change lead time (via pipeline feedback loops)

Track incidents where chaos tests **prevented** future failures—these are the best proof of ROI.

Best Practices Summary

- Treat chaos engineering as **controlled experimentation**, not reckless breaking
- Always define a **steady state** and hypothesis
- Start with **low-risk components** and scale up
- Use **Azure Chaos Studio** for seamless Azure-native injection
- Automate experiments for consistency and coverage
- Pair with **observability tools** to measure system behavior
- Document every experiment and integrate findings into system improvements
- Make chaos engineering a **routine**, not a one-off event

Summary

Chaos engineering is an essential discipline for validating the assumptions that underlie system resilience. On Azure, tools like Chaos Studio provide a powerful foundation for testing failure modes across compute, storage, networking, and service dependencies. When chaos is introduced with intention, structure, and observability, it becomes a source of clarity and strength.

In the next section, we explore how to align your architecture with Azure's evolving roadmap, taking advantage of emerging capabilities while maintaining resilience and backward compatibility.

Evolving with Azure's Roadmap and New Services

Resilient systems are not static—they must evolve in tandem with the platforms on which they run. Azure's cloud ecosystem continues to grow at a rapid pace, introducing new capabilities, services, and paradigms that impact architectural decisions. To future-proof resilience, engineering teams must build systems that can **adapt to change**: new SKUs, API deprecations, pricing shifts, network topologies, regional capacity limits, and security model updates.

This section outlines a practical approach to building **adaptable cloud-native systems** on Azure that can evolve gracefully. It discusses service evolution patterns, observability for platform changes, architectural modularity, integration of preview features, deprecation awareness, and strategies for continuous architecture modernization.

Why Architectural Evolution Matters

Systems that don't evolve accumulate **tech debt** and **operational risk**:

- Reliance on deprecated APIs or SKUs
- Manual configurations that block scaling
- Incompatibility with new Azure regions or service plans
- Missed opportunities to reduce cost or increase performance

Meanwhile, Azure evolves continuously:

- New tiers of services (e.g., Premium, Zone-Redundant, ARM-based)
- Shifting service limits and SLA enhancements

- Introduction of cloud-native platforms like Azure Container Apps, Azure Arc

- Security posture improvements (e.g., managed identities, Private Link)

Building in awareness and capacity for change is a resilience imperative.

Categories of Azure Change

Understanding what evolves helps shape your system boundaries and monitoring focus.

1. **Service**   **Features**

   o New configurations, flags, or protocols

   o Examples: HTTP/3 for Azure Front Door, autoscaling enhancements for App Service

2. **SKU**   **and**   **Plan**   **Changes**

   o Legacy tiers deprecated; newer ones introduced with better SLA

   o Example: Migration from App Service Basic to Premium V3

3. **Regional**   **Expansion**   **and**   **Constraints**

   o Services roll out regionally; capacity is not guaranteed

   o Some features only available in selected regions

4. **API**   **Versions**   **and**   **Deprecations**

   o Azure REST and ARM templates change over time

   o Breaking changes may impact automation scripts

5. **Pricing**   **Model**   **Adjustments**

   o Service meter names, billing units, or discount plans may evolve

   o Example: Pay-as-you-go vs. reserved capacity pricing

6. **Security**   **Standards**   **and**   **Policies**

   o Changes to default TLS versions, encryption requirements, or compliance rules o   Azure Policy may enforce restrictions that break old deployments

---

Principles for Evolution-Ready Architecture

1. Embrace Abstraction and Modularity

Abstract your dependencies on specific services. Use:

- Interface-driven design for storage, compute, identity, and networking

- Internal SDKs/wrappers to encapsulate Azure service calls

- Terraform modules or Bicep templates as reusable units

Example: Storage Abstraction

```
interface IBlobStore {

  upload(file: File): Promise<string>;

  download(id: string): Promise<Buffer>;

}
```

Switching from Azure Blob Storage to another implementation becomes simpler when this boundary exists.

2. Use Infrastructure as Code (IaC) for All Resources

Track Azure resource definitions as version-controlled code using:

- Bicep

- Terraform

- Pulumi

- Azure CLI scripts (with linting and validations)

IaC helps detect:

- API version drift

- Deprecated parameter use

- Regional constraints before runtime

Run validations regularly:

```
az bicep build --file main.bicep
```

3. Stay Aligned with Microsoft's Roadmap

Use official resources to track updates:

- Azure Updates: https://azure.microsoft.com/updates

- Azure Roadmap: https://aka.ms/azureroadmap

- GitHub release notes for SDKs and CLI tools

- Microsoft Learn and Ignite recordings

Subscribe to RSS feeds or use automation to extract change summaries.

4. Design for Progressive Rollout

Test new services in sandbox or isolated tenants:

- Use feature flags or traffic splitting for gradual exposure

- Apply "shadow mode" where new service runs in parallel without impact

- Keep older paths alive until confidence is gained

Use **Azure Deployment Stamps** for per-tenant isolation and regional testing.

5. Avoid Service Lock-In Without a Path Forward

Balance platform benefits with flexibility:

- Prefer open protocols (e.g., OAuth, HTTPS, AMQP, SQL) over vendor-specific SDKs

- Choose services with long-term support and strong adoption

- Document exit strategy for every critical dependency

Monitoring for Azure Platform Drift

Resilient systems require **observability into Azure changes**.

Recommended Practices:

- Enable **Resource Health Alerts** for each key resource type

- Use **Azure Advisor** for upgrade recommendations and deprecated usage

- Query **Activity Logs** for policy enforcement or provider-level changes

KQL Sample – Detect API Version Drift:

```
AzureDiagnostics
| where ResourceProvider == "Microsoft.Web/sites"
| summarize count() by Resource, apiVersion_s
```

Migration and Upgrade Strategies

1. **Canary** **Resources**

   - Use one or more subscriptions to test new versions and SKUs

   - Mirror your production topology in a safe environment

2. **Automation-First** **Upgrades**

   - Script every migration step

   - Use tools like `az resource move`, `bicep`, or `terraform plan` with preview

3. **Downtime-Aware** **vs.** **Zero-Downtime** **Migration**

   - Web apps: use deployment slots or traffic manager routing

   - Databases: leverage geo-replication + failover testing

- Functions: use staging slots and monitor cold start impact

4. **Deprecation** **Tracking**

  - Build a dashboard showing resource types and API versions
  - Use Azure Resource Graph to extract metadata for scale

Case Study: Transitioning to App Service Premium V3

A B2B SaaS provider upgraded from App Service Standard to Premium V3 for improved scalability, VNet support, and cost savings via reserved instances.

Steps Taken:

- Validated feature compatibility (deployment slots, identity)
- Migrated staging apps first using IaC templates
- Ran load tests comparing startup time, cold start, latency
- Reserved capacity for 1 year at discounted rate
- Created rollback slot in case of critical regressions

Outcome:

- 30% cost reduction
- 70% improved cold start performance
- No downtime or customer impact

Team and Process Alignment

Resilience through evolution requires organizational readiness:

- Assign **Azure Change Owners** in your platform team
- Include **Azure Upgrade Reviews** in quarterly architecture reviews

- Bake version checks into CI pipelines

- Tag IaC files with minimum required Azure API versions

Build a **culture of experimentation and evaluation** rather than waiting for incidents to prompt upgrades.

Summary

Azure will continue to evolve. Your architecture must too. By investing in modular design, abstracted dependencies, continuous IaC validation, and a strong awareness of roadmap signals, your systems can remain resilient even as the ground beneath them shifts. Cloud-native resilience isn't just about high availability today—it's about staying relevant, supportable, and secure tomorrow.

In the next and final technical section of this chapter, we'll explore how **sustainability and cost optimization** intersect with resilience and how to build efficient, scalable, and environmentally conscious Azure architectures.

Sustainability and Cost Optimization in Design

As cloud architectures scale in complexity and reach, organizations face increasing pressure to balance performance, availability, and scalability with **economic efficiency** and **environmental responsibility**. A resilient system that burns excessive compute or leaks unused resources is neither sustainable nor cost-effective. Conversely, a highly optimized, green system that lacks fault tolerance will compromise user trust and business continuity.

This section explores how to integrate **sustainability** and **cost optimization** into the architectural DNA of Azure-based systems. We cover principles, strategies, tools, and real-world practices that help align resilience goals with operational efficiency, carbon awareness, and cloud economics.

Why Sustainability and Cost Optimization Matter for Resilience

1. **Resilience Under Cost Pressure**
Cost constraints often lead to under-provisioned infrastructure or rushed architectural shortcuts. Systems designed with built-in efficiency maintain resilience even when budgets tighten.

2. **Green Operations Are Resilient**
Efficient systems reduce operational overhead, energy consumption, and resource waste—key tenets of sustainable engineering. They are easier to maintain, scale, and troubleshoot.

3. Cloud-Native Waste is Real

Common issues include:

- Idle VMs and containers

- Over-provisioned App Services

- Redundant backups

- Unused storage and orphaned disks

- Always-on workloads with bursty usage

Foundational Principles

1. Right-Sizing

Provision resources to meet actual demand—not peak capacity—with headroom for burst scaling. Use autoscaling wherever possible.

- For AKS: Use Horizontal Pod Autoscaler (HPA) and node pool autoscaling

- For App Service: Configure autoscale rules by CPU, memory, or custom metrics

- For Functions: Use Consumption or Premium Plans instead of always-on tiers

Example Bicep for App Service Autoscale:

```
resource autoscale 'Microsoft.Insights/autoscalesettings@2021-05-01'
= {

  name: 'webapp-autoscale'

  location: location

  properties: {

    profiles: [

      {

        name: 'default'

        capacity: {
```

```
    minimum: '1'

    maximum: '5'

    default: '2'

}

rules: [

  {

    metricTrigger: {

      metricName: 'CpuPercentage'

      operator: 'GreaterThan'

      threshold: 70

      timeGrain: 'PT1M'

      statistic: 'Average'

      timeWindow: 'PT5M'

      timeAggregation: 'Average'

      metricNamespace: ''

      dimensions: []

    }

    scaleAction: {

      direction: 'Increase'

      type: 'ChangeCount'

      value: '1'

      cooldown: 'PT5M'

    }

  }
```

```
        ]

      }

    ]

    enabled: true

    targetResourceUri: webApp.id

  }

}
```

2. Serverless and Event-Driven Models

Serverless architectures scale to zero when idle. They reduce resource usage and carbon emissions significantly.

- Replace always-on VMs or WebJobs with Azure Functions or Logic Apps

- Use Event Grid to trigger downstream services only when events occur

- Use Azure Container Apps for microservices that can hibernate and wake on demand

3. Cold Path vs. Hot Path Data Pipelines

Design dual-path ingestion:

- **Hot path**: Real-time, low-latency analytics (e.g., Stream Analytics)

- **Cold path**: Batch processing and archival (e.g., Synapse, Data Lake)

Avoid running all data through the hot path unless necessary. Apply time-window aggregation and tiering strategies.

4. Sustainable Storage Practices

- Enable **lifecycle policies** to tier infrequently accessed data

- Choose ZRS or LRS based on actual durability needs

- Delete orphaned resources: disks, snapshots, unused backups

- Use **immutable blob storage** only where required (e.g., compliance)

Lifecycle Management JSON Example:

```json
{
  "rules": [
    {
      "enabled": true,
      "name": "archiveOldBlobs",
      "type": "Lifecycle",
      "definition": {
        "filters": {
          "blobTypes": ["blockBlob"],
          "prefixMatch": ["logs/"]
        },
        "actions": {
          "baseBlob": {
            "tierToArchive": {
              "daysAfterModificationGreaterThan": 30
            }
          }
        }
      }
    }
  ]
}
```

```
    ]

}
```

Azure Tools for Cost Optimization and Sustainability

Azure Advisor

- Recommends underutilized VMs
- Suggests right-size SKUs and shut-downs for idle resources
- Highlights savings plan opportunities

Azure Cost Management + Billing

- Track usage and spend by resource, region, or tag
- Set budgets and thresholds
- Detect anomalies and forecast usage

Example:

```
Usage
| where ResourceGroup == 'prod-app'
| summarize cost = sum(PreTaxCost) by bin(UsageDateTime, 1d),
ResourceType
```

Microsoft Sustainability Calculator

- Estimate carbon impact of your Azure usage
- Breakdown by service, region, and time period
- Aligns with GHG Protocol standards

Azure Resource Graph

- Query all resources across subscriptions
- Find unused public IPs, unattached disks, zombie VMs

```
Resources
| where type == "microsoft.compute/disks"
| where properties.diskState == "Unattached"
```

Governance for Cost and Sustainability

1. **Tag** **Everything**

   - Environment, Owner, Application, CostCenter, TTL
   - Use Azure Policy to enforce tagging

2. **Define** **Budgets** **per** **Team** **or** **Environment**

   - Prod, staging, dev, and experiments must have cost boundaries
   - Alert via email, webhook, or Teams

3. **Enforce** **Resource** **TTL**

   - Use tags + scheduled Functions to delete resources after expiration

4. **Audit** **Orphaned** **Resources** **Monthly**

   - Use custom scripts or Azure Automation Runbooks

Real-World Example

Context: A logistics company was spending $280,000/year on underutilized Azure VMs and App Services across dev/test environments.

Action Taken:

- Migrated 60% of compute to serverless Functions
- Enabled lifecycle policies for blob storage
- Created Azure Budget alerts and weekly audits
- Adopted Azure Reservations for consistent workloads
- Consolidated test environments into Container Apps with scaling policies

Result:

- 42% cost reduction
- 30% decrease in carbon emissions per Microsoft Sustainability Calculator
- Improved engineering discipline through tagging and governance

---

Design Patterns for Resilient Efficiency

Problem	Resilient Pattern	Sustainable Optimization
Traffic Spikes	Auto-scaling with queue buffer	Function-as-a-Service
Nightly ETL Load	Durable Functions + Batching	Timer-based trigger, blob batching
Static Asset Delivery	Azure Front Door	Long TTL + CDN caching
Stateful Sessions	Redis Cache (Premium)	Eviction policy + max memory tuning
Logs and Diagnostics	Azure Monitor Logs	Retention policies + sampling

Summary

A resilient Azure architecture is not just fault-tolerant—it is **efficient**, **cost-conscious**, and **environmentally aware**. Sustainable cloud engineering improves uptime, reduces waste, and ensures long-term operability. With careful right-sizing, serverless adoption, intelligent automation, and strong governance, teams can build systems that perform exceptionally—without breaking the bank or the planet.

With this final section, we've completed our journey through building and future-proofing resilient architectures on Azure. The appendices that follow contain glossary terms, resources, code snippets, and FAQs to help you implement and extend the concepts from this book in your own environments.

Chapter 12: Appendices

Glossary of Terms

This glossary serves as a quick reference for key concepts, services, and terms related to resilient cloud architecture on Azure. Understanding this vocabulary will reinforce the knowledge gained throughout the book and serve as a foundation for deeper exploration.

A

Active-Active   **Architecture**
A high availability configuration where multiple systems or regions handle traffic simultaneously. Ensures minimal failover time and load distribution.

Active-Passive   **Architecture**
A redundancy model in which one system actively handles traffic while a standby (passive) system remains idle, ready to take over in the event of failure.

Application   **Insights**
A feature of Azure Monitor that provides application performance monitoring, telemetry data, and diagnostics.

Azure   **Advisor**
A personalized cloud consultant that helps optimize Azure deployments across high availability, performance, security, and cost.

Azure   **Automation**
A service that enables you to automate frequent, time-consuming, and error-prone cloud management tasks.

B

Backoff   **Strategy**
A technique to avoid overwhelming a service by spacing out retry attempts. Common types include exponential and jittered backoff.

Bicep
A domain-specific language (DSL) for deploying Azure resources declaratively, simplifying the authoring experience compared to raw ARM templates.

Blob   **Storage**
An Azure Storage service optimized for storing massive amounts of unstructured data.

Bulkhead   **Pattern**
A resilience pattern that isolates components or workloads to prevent cascading failures.

C

Circuit   **Breaker**
A design pattern that stops execution of an operation when repeated failures occur, preventing system overload and allowing recovery.

Chaos   **Engineering**
The practice of deliberately injecting failures into systems to validate their resilience and recovery capabilities.

Cloud-Native
Architectures designed specifically for scalability, fault-tolerance, and continuous delivery in cloud environments.

Cosmos   **DB**
A globally distributed, multi-model Azure database service offering high availability, partitioning, and multi-region writes.

D

Data   **Lake**   **Gen2**
A storage solution built on Azure Blob Storage for big data analytics. Integrates with Hadoop and analytics tools.

Data   **Residency**
The concept that data must reside in a specific location or region to comply with regulatory or legal requirements.

Dead   **Letter**   **Queue**   **(DLQ)**
A queue that stores messages that could not be delivered or processed successfully. Used for debugging and retry mechanisms.

Durable   **Functions**
An extension of Azure Functions that enables building stateful workflows in a serverless compute environment.

E

Event **Grid**
An eventing backplane in Azure used for reactive programming and decoupling services through publish/subscribe patterns.

Event **Sourcing**
A pattern where changes to application state are stored as a sequence of immutable events rather than as direct updates to state.

Exponential **Backoff**
A strategy that increases wait time between retries exponentially to reduce the likelihood of retry storms during service failure.

F

Failover
The process of switching from a failed component, region, or service to a standby or redundant one.

Feature **Flags**
A technique that allows features to be turned on or off in production without deploying new code.

Function **App**
A container for Azure Functions that defines the execution context and configuration settings for one or more functions.

G

Geo-Redundancy
The practice of distributing systems and data across geographically separated regions to ensure continuity during regional failures.

GitHub **Actions**
CI/CD workflows hosted on GitHub that automate development lifecycle tasks such as testing, building, and deployment.

H

Health **Probes**
Mechanisms used by load balancers or orchestrators (e.g., Kubernetes) to determine if an instance is healthy and can receive traffic.

High   **Availability**   **(HA)**

The ability of a system or component to remain accessible and operational for a high percentage of time, often measured by SLA.

I

Idempotency

The property that allows the same operation to be applied multiple times without changing the result beyond the initial application.

Infrastructure   **as**   **Code**   **(IaC)**

Managing and provisioning cloud infrastructure through machine-readable configuration files rather than manual processes.

Ingress   **Controller**

In Kubernetes, a component that manages external access to services, typically via HTTP/HTTPS routing.

K

Key   **Vault**

An Azure service that securely stores and accesses secrets, encryption keys, and certificates.

Kubernetes

An open-source container orchestration platform for automating deployment, scaling, and operations of application containers.

L

Latency

The delay between a request and a response. A key metric in performance and user experience.

Load   **Balancer**

A networking solution that distributes incoming network traffic across multiple servers to improve availability and responsiveness.

M

Managed **Identity**
An automatically managed identity in Azure Active Directory that allows secure authentication without storing credentials in code.

Metrics **Advisor**
An Azure service that uses machine learning to detect anomalies in time-series data.

Monitoring
Collecting and analyzing system metrics and logs to understand performance, detect anomalies, and improve reliability.

N

Network **Security** **Group** **(NSG)**
A firewall used in Azure to control inbound and outbound network traffic to resources within a virtual network.

Node **Pool** **(AKS)**
A set of virtual machines in Azure Kubernetes Service used to run workloads. Each pool can be scaled and configured independently.

O

Observability
The ability to measure and understand the internal state of a system based on outputs such as logs, metrics, and traces.

Outage **Simulation**
The act of deliberately creating a system fault or disruption to test recovery and resilience strategies.

P

Partitioning
A technique for distributing data across multiple servers or containers for scalability and performance.

Private **Link**
Azure service enabling private access to services across a virtual network, enhancing security and reducing data exfiltration risks.

P95   **Latency**
The latency below which 95% of all requests are served. Used to understand worst-case performance for most users.

Q

Queue-Based   **Load**   **Leveling**
A design pattern that introduces queues between components to decouple workload spikes from processing capacity.

R

Region   **Pairing**
Azure's mechanism of pairing regions within a geography for replication and disaster recovery.

Resilience
The ability of a system to recover from failures and continue operating under stress or degradation.

Retry   **Policy**
Rules for retrying operations that have failed due to transient errors, often with backoff strategies.

S

Service   **Bus**
A fully managed enterprise message broker in Azure for reliable message delivery between applications and services.

Service   **Principal**
An identity used by applications, services, and automation tools to access Azure resources securely.

SLAs   **(Service**   **Level**   **Agreements)**
Formal documents defining the expected availability and performance of a service.

Sustainability   **Scorecard**
A metric used to assess the environmental impact and energy efficiency of a cloud architecture.

T

Terraform
An open-source IaC tool that enables provisioning of cloud infrastructure across multiple providers including Azure.

Timeouts
Limits set on the duration a request can take before being canceled. Used to avoid resource lockup.

U

Unattached **Resources**
Azure resources that are no longer linked to an active workload (e.g., orphaned disks), often targeted for cleanup.

Uptime
A measure of system availability over a period, often expressed as a percentage (e.g., 99.95%).

V

Virtual **Network** **(VNet)**
Azure's logical isolation of the cloud network, allowing resources to securely communicate with each other and on-premises.

Virtual **Machines** **Scale** **Sets** **(VMSS)**
An Azure compute resource that allows you to deploy and manage a set of identical, auto-scaling VMs.

W

Workbooks **(Azure** **Monitor)**
Interactive dashboards for visualizing telemetry data, diagnostics, and metrics across Azure services.

Z

Zone-Redundant **Services**
Services deployed across multiple availability zones in a region to provide higher availability and fault tolerance.

This glossary should serve as a living reference to deepen your understanding of resilient cloud design. For deeper dives, consult the documentation links provided in the Resources section of this book.

Resources for Further Learning

The field of cloud resilience is dynamic, fast-evolving, and interconnected with many other domains such as distributed systems, DevOps, security, observability, and systems design. While this book provides a comprehensive foundation for designing resilient architectures on Azure, continuing education is key to mastering this discipline. This section provides a curated collection of high-quality resources for deepening your understanding, staying updated on Azure innovations, and connecting with the broader community.

1. Official Microsoft Documentation

The most authoritative and up-to-date source for Azure services and architectural guidance.

Azure Architecture Center

- **URL:** https://aka.ms/AzureArchitecture

- Offers reference architectures, design patterns, and best practices.

- Particularly useful are the "Resiliency checklist" and "Well-Architected Framework" sections.

Azure Well-Architected Framework

- **URL:** https://learn.microsoft.com/en-us/azure/architecture/framework/

- Covers five pillars: Cost Optimization, Operational Excellence, Performance Efficiency, Reliability, and Security.

- Includes assessments and recommendations.

Azure Resiliency Overview

- **URL:** https://learn.microsoft.com/en-us/azure/availability-zones/resiliency-overview

- Describes the built-in availability, redundancy, and failover features of Azure.

Azure Status and Health

- **URL**: https://status.azure.com

- Real-time information about Azure services' availability and historical incidents.

---

2. Microsoft Learn Modules

Self-paced, hands-on training modules that offer practical learning paths.

Recommended Modules:

- **Designing Resilient Applications on Azure**
  https://learn.microsoft.com/en-us/training/modules/design-for-availability-reliability/

- **Architecting Cloud-Native Apps on Azure**
  https://learn.microsoft.com/en-us/training/paths/cloud-native-apps/

- **Automate Azure Tasks using ARM Templates and Bicep**
  https://learn.microsoft.com/en-us/training/modules/intro-to-infrastructure-as-code/

- **Design for Efficiency and Operations**
  https://learn.microsoft.com/en-us/training/modules/design-for-efficiency-operations/

---

3. Books and Publications

Recommended Books:

- **"Designing Distributed Systems" by Brendan Burns**
  A practical guide from a Kubernetes co-founder on building scalable, fault-tolerant systems.

- **"Site Reliability Engineering" by Google**
  Introduces SRE concepts that are widely applicable in cloud resilience practices.

- **"The Art of Scalability" by Abbott & Fisher**
  Deep insights on growth, resilience, and architecture at scale.

- **"Building Microservices" by Sam Newman**
  Valuable for understanding resilient communication patterns and service boundaries.

Azure-Specific Publications:

- **Microsoft Azure Essentials Series**
  Covers topics such as cloud design patterns, Azure fundamentals, and enterprise development.

- **Cloud Design Patterns eBook (MSDN)**
  https://docs.microsoft.com/en-us/azure/architecture/patterns/

4. Community and Expert Blogs

Follow Azure practitioners, engineers, and solution architects for practical guides and real-world scenarios.

Notable Blogs:

- **Scott Hanselman**
  https://www.hanselman.com/

- **Mark Russinovich (Azure CTO)**
  https://techcommunity.microsoft.com/t5/azure-architecture/bg-p/AzureArchitecture

- **Microsoft Tech Community**
  https://techcommunity.microsoft.com/

- **Troy Hunt (Security Focus)**
  https://www.troyhunt.com/

- **Jeremy Likness (Azure Developer Relations)**
  https://www.linkedin.com/in/jeremylikness/

5. GitHub Repositories and Open Source Projects

Leverage real-world templates, samples, and tools from Microsoft and the community.

Repositories:

- **Azure Quickstart Templates**
  https://github.com/Azure/azure-quickstart-templates

- **Azure Architecture Center GitHub**
  https://github.com/mspnp

- **Azure** **Bicep** **Samples**
  https://github.com/Azure/bicep

- **Microsoft** **Azure** **SDKs** **and** **Tools**
  https://github.com/Azure/azure-sdk

---

6. Conference Talks, Videos, and Podcasts

Explore visual and auditory learning formats.

Conferences:

- **Microsoft** **Ignite**

- **Microsoft** **Build**

- **Azure** **Open** **Source** **Day**

- **KubeCon** **+** **CloudNativeCon**

YouTube Channels:

- **Azure** **Friday**
  https://www.youtube.com/c/AzureFriday

- **Microsoft** **Azure**
  https://www.youtube.com/c/MicrosoftAzure

Podcasts:

- **Azure** **DevOps** **Podcast**

- **The** **Cloudcast**

- **Software** **Engineering** **Daily**

- **Screaming** **in** **the** **Cloud**

---

7. Learning Platforms

Courses from expert instructors for in-depth technical skill building.

- **Pluralsight** – Many Azure courses across architecture, DevOps, networking, and data

- **LinkedIn Learning** – Great for short refreshers and leadership-skills development

- **Udemy** – Affordable training on Azure certifications, Kubernetes, Bicep, Terraform, etc.

- **Coursera** – Partnerships with Microsoft and universities for credentialed learning

8. Certifications

Validate your skills and deepen your expertise with role-based certifications:

Microsoft Certifications:

- **AZ-305**: Designing Microsoft Azure Infrastructure Solutions

- **AZ-400**: Designing and Implementing Microsoft DevOps Solutions

- **AZ-500**: Microsoft Azure Security Technologies

- **SC-100**: Microsoft Cybersecurity Architect

- **DP-420**: Designing and Implementing Cloud-Native Applications using Azure Cosmos DB

9. Newsletters and Community Updates

Stay updated on Azure changes and best practices.

- **Azure Updates RSS Feed**
  https://azure.microsoft.com/en-us/updates/

- **Azure Weekly Newsletter**
  https://azureweekly.info/

- **Cloud Skills Weekly (by ACloudGuru)**
  https://acloudguru.com/blog

Summary

Resilience is a journey, not a destination. The more you learn, the more context you gain to design systems that are not only technically robust but aligned with user needs, business constraints, and platform realities. This resource guide will help you sharpen your edge, build communities of practice, and stay ahead in the ever-evolving world of cloud resilience on Azure.

Sample Projects and Code Snippets

To bridge the gap between theory and practical implementation, this section presents sample projects and code snippets that demonstrate resilient design patterns using Azure services. These examples provide a foundation for hands-on experimentation, prototyping, or direct integration into production systems.

Whether you're building fault-tolerant APIs, implementing event-driven pipelines, or designing for high availability, these samples highlight key strategies for resilience across compute, storage, messaging, and observability.

Sample Project 1: Resilient API with Azure API Management and Azure Functions

Goal: Create a highly available, fault-tolerant API using Azure Functions behind Azure API Management, with retries, circuit breakers, and health checks.

Architecture Overview:

- Azure API Management (APIM) for gateway and throttling
- Azure Functions (Premium Plan) for business logic
- Azure Application Insights for monitoring
- Azure Key Vault for secrets
- Cosmos DB (with retry logic) as backend data store

Function App with Retry Logic

```
public static class GetCustomerFunction
{
    [FunctionName("GetCustomer")]
    public static async Task<IActionResult> Run(
```

```
        [HttpTrigger(AuthorizationLevel.Function,  "get",  Route  =
"customer/{id}")] HttpRequest req,

    string id,

    ILogger log)

  {

    int maxRetries = 3;

    int delayMs = 200;


    for (int i = 0; i < maxRetries; i++)

    {

      try

      {

        var          customer          =          await
customerService.GetByIdAsync(id);

        return new OkObjectResult(customer);

      }

      catch  (CosmosException  ex)  when  (ex.StatusCode  ==
HttpStatusCode.TooManyRequests)

      {

        log.LogWarning($"Retry  {i  +  1}  after  429:
{ex.Message}");

        await Task.Delay(delayMs * (i + 1));

      }

    }


    return new StatusCodeResult(503);
```

```
    }

}
```

API Management Policy Snippet

```
<inbound>

    <base />

    <set-backend-service                                    base-
url="https://myfunction.azurewebsites.net/api/" />

    <retry    condition="@(context.Response.StatusCode    ==    503)"
count="3" interval="2" />

</inbound>
```

Sample Project 2: Event-Driven Resilience with Azure Service Bus

Goal: Design a decoupled microservices architecture using Azure Service Bus with retry handling, dead-letter queues, and message durability.

Components:

- Producer: ASP.NET   Core   API
- Consumer: Azure   Function   triggered   by   Service   Bus
- Storage: Azure   SQL   Database
- Monitoring: Azure   Monitor   +   Log   Analytics

Producer: Sending Message to Queue

```
var client = new ServiceBusClient(connectionString);

var sender = client.CreateSender("orders");


var message = new ServiceBusMessage(JsonSerializer.Serialize(order));
```

```
message.MessageId = Guid.NewGuid().ToString();

message.ContentType = "application/json";

await sender.SendMessageAsync(message);
```

Consumer with Retry and Dead-Letter

```
[FunctionName("ProcessOrder")]

public async Task Run(

    [ServiceBusTrigger("orders",            Connection            =
"ServiceBusConnection")] ServiceBusReceivedMessage message,

    ServiceBusMessageActions messageActions,

    ILogger log)

{

    try

    {

        var order = JsonSerializer.Deserialize<Order>(message.Body);

        await orderService.Process(order);

    }

    catch (Exception ex)

    {

        log.LogError(ex, "Failed to process message");


        if (message.DeliveryCount > 3)

        {

            await      messageActions.DeadLetterMessageAsync(message,
"Max retries exceeded");
```

```
        }

        else

        {

            throw;

        }

    }

}
```

Sample Project 3: Geo-Redundant Web App with Traffic Manager

Goal: Deploy a resilient web application across two Azure regions with automatic failover.

Tools:

- Azure   App   Service   (Region   A   and   B)
- Azure   Traffic   Manager   (Priority   routing)
- Azure   Front   Door   (optional   for   CDN   and   WAF)

Traffic Manager Configuration:

```
{

  "routingMethod": "Priority",

  "endpoints": [

    {

      "name": "primary",

      "target": "app-primary.azurewebsites.net",

      "priority": 1

    },
```

```json
  {

    "name": "secondary",

    "target": "app-secondary.azurewebsites.net",

    "priority": 2

  }

 ]

}
```

Health probes monitor /healthz endpoint to detect downtime and reroute traffic accordingly.

Sample Project 4: Durable Functions for Workflow Resilience

Goal: Use Durable Functions to implement a multi-step workflow that resumes from failure.

Use Case: Order Fulfillment Workflow

```csharp
[FunctionName("OrderWorkflow")]

public static async Task<OrderResult> RunOrchestrator(

    [OrchestrationTrigger] IDurableOrchestrationContext context)

{

    var order = context.GetInput<Order>();

    await context.CallActivityAsync("ChargePayment", order);

    await context.CallActivityAsync("ReserveInventory", order);

    await context.CallActivityAsync("SendConfirmation", order);

    return new OrderResult { Status = "Completed" };

}
```

Activities are replayable and state is checkpointed. If one step fails, the workflow can retry or resume from the failed activity.

Sample Project 5: Resilience Observability with Azure Monitor and Workbooks

Goal: Create a unified observability dashboard using Azure Monitor Workbooks.

Metrics to Track:

- Function failure rate

- Service Bus dead-letter message count

- App Service response time (P95)

- Cosmos DB RU consumption

KQL Queries for Workbook

```
AzureDiagnostics

| where Resource == "myFunctionApp"

| where OperationName == "FunctionExecution"

| summarize FailureCount = count() by bin(TimeGenerated, 5m),
resultType
```

```
AzureMetrics

| where Resource == "myCosmosDB"

| where MetricName == "TotalRequests"

| summarize avg(TotalRequests) by bin(TimeGenerated, 5m)
```

Workbooks allow you to visualize the correlation between metrics and alerts, and share insights with stakeholders.

Sample Project 6: Infrastructure as Code (IaC) for Resilience

Goal: Use Bicep to deploy resilient infrastructure in Azure.

Example: High Availability Web App

```
resource appPlan 'Microsoft.Web/serverfarms@2022-03-01' = {

  name: 'webAppPlan'

  location: 'westeurope'

  sku: {

    name: 'P1v2'

    tier: 'PremiumV2'

  }

  properties: {

    zoneRedundant: true

  }

}


resource webApp 'Microsoft.Web/sites@2022-03-01' = {

  name: 'myWebApp'

  location: 'westeurope'

  properties: {

    serverFarmId: appPlan.id

    httpsOnly: true

  }

}
```

Add alerts, autoscaling, and backups as additional modules.

Summary

These sample projects and code snippets provide a blueprint for implementing resilience using Azure-native tools and services. Adapt them to your organization's context, and extend them with your own configurations, pipelines, and architectural constraints.

Remember: resilience isn't a single decision—it's a system of interdependent practices that span development, deployment, infrastructure, and operations. These examples will help you begin that journey with clarity and confidence.

API Reference Guide

This section provides a practical reference for working with key Azure services related to resilient architectures. It includes REST APIs, SDK usage, CLI commands, and resource definitions commonly used in automation, observability, and deployment. This is not an exhaustive specification but a focused, hands-on guide to implementing and managing resilience features programmatically.

Azure Resource Manager (ARM) API Basics

Azure's control plane APIs use the RESTful ARM (Azure Resource Manager) model to provision and manage resources. Most interactions follow a consistent pattern:

Endpoint Structure:

```
https://management.azure.com/subscriptions/{subscriptionId}/resource
Groups/{resourceGroupName}/providers/{resourceProvider}/{resourceTyp
e}/{resourceName}?api-version={version}
```

Common Headers:

```
Authorization: Bearer <token>

Content-Type: application/json
```

Access Token (Azure CLI):

```
az account get-access-token --resource=https://management.azure.com
```

1. Azure App Service

Create App Service Plan:

```
az appservice plan create \

  --name myPlan \

  --resource-group myRG \

  --sku P1v2 \

  --is-linux \

  --location westeurope
```

Deploy a Web App:

```
az webapp create \

  --resource-group myRG \

  --plan myPlan \

  --name myWebApp \

  --runtime "DOTNETCORE:6.0"
```

Configure Backup:

```
az webapp config backup create \

  --resource-group myRG \

  --webapp-name myWebApp \

  --backup-name dailyBackup \

  --container-url <sas-container-url>
```

Enable Always On:

```
az webapp config set \

  --resource-group myRG \

  --name myWebApp \

  --always-on true
```

---

2. Azure Functions

Create Function App:

```
az functionapp create \

  --resource-group myRG \

  --consumption-plan-location westeurope \

  --runtime dotnet \

  --functions-version 4 \

  --name myFuncApp \

  --storage-account mystorageacct
```

Get Function Host Keys:

```
az functionapp function keys list \

  --resource-group myRG \

  --name myFuncApp \

  --function-name HttpTrigger1
```

Invoke Function (REST):

```
curl -X POST https://myFuncApp.azurewebsites.net/api/MyFunction \

  -H "x-functions-key: <function-key>" \
```

```
-H "Content-Type: application/json" \

-d '{"name": "Azure"}'
```

---

3. Azure Service Bus

Create Namespace and Queue:

```
az servicebus namespace create \

  --resource-group myRG \

  --name myNamespace \

  --location westeurope \

  --sku Standard


az servicebus queue create \

  --resource-group myRG \

  --namespace-name myNamespace \

  --name myQueue \

  --max-size 1024 \

  --enable-dead-lettering-on-message-expiration true
```

Send Message (Python SDK):

```python
from azure.servicebus import ServiceBusClient, ServiceBusMessage


conn_str = "<conn-string>"

queue_name = "myQueue"

client = ServiceBusClient.from_connection_string(conn_str)
```

```python
with client:

    sender = client.get_queue_sender(queue_name)

    with sender:

        message = ServiceBusMessage("Hello, Azure!")

        sender.send_messages(message)
```

---

4. Azure Cosmos DB

Create Cosmos DB Account (CLI):

```
az cosmosdb create \

  --name myCosmosDb \

  --resource-group myRG \

  --kind GlobalDocumentDB \

  --locations          regionName=westeurope          failoverPriority=0
isZoneRedundant=false \

  --default-consistency-level Session
```

Enable Multi-Region Writes:

```
az cosmosdb update \

  --name myCosmosDb \

  --resource-group myRG \

  --enable-multiple-write-locations true
```

Create SQL Container (Python SDK):

```python
from azure.cosmos import CosmosClient, PartitionKey


url = "<endpoint>"

key = "<primary-key>"


client = CosmosClient(url, credential=key)

database = client.create_database_if_not_exists("OrdersDB")

container = database.create_container_if_not_exists(

    id="Orders",

    partition_key=PartitionKey(path="/orderId"),

    offer_throughput=400

)
```

---

5. Azure Monitor (Log Analytics)

Query Logs (KQL via REST):

```
POST https://api.loganalytics.io/v1/workspaces/{workspaceId}/query


Headers:

Authorization: Bearer <token>


Body:

{

  "query": "AzureDiagnostics | where TimeGenerated > ago(1h)"
```

```
}
```

List Alerts (CLI):

```
az monitor alert list \

  --resource-group myRG \

  --query "[].{Name:name, Enabled:enabled, Severity:severity}"
```

Create Alert Rule for CPU:

```
az monitor metrics alert create \

  --name HighCPU \

  --resource-group myRG \

  --scopes
/subscriptions/<sub>/resourceGroups/myRG/providers/Microsoft.Web/sit
es/myWebApp \

  --condition "avg Percentage CPU > 75" \

  --window-size 5m \

  --evaluation-frequency 1m \

  --severity 2
```

---

6. Azure Storage

Upload File to Blob Storage:

```
az storage blob upload \

  --account-name mystorageacct \

  --container-name mycontainer \

  --file ./sample.json \
```

```
--name sample.json \

--auth-mode login
```

Set Lifecycle Management Policy:

```json
{

  "rules": [

    {

      "enabled": true,

      "name": "moveToCool",

      "definition": {

        "actions": {

          "baseBlob": {

            "tierToCool": { "daysAfterModificationGreaterThan": 30 }

          }

        },

        "filters": {

          "blobTypes": ["blockBlob"],

          "prefixMatch": ["archive/"]

        }

      }

    }

  ]

}
```

Apply policy using the Azure CLI or ARM template deployment.

7. Azure Bicep Example for Resilient Deployment

```
resource appPlan 'Microsoft.Web/serverfarms@2021-03-01' = {

  name: 'resilientPlan'

  location: 'westeurope'

  sku: {

    name: 'P1v2'

    tier: 'PremiumV2'

  }

}



resource webApp 'Microsoft.Web/sites@2021-03-01' = {

  name: 'resilientWebApp'

  location: 'westeurope'

  properties: {

    serverFarmId: appPlan.id

    httpsOnly: true

  }

}
```

Deploy with:

```
az deployment group create \

  --resource-group myRG \

  --template-file main.bicep
```

Summary

This API reference provides the practical syntax and examples you'll use regularly to build, configure, and monitor resilient systems on Azure. Combine these calls with infrastructure as code, CI/CD pipelines, and observability tooling to create self-documenting and self-healing systems that are scalable, secure, and maintainable.

Use this guide as a foundation and extend it with your own libraries, templates, and scripts based on your specific stack and organizational standards.

Frequently Asked Questions

In this section, we address some of the most commonly asked questions by architects, engineers, and DevOps professionals working with resilient systems on Azure. These questions span strategy, implementation, tooling, and best practices. Use this section as a reference to clarify your understanding or guide architectural decisions during real-world projects.

Q1: What is the difference between high availability and resilience?

High Availability (HA) refers to designing systems that are continuously operational, usually with minimal downtime and strong uptime guarantees (e.g., 99.95%).

Resilience, on the other hand, refers to the system's ability to recover from failures, adapt to unexpected conditions, and maintain acceptable levels of performance even during disruptions.

While HA is a **subset** of resilience, true resilience includes:

- Recovery from transient and regional failures
- Handling dependency outages gracefully
- Automatic failovers and retries
- Chaos testing to validate recovery paths

Q2: How can I simulate a regional outage in Azure for testing?

You cannot directly shut down a region in Azure (obviously), but you can simulate a regional outage using several techniques:

- **DNS-level failover** with Azure Traffic Manager by disabling a regional endpoint.

- **Using Chaos Studio**, apply network faults, shutdown VMs, or simulate node failures.

- **Disrupt service dependencies** in a specific region (e.g., stop a database or disable access to Key Vault).

- Use **az network watcher** to restrict connectivity.

Ensure you have multi-region deployments with replicated data and failover strategies before testing. Monitor the impact through Application Insights or Log Analytics.

Q3: What are best practices for implementing retries without causing cascading failures?

Retrying failed operations is essential, but doing so without structure can lead to retry storms and degraded performance.

Best practices include:

- Use **exponential backoff** with **jitter**.

- **Cap the maximum number of retries** (e.g., 3–5).

- Ensure **idempotency** of operations.

- Use libraries that support built-in retry logic:

  - Polly (for .NET)

  - Axios Retry (for JavaScript/Node)

  - Resilience4j (Java)

Example in .NET using Polly:

```
var policy = Policy
  .Handle<HttpRequestException>()
  .WaitAndRetryAsync(3, retryAttempt =>
    TimeSpan.FromSeconds(Math.Pow(2, retryAttempt)));
```

Q4: How do I manage secrets securely and resiliently in Azure?

Use **Azure Key Vault** with managed identity integration. Resilient secret management involves:

- Using **retry logic** for secret fetches.

- Caching secrets in memory with short TTL.

- Monitoring Key Vault availability via **Diagnostic Settings**.

- Enabling **soft-delete** and **purge protection**.

When using Key Vault in production, always integrate with **Azure Role-Based Access Control (RBAC)** instead of storing secrets in code or configuration files.

Q5: What is the role of Azure Availability Zones in resilience design?

Availability Zones (AZs) are **physically separate datacenters** within a single Azure region. They protect against datacenter-level failures.

Design considerations:

- Use **zone-redundant services** like Azure SQL, App Gateway, or Cosmos DB.

- Deploy **virtual machines and Kubernetes nodes** across multiple zones.

- Combine AZs with **geo-redundant replication** for regional resilience.

Availability Zones are critical for applications with strict uptime requirements (e.g., 99.99% SLA).

Q6: When should I use active-active vs. active-passive architecture?

Use **active-active** when:

- You require high performance and minimal recovery time.

- Your app supports horizontal scaling and stateless workloads.

- You want to distribute traffic geographically for latency optimization.

Use **active-passive** when:

- Budget constraints limit resource duplication.
- You have stateful services that require complex synchronization.
- Failover time (RTO) in the range of minutes is acceptable.

Azure Traffic Manager and Front Door can support both architectures via weighted or priority routing.

Q7: How can I ensure database resilience in Azure?

Azure offers resilience features for databases like:

- **Geo-replication** (e.g., Cosmos DB, Azure SQL).
- **Automatic failover groups** (Azure SQL).
- **Zone redundancy** (Premium tiers).
- **Backups and point-in-time restore**.

Best practices include:

- Design for **eventual consistency** where possible.
- Separate read/write operations using **read replicas**.
- Monitor **DTU/Request Unit** usage and set thresholds.
- Handle **429 errors** with retry logic and graceful degradation.

Q8: What's the difference between Azure Front Door and Azure Traffic Manager?

Feature	Azure Front Door	Azure Traffic Manager

Layer	Layer 7 (HTTP/HTTPS)	Layer 4 (DNS)
Failover Speed	Real-time	DNS TTL-based (slower)
SSL Offload	Yes	No
Caching	Yes (Global CDN)	No
Geo Routing	Yes	Yes
Protocol Support	HTTP, HTTPS	Any (via DNS routing)

Use **Front Door** for low-latency web apps, WAF, and global load balancing. Use **Traffic Manager** for hybrid apps and protocol-agnostic routing.

Q9: What is the difference between Zone Redundant and Geo-Redundant services?

- **Zone Redundant**: Resilience within a single region across multiple availability zones (e.g., App Service Premium V3).

- **Geo-Redundant**: Data is replicated across geographically distant Azure regions (e.g., GRS storage, Cosmos DB with multi-region writes).

Use both for critical systems: zone redundancy for local failures, geo redundancy for regional outages.

Q10: How do I audit resilience configurations in my Azure subscription?

Use **Azure Resource Graph** and **Azure Policy** to assess and enforce resilience standards.

Example query to find non-Zone-Redundant App Services:

```
| where type == "microsoft.web/serverfarms"

| where properties.zoneRedundant != true
```

Example Azure Policy for enabling geo-redundant storage:

```
{

  "if": {

    "allOf": [

      {

        "field": "type",

        "equals": "Microsoft.Storage/storageAccounts"

      },

      {

        "field": "sku.name",

        "notEquals": "Standard_GRS"

      }

    ]

  },

  "then": {

    "effect": "audit"

  }

}
```

Summary

This FAQ provides clear and concise answers to the practical concerns teams face when building resilient systems in Azure. Whether you're new to the cloud or refining enterprise-grade architectures, use these answers as tactical guidance to enhance system reliability, manage costs, and ensure operational excellence.

The appendices conclude here. You're now equipped with a comprehensive, actionable, and resilient framework for modern architecture on Azure. Use it to design with confidence, fail gracefully, and recover quickly—every time.

www.ingramcontent.com/pod-product-compliance
Lightning Source LLC
LaVergne TN
LVHW051427050326
832903LV00030BD/2948